Interpreting Child Sacrifice Narratives

Also Available from Bloomsbury

Martyrdom and Sacrifice in Islam, Meir Hatina
Not Sparing the Child, Edited by Daphna Arbel, Paul C. Burns,
J. R. C. Cousland, Richard Menkis and Dietmar Neufeld
Sacrifice in Pagan and Christian Antiquity, Robert J. Daly

Interpreting Child Sacrifice Narratives

Horror and Redemption

Benjamin Beit-Hallahmi

BLOOMSBURY ACADEMIC
LONDON • NEW YORK • OXFORD • NEW DELHI • SYDNEY

BLOOMSBURY ACADEMIC
Bloomsbury Publishing Plc
50 Bedford Square, London, WC1B 3DP, UK
1385 Broadway, New York, NY 10018, USA
29 Earlsfort Terrace, Dublin 2, Ireland

BLOOMSBURY, BLOOMSBURY ACADEMIC and the Diana logo are trademarks of
Bloomsbury Publishing Plc

First published in Great Britain 2023
This paperback edition published in 2024

Copyright © Benjamin Beit-Hallahmi, 2023

Benjamin Beit-Hallahmi has asserted his right under the Copyright, Designs and Patents Act, 1988, to be identified as Author of this work.

For legal purposes the Acknowledgments on p. vii constitute an extension of this copyright page.

Cover design: Tjaša Krivec
Cover image: The Sacrifice of Isaac, Michelangelo Merisi da Caravaggio, 1603, oil on canvas, 104 x 135 cm © classicpaintings/Alamy Stock Photo

All rights reserved. No part of this publication may be reproduced or transmitted in any form or by any means, electronic or mechanical, including photocopying, recording, or any information storage or retrieval system, without prior permission in writing from the publishers.

Bloomsbury Publishing Plc does not have any control over, or responsibility for, any third-party websites referred to or in this book. All internet addresses given in this book were correct at the time of going to press. The author and publisher regret any inconvenience caused if addresses have changed or sites have ceased to exist, but can accept no responsibility for any such changes.

A catalogue record for this book is available from the British Library.

Library of Congress Control Number: 2022945037

ISBN: HB: 978-1-3502-3672-1
PB: 978-1-3502-3676-9
ePDF: 978-1-3502-3673-8
eBook: 978-1-3502-3674-5

Typeset by Newgen KnowledgeWorks Pvt. Ltd., Chennai, India

To find out more about our authors and books visit www.bloomsbury.com and sign up for our newsletters.

Contents

Preface		vi
Acknowledgments		vii
Prologue		1
1	Exploring Religion	7
2	The Enlightenment View of Religion	15
3	The Satanism Craze: Looking at an Imaginary Religion	23
4	Proximal Explanations for the Satanism Craze: Social Context	57
5	Possible Genealogies of Recent Satanism Narratives	71
6	A Child Is Being Sacrificed	87
7	Sacrifice Fantasies	99
8	Human Sacrifice in West Asian Heritage	117
9	The Binding	139
10	The Binding of Jesus	163
11	In Remembrance of a Mythical Sacrifice	173
12	Genital Mutilation and Child Sacrifice Fantasies	187
13	An Infanticidal Impulse and the Oedipal Paradox	195
14	Conclusion: Back to the Present	207
References		217
Index		251

Preface

Horrifying ideas about human sacrifice, child sacrifice, and a father offering his beloved son to the gods appear in some religious traditions, starting with the Greeks and the Hebrews, but similar stories made a claim for our attention more recently.

This happened when narratives about an underground religion devoted to Satan, which demands and carries out child sacrifice, appeared in the United States in the late twentieth century and became the subject of media reports, supported by some mental health professionals. Looking at these modern fantasies leads us back to ancient stories, which in some cases are considered by believers to be the height of religious devotion.

The book examines connections between Satanism stories in the 1980s and other child sacrifice fantasies. These include the Blood Libeli and Eastern Mediterranean (Greek, Phoenician, and Hebrew) narratives of child sacrifice, best known in the myths of Isaac, Ishmael, and Jesus. These connections may seem obvious to some, but no one has spelled them out before. The absurdity of shocking narratives being told about nonexistent Satanists recently contrasts with our attitude toward ancient stories held sacred by established religions.

The current book draws on my earlier work, published as *Flesh and Blood: Interrogating Freud on Human Sacrifice, Real and Imagined* (Leiden: Brill, 2019).

In preparing this book, I had an opportunity, which I appreciate very much, to expand, revise, and rewrite my earlier interpretations, something rarely given to an author.

Acknowledgments

I first encountered the phenomenon of contemporary Satanism stories through a brilliant presentation by David Bromley I heard in Solvang, California, in 1991. When the session was over, I told him that one day I would like to apply psychoanalytic ideas to these strange and perennial fantasies. Later, in April 1992, I had the good fortune of meeting Sherrill Mulhern at a conference in Lyon, France. She has been a major source of ideas and materials. More work on the topic was done when I was a visiting professor at King's College, London, during 1994–5. This was made possible by Peter Clarke. During my stay in London, I had a chance to learn from Jean La Fontaine, among others.

While writing this book, I must gratefully acknowledge important suggestions made, and important materials provided, by Moshe Almagor, Yaacov Ariel, Haya Bar-Itzhak, Yoram Bilu, Michael P. Carroll, Yaacov Ben-Cnaan, Peter Collett, Heath Dewrell, Asbjørn Dyrendal, Avshalom Elitzur, Rachel Erhard, Jay Feierman, Mark Finn, David Frankfurter, Yerach Gover, Ariela Keysar, Barry Kosmin, Etan Levine, Roland Littlewood, Zvi Lothane, Harriet Lutzky, Michael Nielsen, Richard Noll, Ray Paloutzian, Dick Peterson, Jerry Piven, Amiram Raviv, Roy A. Rosenberg, Henry Rosenfeld, Marilyn Safir, Richard Schuster, Eli Somer, Jason Tatlock, Roger van Zwanenberg, Jeffrey S. Victor, Dan Wassermann, and Scott Wetzler. Two anonymous readers helped greatly with the manuscript.

Institutional support has been provided by the Centre d'Etudes Transdisciplinaires of the CNRS in Paris, the Department of Psychology at the University of Haifa, the Library of the University of Haifa, and the Research Authority at the University of Haifa.

Ralph W. Hood Jr. has been a good friend for many decades and his encouragement led to the writing of this book.

Many conversations with Aram Schlosberg helped me immensely.

My wife Zmira, as always, has shown more patience than I deserve.

Prologue

The human experiences addressed in this book are not real acts of bloody sacrifice, but fantasies about such acts, which are real for those sharing them, whether they are secular individuals who have confidence in stories about Satanists or religious believers who hold true ancient fantasies about Isaac, Jesus, or Ishmael.

The common denominator is the fantasy about children being offered to the gods by their parents, whether the god is YHWH, Zeus, or Satan.

Why do individuals find such stories compelling? In the case of religious fantasies, they are supported by institutions and by direct socialization. What you learned and celebrated at your mother's knee is naturally internalized. Original, novel fantasies without social support are another case altogether. Modern Satanism narratives competed with others for attention and acceptance, possibly with the help of nontraditional entrepreneurs.

The universe for this book is religion, which induces love and loyalty, as well as real conflicts. It has been said, wisely, that religion is fiction with authority (Boyer, 2008). Does this imply that the power of authority will make any fiction attractive, or at least acceptable, to its adherents? Many religious narratives seem implausible and incoherent to us, but tradition, represented by actual engagement and power, attempts (often with great success) to offer plausibility and coherence. Once a story is canonized, it has behind it and around it the power of identity and institutions.

Conscious identity and unconscious identification may lead individuals to affirm less palatable doctrines or narratives and defend them. Moreover, within a particular tradition, mythological stories become part of the individual construction of human history, even individual autobiography. (I may think of the mythological story about Jesus, which I learned as a child, as a chapter in ancient history.) The ardent believer may even think of himself as living in continuity with Abraham or Jesus. We also discover that some themes are found almost everywhere, and we tend to interpret this as reflecting universal human concerns (Brown, 1991).

Both traditional narratives and stories disseminated by informal sources raise the question of the needs they satisfy. How do they gratify or empower those who are exposed to them? We can ask the same questions about both modern Satanism stories and ancient mythical narrative.

Intuitively, we think that stories must satisfy significant needs to be accepted by an audience. Fantasies that humans find inspiring, attractive, or consoling will make the grade. Another relevant factor, which this book addresses, is that of contributing to self-esteem through belonging to an elect group and the experience of moral superiority. Belief in superiority is naturally rewarding.

A related question is why and how a particular narrative was first created, and what was its original source. I will naturally ignore any religious claims about origins.

Was there an original author who invented a plot and presented it to his family or clan? Does somebody own the rights to the Binding of Isaac story? As we shall see, the Binding story is probably just a late version of a well-known template, which was preceded by powerful accounts and later morphed into the Crucifixion myth and the Ishmael myth.

Folklore scholars taught me how easily stories travel and how cultural borders do not exist. As we examine some ancient narratives, this will be obvious.

What is my starting point?

I trust that all readers will discover my preferences and biases soon enough.

I am not interested in moral judgments. Is YHWH a cruel God? Does the Bible endorse violence and cruelty? (Collins, 2003). Such are not my concerns.

The book is guided by hypotheses about love, violence, self-esteem, ideas of election, moral superiority, and insecurity.

Much of the interpretation of narratives will focus on traditional texts, which direct us to religion as praxis, reflecting a universal fantasy about fruitful contacts with the spirit world.

We are faced with challenging narratives, which focus on child sacrifice by fathers seeking existential security (survival) as a unique form of imaginary negotiations with powerful spirits. These texts have enjoyed a privileged position in Western culture, inspired by Christianity. The decline of religion has diminished their authority, but it is still experienced by many. The narratives in the texts give rise to powerful images, which create affective responses as we identify with the protagonists, the text, and its context.

The Bible, just like "Greek mythology," is an anthology of mostly fragmentary texts, sanctified (for believers) by the authors' claims, and not one unified work. Much effort was taken to present a dominant position on ritual or child sacrifice, but multiple voices remain in the final text.

Questions about the dating of the fragments and the creation of the final text are the concern of Bible scholars and historians, and I will rely on their work. In this book, the main concern is with the messages and their reception and preservation over hundreds and thousands of years. Why were certain narratives selected to become centerpieces of mythology, worship, and identity? How did the firstborn sacrifice motif become a centerpiece of Judaic or Christian mythology?

We are far removed from those who created the ancient stories, but the stories are kept alive today in the minds of the believers, by clergy, and the rituals commemorating them.

The most common attitude toward mythology today is one of culturally biased underestimation of the power of the imagination. One's attitude to any given scripture is usually predictable and depends on social learning and identity. Educated Westerners often don't believe in Noah's flood, but many of them do regard as factual stories the Exodus from Egypt, the Israelite conquest of Canaan, the kingdom of David and Solomon, and the building of Solomon's Temple. Similar stories in other traditions, be they European or Asian, are rightly regarded as fictional. The common notion is that the Bible does have not only its mythological parts but also its factual narratives.

Some readers have tried to secularize religious tales, supposedly judging them based on evidence and suggesting that "collective memory" may be at work. Another famous way of rationalizing mythology is the "kernel of truth" idea. "Every myth is based on a kernel of truth." This famous old kernel is supposed to be hard at work with Adam and Eve or with Cain and Abel. But mythology starts, and ends, with a kernel of fiction.

Religious texts are works of fiction, which reflect the beliefs and imaginations of their authors, and not any historical events. They can teach us about their authors' imagination and beliefs, not about history. They are written to convey religious messages about revelations, miracles, and heroes. Discussions about the reliability of scriptures as historical sources reflect either naïveté or ignorance, or both.

Scriptures are not even reliable reports on ancient religious practices. Mythologies offer us fairy tales presented with a validating meta-representation, but they must be fairy tales to remain accessible to both children and adults. Most believers, after all, have learned all they know about their religion as children.

The heroes of the Hebrew Bible as well as those of New Testament, from Abraham to Moses and David, are fictional, as shown by their mythical exploits. Similar stories are told in all cultures about the great men of yore. Yet, within Western culture, Biblical mythology still enjoys a privileged status. Western media show not only deference, but also reverence, and they regularly refer to "Abraham," "Jesus," or "Moses" as real people, and numerous books tell us about their inner lives and psychological problems. There are hundreds of books describing the lives of Abraham, Moses, or Jesus (or rather "Abraham," "Moses," or "Jesus").

The nineteenth century was an age of optimism about uncovering evidence for the historicity of Christian mythology. The Palestine Exploration Fund (PEF), founded in London in 1865, embodied the dream of proving the Bible true with the help of archeological explorations. When it held an exhibition of "Biblical objects" in 1869, the PEF already had to admit that no artifacts related to any Bible stories had been found (Bar-Yosef, 2005). The future failure of academic studies and archeological knowledge to support religious beliefs and the great disappointments involved were evident to some observers by the end of the nineteenth century (White, 1896).

We know almost nothing about the actual beginnings of Hinduism, Buddhism, Islam, Christianity, and Judaism. Reading the scriptures and traditions of various religions will just expose us to legends and fiction. Archaeological finds tell us much about the reality of religion in ancient times, which is totally unlike "official" claims. Thus, we know that Israelite temples, altars, and sacrifice rules are identical to "Canaanite" ones (Kamlah and Michelau, 2012). This is acknowledged today even by Evangelical scholars (Arnold, 2017).

We may be able to know something about how religious traditions are formed if we look at Mormonism, a very young religion where we have scriptures, together with much historical documentation. We know exactly how scriptures are written. See the case of Joseph Smith Jr., who made up 500 pages of boring stories with the help of the King James Bible and some helpful friends. There is no reason to assume that the authors of the Bible were sitting with documents and recordings and checking the authenticity of reports before writing down their narratives.

Take John Ballou Newbrough (1828–1891), a dentist and spiritualist from New York City, who in 1882 published OAHSPE: A New Bible, which he said was dictated to him by angels. It contained a 78,000-year history of the earth, as well as "occurrences in the spiritual world" during the same time. During the Kosmon Era, which started in the nineteenth century, the world will be transformed into a heavenly kingdom. Newbrough may seem to us like a totally ridiculous figure but is no different from all other authors of holy books.

There is one undisputed historical fact about all scriptures, whether from New York City or from West Asia: They have been composed by real human beings, guided by human imagination and beliefs, during different periods over the past 5,000 years. Religious texts, and unwritten traditions, make a demand, or at least an invitation, on readers and listeners, to receive the Good News and join a community of believers with joy, confidence, and loyalty.

Staubli (2015) reminds us, if we need such a reminder, that what is ascribed to the gods in sacrifice scripts are human projections. The acts, intentions, and emotions attributed to gods and to human actors in sacrifice narratives are obviously human concerns projected on a cosmic screen (Beit-Hallahmi, 1989). Our impressions of the humans who created ancient traditions come from what they projected on their gods, through a process that was only partly conscious. Both real sacrifices, that is, any real offering of objects or energy, or fantasies about sacrifice come from the same human brain.

The texts speak to us today and have been speaking to believers for millennia, as part of tradition, where the narratives have been persuasive and foundational, whether about Isaac, Ishmael, or Jesus. The narratives are seemingly approachable, because we know them so well, and they are part of cultural legacy. Such texts are the most direct expression of the ancient minds at work, and what they held dear.

As indicated, I am going to (repeatedly) ask the same questions about both ancient and modern narratives. Sacrifice narratives, whether in the Hebrew Bible, the New Testament, or coming from somebody telling us about the Satanic underground will move us to react, whether by identification with a belief system, or, as we identify with the victims, by horror.

The argument of this book is that we can interpret ancient ideas because we still share much with them. What hasn't changed in 200,000 years is the human brain and basic religious ideas. We still share our ancestors' existential insecurity and wishes for a stable world. The existential insecurity hypothesis suggests that it accounts for the appearance of religious ideas and for historical changes in religiosity levels (Norris and Inglehart, 2004). One does not have to be uniquely pessimistic to recognize the prevalence of insecurity, anxiety, and victimization in so many human lives, and in so many cultures.

The journey presented in this book starts with the image of the killing father, the starting point in both the Satanism Craze and mythological sacrifice. The major human experiences that emerge from child sacrifice fantasies are love, pain, grief, vulnerability, paternal authority, and submission. Crisis, be it a plague, famine, or imminent defeat starts with human culpability. Whether the transgression is public or private, atonement, as ordered by the spirits, must be offered. Imaginary solutions will express the inability of directly overthrowing authority.

Humans are preoccupied with choosing the right victim for sacrifice, because the wrong choice, we are told, will doom us. In the case of sacrifice to the spirits, the exchange is, in most cases, judged to be a success. The local culture will reassure us that the sacrificial transaction is successful, and offering the child was the correct move. Justice is served, and the cosmic order saved. Ambivalent plots about the triumph of father and son together express children's helplessness and hopes for unconditional parental love. In the case of Satanism, despair wins over hope, and the cry for justice will never be answered.

1

Exploring Religion

Humans use their imagination to their own satisfaction, managing to drive away, or at least push aside, anxiety and the awareness of inevitable death, as ideas and practices seem plausible and satisfying within a community of believers. Fantasies may be dark and violent, but while there are no gods listening to prayers or savoring bloody sacrifice, humans seem to enjoy the practices and the dreams. Violence is at the center, with real and imagined sacrifice, bloody mythology, and apocalyptic dreams of total world destruction.

Actions may be deliberate and cold-blooded; not personal but guided by traditions and beliefs about negotiating with gods and spirits. Blood rituals may seem bizarre and shocking if you are an outsider. To the initiated, they offer belonging, safety, and relief. They preserve a world order at the cost of human or animal lives, or just a fantasy of someone being killed for our sake.

Some of the discussions in this book are about an imagined religion, invented by deluded or evil modern psychotherapists. This modern variant also turns out to be tied to historical religions and real rituals, and not only because all religious claims are invented as well.

The Phenomenon

"Religion" is an abstraction, and the frequent use of this term, rather than of specific reference to a specific religion such as Islam or Christianity, is an indication of growing secularization. There may be as many as 50,000 religions in this world, all engaged in trying to prove their uniqueness and superiority. Their followers number in the billions and comprise most of humanity, busy holding on to many concrete traditions and practices.

Fortunately, the seeming cacophony of competing belief systems can be summarized through its common essence. There are local religious systems, known as Islam, Buddhism, Hinduism, or Christianity, but humans really have just one religion. The irreducible belief core common to all religions contains the notion of spirits inhabiting an invisible world, including gods, angels, demons, and human souls, as well as ideas about our relationship with them (Beit-Hallahmi, 1989, 2015; Beit-Hallahmi and Argyle, 1997). Some authors discuss "magic" or "paranormal beliefs" as separate from religion, but "magic" and "paranormal beliefs" are predicated on invisible spirit entities that are independent of physical bodies.

Religion is not about abstract philosophizing, but about actual faith in invisible creatures and spirits. Millions of shrines, in homes and dedicated places of worship, where humans engage in acts conceived of as communication with spirits, giving thanks for help delivered or asking for future support. The practice of religion involves imaginary transactions with spirits great and small, and humans making concrete sacrifices and believing in being rewarded.

Fantasies about Spirits and Contacts

The human imagination in all cultures extends the boundaries of community beyond the living, and beyond mere mortals. There is a community of the living and the dead, the mortals, and the saints, all united in faith and certainty. The essence of religious rituals and beliefs has not changed over the past 200,000 years. Whether it is an ancestor who died not too long ago or a god who created the universe, humans negotiate with the spirits to ensure life and prosperity. Transactions with invisible powers are central to all human cultures, whether referred to as witchcraft, magic, or worship.

The range of collective religious actions is immense and ever-fascinating—from Cargo Cults, Third World salvation movements, which express frustration and despair, to seemingly modern searches for the soul by way of the Society for Psychical Research.

Fantasies about the afterlife, both official (as relayed by doctrine) and unofficial (invented by individuals), are an inevitable part of religious discourse. Discussing demons, ghosts, and communication with the dead are the hallmark of religions all over the world.

Religious praxis, carried out in various settings, consists of not only communicating with spirits but also continuously negotiating and bargaining with them. The assumption is one of mutuality between two parties. Humans negotiate with their environment, which includes negotiating with the spirits that surround us.

The ancient Romans summarized this implied contract in the formulae *do ut des* ("I give that you might give"). Emile Durkheim, in his *The Elementary Forms of the Religious Life*, regarded the *do ut des* formula as the best description of the relationship between deities and worshippers. Max Weber similarly stated that

> whether sacrifice is offered as barter, bribe, homage, or tribute, man expects some results—material or immaterial, direct or indirect, in this world or hereafter. (1920/1993: 211)

The same idea is spelled out in what children in some countries are taught about Santa (Santa Claus, Saint Nicholas, or Father Christmas). The story is about an invisible entity that can watch human acts and reward good behavior. The Santa formula is the essence of religious praxis. Whether it's an ancestor, a saint, or a god, the powers are there to watch us and affect our fate through reward or punishment.

Every religion proposes an imaginary structure surrounding us, which gives meaning to nature, history, and personal destiny. Within this structure there is a moral order, satisfying our conscious need for justice and providing an illusion of cohesion. Authority and tradition are maintained, and members are resocialized by rituals that celebrate imaginary vindications of the group's worldview.

Particular religions become the focus of social identity and claims of collective uniqueness and superiority are attached to each religious collectivity. This means that, starting in childhood, individuals are immersed in beliefs and assumptions that form part of their life experience. Beliefs about the end of life or the end of the world and the birth of a new cosmic order are central to some people.

The power of identity grows out of the support we experience in small, intimate groups, and its effects provide a reason to think that our species is powerfully predisposed toward in-group favoritism from childhood on. Group loyalty is maintained at a high cost because a lack of loyalty threatens survival. This is reflected in a well-known observation:

> It is always possible to bind together a considerable number of people in love, so long as there are other people left over to receive the manifestations of their aggressiveness. (Freud, 1921: 72)

And Freud reiterates as follows:

> A religion, even if it calls itself the religion of love, must be hard and unloving to those who do not belong to it. Fundamentally indeed every religion is in the

same way a religion of love for all those whom it embraces; while cruelty and intolerance towards those who do not belong to it are natural to every religion. (Freud, 1921: 128)

Externalizing aggression strengthens group cohesion and creates what is known as scapegoating.

Moreover, identification with the group is rewarded by a boost to self-esteem:

Anyone who believed in this God had some kind of share in his greatness, might feel exalted himself ... since one can scarcely claim to assist God in the administration of the world, the pride in God's greatness fuses with the pride in being chosen by him. (Freud, 1939: 112)

Universals in Religion

Universals are found when the same basic psychological processes are expressed in individual imaginative products (dreams, stories, daydreams), and in cultural imaginative products (art, literature, folklore, wit, religion, law, science), because they are basic and central to human experience. Universal themes in religious mythology are the result and reflection of the psychic unity of mankind, which in turn is the consequence of common psychological structures and universal early experiences, shared by all mankind.

The denial of death and the belief in immortality, or at least resurrection, are universal (Becker, 1973; Brown, 1991). Burials constitute the oldest nonutilitarian activity recorded in human evolution, and burials may be the first evidence of religious ideas. Archeologists suggest that only ideas about death as a transition can explain intentional burials. The oldest burials are found in the Middle Paleolithic in West Asia (Ronen, 2012). What we find in them are grave goods, that is, articles left with the body, mostly food. The investment in grave goods is interpreted as reflecting a wish to help the dead person survive, so to speak, in this new stage of existence.

These early humans already thought that death was not the end, and the difference between one bowl of food left with a dead child 100,000 years ago and the tombs of Egyptian pharaohs 5,000 years old is just quantitative. The belief animating both is identical: We must invest in creating the right future for the dead.

Burial customs and a belief in immortality are other common examples of denial with the help of a wish-fulfilling fantasy as a reaction to depressive affect ...

> Wish fulfilling fantasies like those just described, which buttress denial, can as well be considered under the heading of undoing: ... immortality "undoes" death. (Brenner, 1975: 22)

This description by a psychoanalyst parallels the observations offered by two biologists:

> The active manner of dealing with existential fears in the form of a meanwhile ritualised form of burial helped our ancestors to conceptualise the existential threat symbolically, allowed them to wrest control of the situation through their own actions, and thus allowed them to gain an inner distance to the events. (Wunn and Grojnowski, 2016: 117)

Moreover, religion suggests that only through death we can join the gods. The world of the spirits and gods is where we move to, as souls, when we die, according to most believers. It is significant that only after crossing over to the afterlife we are supposed to know more about life and death than before. The world of the dead turns out to be the world of truth and faith.

Humans have invested not only in the future of the dead but also in temples, priesthoods, and rituals used by the living. In economic terms, the investment has been huge, often a real burden on society, and the returns have not been material. The returns on this investment have been in imagined good fortune. The priests and the believers have believed, and we can hear this every day, that sacrifices, prayers, and true faith not only provide protection from death and misfortune for the believers but also maintain societal and cosmic order.

Interpreting Religion

The first question for the psychology of religion is that of the origin of religious ideas of any kind. Psychologists naturally point to the internal psychic landscape as the source of religious ideas, while sociologists and anthropologists point to the social landscape as the likely origin.

Cross-cultural regularities point to an apparent universal psychological readiness, which creates the universal plausibility of religious ideas. We assume that religion first appears, or is learned and embraced, through the operation of ordinary, automatic, cognitive processing. Several natural mechanisms create the capacity for developing supernaturalist ideas, as well as the readiness to accept these ideas once they have been created. Humphrey describes the appearance of unique cognitive skills that took place 100,000 years ago. These were "counterfactual reasoning, mental simulation, time travel and theory of mind" (2018: 2).

This evolutionary-cognitive approach tells us why and how religious ideas are so natural to humans:

> The explanation for religious beliefs and behaviors is to be found in the way all human minds work ... Our minds are prepared because natural selection gave us particular mental predispositions. (Boyer, 2001: 2)

Religious ideation is natural and intuitively plausible because of innate mechanisms that lead us to imagine reality in terms of egocentric, anthropocentric, animistic, and teleological processes, and to interpret events through intentionality and design (Beit-Hallahmi, 2015). It seems that the search for causality is an overriding force, but in humans, causality is conceived in an egocentric and anthropocentric way.

The root metaphor of animism, as Pepper (1942) suggested, is the human being. Anthropomorphic thinking is its sole explanation. Every event in nature comes about just as we feel our own behavior does, as the result of a wish or conscious intention. This is a direct projection of human conscious experience. We infer intentions from observing any action, and these are directed at us. Humans find themselves at the center of all causal chains they can think of, and this is reflected in their animism. When rain spoils our plans for an outing, we take it personally. When the skies are blue, modern humans say that the universe is smiling at them.

After raising the question of origin, the next issue is that of the actual substance of beliefs, narratives, and rituals. The historical origin of a myth or a ritual can rarely be uncovered, but we may try to assess their psychological significance for those who created them.

The historical (or prehistorical) events that led to the creation of specific religious taboos, beliefs, or rituals cannot be reconstructed. We cannot go back in time thousands of years. What can be done is to propose ahistorical psychological factors that played a role in the development of religious traditions. At some point, practices and beliefs become institutionalized and gain the status of identity markers. Institutionalization is selective, and we may ask and speculate about the reasons particular acts or ideas are selected and preserved.

More recent events could not have been predicted or understood more easily than ancient ones. No one could have predicted the modern epidemic of stories about the underground Satanic religion, which was killing thousands of children in the late twentieth century in the United States and some other countries.

Could we be sure that Satanic sacrifice stories will not come back to haunt us in the future?

Researchers using the evolutionary-cognitive approach to religion, while describing the basic mechanisms that make religious ideas attractive and natural, do not analyze concrete rituals. Offering explanations for the formation of concrete behaviors is often speculative, but so are references to prehistorical evolutionary processes.

Before Interpretation

Do we need to assume unconscious factors or processes in the making of religious beliefs and practices?

The conscious message in all religions is attractive and powerful. It includes the promise of a good life and good afterlife for the believers. The conscious message is positive, sweet, banal, and attractive. What is there to explain?

What we find in actual religions is not just the good news of salvation and afterlife, but a lot of extra baggage. So, why do we need stories about unusual events, such as virgin birth, child sacrifice, or shocking practices of genital mutilation? Where do they come from? Practices and rules we may find costly, or shocking, are part of human history and the history of every religion. Human projection creates evil demons and divine wrath, balanced by positive wishes for a blissful existence in heaven. Childhood fears and nightmares create a pantheon populated by demons and angels to protect us.

2

The Enlightenment View of Religion

The starting point of all studies of religion is viewing it as a mental (and social) construction. The process of mental construction involves externalization, objectification, and internalization of the externalized and objectified objects. Objectification is the process by which the externalized fantasies gain a life of their own and appear to be independent of the individuals, and the society, that created them. The products of human creativity become part of the reality, to be taken for granted. In the process of internalization, individuals learn the externalized social products and assume them as part of their consciousness.

All religions demand our attention as objects, without respect or hesitation. One issue is cultural identity and bias. Non-Western religions can be dissected and ridiculed by Westerners, but establishment religions, mainly Christianity, are another matter. Religious traditions, which are part of culture and identity, are, to many, above and beyond examination.

Even in a secular age, research on religion involves politics, in the sense of power in society. Religion examined and explained is religion diminished. When religion is treated as a natural or historical phenomenon to be explained, believers can only perceive it as a threat. A secular gaze at religion is always consequential, because of the reality of political struggles that are not only a matter of history but of our present and future. Religion affects us not only as ideas but also as institutions and political power.

The creation of academic psychology and then of nonacademic psychoanalysis was part and parcel of modernity and the Enlightenment project, both characterized by secularization. *Sapere aude*, dare to know, was the slogan. Sigmund Freud, born in 1856, was one of many Enlightenment thinkers who looked at modern society and culture with extreme sobriety, ready to reexamine and undermine received wisdom. Karl Marx, born in 1818, presents a projection theory of religion in 1844, when he stated that in religion the spontaneous activity of human fantasy, of the human brain and heart, reacts independently as an alien activity of gods or devils upon the individual. (quoted in Fromm, 1961: 82)

Psychoanalytic ideas have been the consequences and reflections, but not the causes, of historical changes. Freud's work followed it and was part of larger cultural changes. One man's work will have no impact without an eager audience.

What characterizes the Freudian sensibility is the detection of conflict, not just as a metaphor. The family, locus of love and devotion, is a battlefield, but it only reflects the reality of both individual psyches and human society as a whole. This is the source of what must be called the tragic dimension in psychoanalytic literature, a deep recognition of human limitations and a realistic approach to one's chances of achieving happiness. The prevalence of internal and interpersonal conflict in humans leads to struggle, adjustments, and compromises.

Reading Freud

Freud's writings, even when most speculative, are anchored in a biological model, or a biological analogue, which we find intuitively attractive and persuasive.

Few will argue with the assumption that the organism is most open to influence during childhood, and that the impact of early learning will be long-lasting. We all agree with the notion that what is sensitive during critical periods is the central nervous system, and we have much anatomical evidence to support that thesis.

Our style of dealing with the world starts with the small child and its (mis)understanding of sex, birth, and the family, with the resulting confused ideas that stay with us for life.

Freud's theoretical explanation for the origin and existence of religion is based on presumed universal experiences and processes: the universal experience of helplessness, the tendency for compensation through fantasy, and the impact of early relations with protective figures (Freud, 1910). Freud directs us to search for the origins of all intense emotional experiences in early and archaic experiences of vulnerability. Infancy and childhood are filled with unfulfilled desires on the one hand and fears and anxieties on the other. What is intense, profound, and universal in human behavior must have its origins in early experience. There is only one religion as there is only one humanity, one childhood, one helplessness, one dependence, mother and father. The intensity of universal helplessness created the psychological reality in which people could not imagine a world without parents. (Adults may also experience helplessness, sometimes when it is felt due to objective conditions, or strictly because of their own personality.)

Jean Piaget, like Freud, found the roots of religion in actual childhood experiences and in childhood fantasies. He also stated, in agreement with Freud, that young children believe that parents and adults, in general, are omniscient and omnipotent:

> The child in extreme youth is driven to endow its parents with all of those attributes which theological doctrines assign to their divinities—sanctity, supreme power, omniscience, eternity, and even ubiquity. (Piaget, 1929: 378)

Both Freud and Piaget described the disillusionment children undergo on discovering their parents' human limitations. Piaget expressed the notion that God is a parent who helps to account for the structure of this world:

> The child begins by attributing the distinctive qualities of the divinity—especially omniscience and almightiness—to his parents and thence to men in general. Then, as he discovers the limits of human capacity, he transfers to God, of whom he learns in his religious instruction, the qualities which he learns to deny to men. (Piaget, 1929: 268)

Piaget stated that at age six, children come to see humans as fallible, subject to limitations, and thus distinct from God who retains the extraordinary properties bestowed earlier. This suggestion has been supported by research across cultures.

Childish stories console, support, and offer imaginary rewards. This view of religion has been consistently expressed by Enlightenment writers. Baron d'Holbach (1723–1789) described the origins of religion in the infantile helplessness and dependence of the parents, just like Freud in 1927 (Manuel, 1983).

Historically, recent and unexpected developments in modern culture direct us to examine closely religious phenomena that first appeared thousands of years ago and survived in various forms. They may be ignored by students of religion, but then we are forced to realize that in human culture, old ideas, born out of fear and helplessness, stay alive.

Some religious apologists point to the universality of religious ideas as an indication of some underlying validity (Johnson, 1977). The classical psychoanalytic interpretation of religion does not come to praise religion but to bury it, analyzing it in every sense of the word. The analysis is intended to be emancipatory, liberating from illusions. Demystification, which is the opposite of the apologetic impulse, is its final goal. It is a "reductionist" approach, which takes religion as a phenomenon to be examined, and only that. Analysis demands taking the stand of the observer, and this is the normal stand in psychology.

Freud holds our attention because of subversive, counterintuitive insights that leave us often with a sense of wonder and amazement. As has been noted many times, Freud was a promiscuous interpreter, and a collector of fascinating observations. The issue that should concern us is whether all the observations are equally representative, or representative at all.

In every case, when dealing with religion Freud will direct us to the real thing, that is, the actual, communicated, content of religious beliefs, narratives, and rituals. The academic psychology of religion often does not analyze such communications. At the observed behavior level, believers tell us that they are engaged in celebrating their god by drinking his blood. This is the conscious message, and it is rarely deconstructed.

In *Totem and Taboo* (1913), Freud started dealing with death as a factor in the formation of religious ideas. Beyond his notion of the primal crime, which led to the creation of guilt, morality, and culture, he first suggested that encounters with death, together with ambivalence about the departed, led to the invention of evil demons, which were the precursors of all divinities: "Spirits and demons ... are only projections of man's own emotional impulses. He turns his emotional cathexes [investments of psychic energy] into persons, he peoples the world with them and meets his internal mental processes again outside himself" (1913a: 92).

In the middle of the First World War, Freud explained the beginning of religion as a defense against the reality of death:

> It is beside the body of someone he loved that he invented spirits ... memory of the dead became the basis for assuming other forms of existence and gave him the conception of life continuing after apparent death ... What came into existence beside the dead body of the loved one was not only the doctrine of the soul, but the belief in immortality and a powerful source of man's sense of guilt. (Freud, 1915: 294–5)

Realizing the meaning of death leads to the creation of a belief system based on immortality, guilt, and restraints on violence. Contrary to what Freud wrote in *Totem and Taboo*, only two years earlier, here the beginning of religion is a result of the encounter with the death of loved ones, not the result of any "original sin" against the Great Father.

Explaining Religious Beliefs

The basic Freudian way of looking at religion is defined by rejections: first, being secular and rejecting any claims about the spirit world, then rejecting conscious and explicit or "official" explanations for customs and practices. This, in turn, leads to assuming the projection of internal psychic processes and the centrality of childhood, which determines the infantile nature of religious ideation. Above all, human existence is marked by helplessness and deprivation, producing end-time visions, both violent and comforting.

Once we reject all religious explanations, then projection is the only logical solution. If it's not out there in heaven, and is felt so strongly and vividly, it must be the result of internal scripts. What else could it be? Projection of internal processes is the concept we use to explain the specific content of cultural externalizations.

In 1901, Freud presented this description of projection as the source of religious ideation:

> In point of fact I believe that a large part of the mythological view of the world, which extends a long way into the most modern religions, is nothing but psychology projected into the external world ... One could venture to explain in this way the myths of paradise and the fall of man, of God, of good and evil, of immortality, and so on, and to transform metaphysics into metapsychology. (Freud, 1901: 258–9)

The basic moral stand is against projection, against externalization of undesirable traits and drives, because the demons are inside each one of us, and outside there is only harsh reality and death.

Freud lived in Vienna between 1860 and 1938 and felt oppressed by its Roman Catholic majority. He delayed the publication of *Moses and Monotheism* because of fear. In 1910, 93.7 percent of Austrians were Catholics, and 2.9 percent were Jewish. In the twenty-first century, with nominal Catholics down to 64.2 percent, 16.9 percent opting for no religion, and about two thousand Jews, it's hard to imagine Freud's Vienna. Still, Freud was able to publish his views of religion, and the world knew where he stood. He was able to declare himself an atheist, which is one indication of historical secularization and its effects being felt even in Catholic Vienna.

Freud sounds much like Karl Marx when recording his impressions during a visit to Rome in 1901:

> I found almost intolerable the lie of salvation which rears its head so proudly to heaven. (Masson, 1985: 449)

Religious salvation is a lie and should be exposed as such. Even if it does bring subjective relief, in the eyes of such critics as Freud and Marx it dooms humanity to eternal suffering, because real salvation is truth and nothing but the truth. Enlightenment is a judgmental, moral project of advancing toward emancipation, with a utopian vision of a future world where all are educated, independent, and mature, and can face reality without illusions.

In *The Future of an Illusion* (1927), Freud described religion as false consciousness:

> We tell ourselves how lovely it would be, would it not, if there were a God who created the universe and benign Providence, a moral world order, and life beyond the grave, yet it is very evident, is it not, that all of this is the way we should inevitably wish it to be. And it would be even more remarkable if our poor, ignorant bondsman ancestors had managed to solve all these difficult cosmic questions. (Freud, 1927: 47)

Freud also presents a cognitive analysis of human animism:

> Impersonal forces and destinies cannot be approached; they remain eternally remote. But if the elements have passions that rage as they do in our own souls, if death itself is not something spontaneous but the violent act of an evil Will, if everywhere in nature there are Beings around us of a kind that we know in our own society, then we can breathe freely, can feel at home in the uncanny and can deal by psychical means with our senseless anxiety. (Freud, 1927: 20–1)

By the time Freud came to write *Civilization and Its Discontents* (1930), however, his views on religion had undergone one important, possibly dramatic, modification. No longer satisfied with the word "illusion" to describe religion, Freud now termed it a delusion.

"A special importance," Freud wrote, "attaches to the case in which this attempt to procure a certainty of happiness and a protection against suffering through a delusional remolding of reality is made by a considerable number of people in common." He then poignantly added, "The religions of mankind must be classed among the mass delusions of this kind" (Freud, 1930: 81).

We often see references to the "truth claims" of religion and religions. There have been suggestions that social scientists, including psychologists, are not qualified to pass judgment on religious "truth claims." Many social scientists in the United States have largely embraced the idea that "empirical science can say nothing definitive about the truth or falsity of religious belief" (Johnson, 1977: 368). According to Talcott Parsons, one of the leading sociologists of the twentieth century, religion refers to "aspects of 'reality' ... outside the range of scientific investigation and analysis" (Parsons, 1937: 421). In the real world, millions of individuals pass judgment on religious claims every day, while never being asked about qualifications. They usually tell us without hesitation that the truth claims of all religions, except theirs, are laughable, and then sing the praises of the one true revelation, which, in 99.99 percent of cases, they grew up with.

The way Freud regarded the truth claims of all religions can be summed up in one word: nonsense (Blass, 2004). Whether it is the "truth claims" about Zeus, YHWH, Krishna, Jesus, or Osiris, he thought that they could be rejected without much contemplation of consideration.

Where I think we should part ways with Freud, Johnson, and Parsons is their use of "science" and "scientific," as if they should have anything to do with our judgment of religious claims. Do we need to know anything about science to assess the stories about the miracle performed by Krishna, or by YHWH, or the resurrection of Osiris, or Jesus, or the creation stories in Genesis? Do we need to know chemistry, or physics? There is no need to get science involved. Simple common sense will do.

Freud's Impatience

Freud was impatient with humanity, telling fellow humans to give up illusions and grow up as soon as possible. The material discussed in this book is directly pertinent to Freud's supposed biases in observing humanity. Look at the way bizarre fantasies are so attractive to so many, as reflected in stories about a nonexistent Satanic religion or the bloody rituals of real religions, and ask yourself: Was Freud leading us astray?

> The whole thing [religion] is so patently infantile, so foreign to reality, that to anyone with a friendly attitude to humanity it is painful to think that the great majority of mortals will never be able to rise above this view of life. (Freud, 1930: 74)

Religion is infantile in more than one sense.

1. The ideas are childish, and (in adults) demonstrate a regression in thinking mode. Religious ideas are obviously unacceptable for a grown-up mind. As Sartre (1967: 154) says, "Because it is childish, nothing touches a child more closely."

2. Religious ideas were developed as a result of early experience and are a reflection of childhood realities:

> When the growing individual finds that he is destined to remain a child forever, that he can never do without protection against strange superior powers, he lends those powers the features belonging to the figure of his father; he creates for himself the gods whom he dreads. (Freud, 1927: 30)

Atheist intellectuals are impatient with the way individuals stay loyal to religious identities inherited from parents even when they no longer believe or practice anything related to those identities. They don't understand the power of identity, the sense of belonging, and the feeling of superiority and certainty. These intellectuals are willing to give up such an identity because they have an individual sense of superiority and certainty thanks to their intelligence and intellectualism. Like Sigmund Freud and Jean Piaget, they were admired as children for their talents and did not need group belonging to support their self-esteem. Such intellectuals are rarely committed nationalists and may be suspicious of most ideologies.

If they dream of changing humanity's fate, it is, for Piaget or Freud, by increasing knowledge about human desires and capacities. Does increasing psychological knowledge work? We must be unsure.

3

The Satanism Craze: Looking at an Imaginary Religion

To illustrate the belief system that characterized those committed to the fantasy of a Satanic underground in the late twentieth century, I have selected the following episode, which will take you right into the deep end of the phenomenon.

On Thursday, June 25, 1992, hundreds of mental health professionals from the Washington, DC, area gathered in Alexandria, VA, for the Fourth Annual Eastern Regional Conference on Abuse and Multiple Personality. They were scheduled to listen to D. Corydon Hammond, arguably one of the world's leading authorities of hypnosis. Hammond holds a PhD in counseling psychology from the University of Utah; is a diplomate in clinical hypnosis, the American Board of Psychological Hypnosis; is a diplomate in sex therapy, the American Board of Sexology; and is the winner of numerous professional awards.

The University of Utah Medical School's official website tells us that "Dr. Hammond is a psychologist with advanced specialties in neurofeedback (EEG biofeedback), quantitative EEG brain mapping, clinical hypnosis, and marital and sex therapy. He has been President of the International Society for Neurofeedback & Research and of the American Society of Clinical Hypnosis."

Hammond's topic for the session was "Hypnosis in MPD and Ritual Abuse." What he presented has become known as *The Greenbaum Speech*, and the full text can be found by Googling that title (Hammond, 1992). An audio recording is also available, so the accuracy of the text can be checked.

To appreciate the Satanism Craze and the content of assertions about "ritual abuse," here are a few paragraphs I have selected, and a few comments:

> So I have gone from someone kind of neutral and not knowing what to think about it all to someone who clearly believes ritual abuse is real and that the people who say it [is not] are either naive like people who didn't want to believe the Holocaust or—they're dirty. [Applause] ... Myself, as well as a few others

that I've shared it with, were hedging out of concern and out of personal threats and out of death threats. I finally decided to hell with them. If they're going to kill me, they're going to kill me. (Hammond, 1992: 4)

What are the secrets that Hammond is risking his life by sharing with his audience?

At the end of World War II, before it even ended, Allen Dulles and people from our Intelligence Community were already in Switzerland making contact to get out Nazi scientists. As World War II ends, they not only get out rocket scientists, but they also get out some Nazi doctors who have been doing mind-control research in the camps. They brought them to the United States. Along with them was a young boy, a teenager, who had been raised in a Hasidic Jewish tradition and a background of Cabalistic mysticism ... But he saved his skin by collaborating and being an assistant to them in the death-camp experiments. They brought him with them. They started doing mind-control research for Military Intelligence in military hospitals in the United States. The people that came, the Nazi doctors, were Satanists. Subsequently, the boy changed his name, Americanized it some, obtained an M.D. degree, became a physician and continued this work that appears to be at the center of Cult Programming today. His name is known to patients throughout the country. (Hammond, 1992: 4) [The boy's original name was Greenbaum, and became Green.]

What they basically do is they will get a child and they will start this, in basic forms, it appears, by about two and a half after the child's already been made dissociative ... early programming took place on a military installation. That's not uncommon. I've treated and been involved with cases who are part of this original mind-control project as well as having their programming on military reservations in many cases. We find a lot of connections with the CIA. (Hammond, 1992: 5-6) [What follows is an explanation of different personalities created by Satanic programming.]

Alphas appear to represent general programming, the first kind of things put in. Betas appear to be sexual programs. For example, how to perform oral sex in a certain way, how to perform sex in rituals, having to do with producing child pornography, directing child pornography, prostitution. Deltas are killers trained in how to kill in ceremonies. There'll also be some self-harm stuff mixed in with that, assassination and killing. Thetas are called psychic killers. (Hammond, 1992: 8)

I've found, for example, in one case that Zeta had to do with the production of snuff films that this person was involved with. With another person, Omicron had to do with their linkage and associations with drug smuggling and with

> the Mafia and with big business and government leaders. (Hammond, 1992: 9) [There are no "Snuff films." See Wax (2021), and Snuff Films | Snopes.com at https://www.snopes.com.]
>
> The way you create Manchurian Candidates is you divide the mind. It's part of what the Intelligence Community wanted to look at. If you're going to get an assassin, you're going to get somebody to go do something, you divide the mind. (Hammond, 1992: 12)
>
> My best guess is that the purpose of it is that they want an army of Manchurian Candidates, tens of thousands of mental robots who will do prostitution, do child pornography, smuggle drugs, engage in international arms smuggling, do snuff films, all sorts of very lucrative things and do their bidding and eventually the megalomaniacs at the top believe they'll create a Satanic Order that will rule the world. (Hammond, 1992: 19)

Hammond shares with the audience, and with us, information that had supposedly been gathered from his clinical work, using hypnosis. Reading these paragraphs, you will realize that the speaker offers us a collection of delusional stories. He probably invents various bits and pieces and then miraculously finds them in his clients' hypnotic speech. So much for the value of "clinical hypnosis."

His musings about the Second World War and "cabalism," and especially his story about Greenbaum/Green may raise suspicions of anti-Semitism. Nothing of the kind seems justified to me. Hammond is not an anti-Semite; he is a profound and terminal ignoramus, a devout customer of conspiracy theories and urban legends about "snuff films" and "Manchurian Candidates." What he says about "cabalism" and the books he recommends to his audience are laughable. Despite his formal training and his many awards, Hammond doesn't know the first thing about psychology or psychopathology, as shown by his conceptions of dissociation and multiple personality ("If you're going to get an assassin, you're going to get somebody to go do something, you divide the mind").

Anybody using the term "mind control" is telling us that he is not really an academic. It is a vulgar media term, like "brainwashing," which has never gained any standing in academic discourse. Those referring to projects such as MKUltra to show that government agencies believed in trying to arrive at "mind control" techniques merely remind us that stupidity does play a role in many official decisions (Marks, 1991). During the Cold War, both the USSR and the United States allocated resources to various attempts to develop "telepathy" or "mind control." All these attempts were a total waste. Neither side developed any special abilities, and the story ended with the end of the USSR.

The most significant thing about the Greenbaum Speech is the reception it gets from its audience of credentialed mental health professionals. Before we wonder about the many times he is applauded and the standing ovation at the end, we should remember that this is a crowd that signed up for a Conference on Abuse and Multiple Personality.

Hammond was not the only one reporting on death threats from Satanists. Ronald Fox, who served as president of the American Psychological Association in 1994, reported on psychologists being threatened by Satanists (Fox, 1995). I can happily report to you that, as of 2022, no psychologists or psychiatrists have ever been assaulted or molested by Satanists.

Hammond's reference to Holocaust denial was not unique. In 1989, psychiatrist Richard Kluft expressed concern about a "hidden holocaust" perpetuated by a Satanic religion (Kluft, 1989: 192). Another psychiatrist, S. L. Bloom (1994), compared denying the reality of Satanism to denying the Holocaust. In 1996, at the NATO Advanced Study Institute on Recollections of Trauma, a leading trauma researcher told me I was just like Holocaust deniers because I considered Satanism allegations pure fantasies.

The story of Dr. Hammond exposing Cult Programming of multiple personalities and the coming Satanic world order is a good way of introducing a shocking and tragic episode involving mental health professionals who, in the last decades of the twentieth century, created an imaginary universe of nonexistent monsters.

A significant aspect of the Satanism Craze was the involvement of women, scripted by the creators of this horror show as both victims and perpetrators. Ninety-nine percent of those who were involved in "recovered memories," or Multiple Personality Disorder (MPD), and gave us their first-person accounts of witnessing Satanic rituals were women. If Oedipal dynamics are involved, we would have predicted that they would accuse their mothers, and this is indeed the case. Women therapists had also been active in the Satanism movement, because they were more likely to believe in MPD, repressed memory, and Satanic Ritual Abuse (SRA) (Bottoms and Davis, 1997).

What we are going to discover is that the delusional ideas at the heart of the Satanism Craze came from a small group of psychiatrists and psychologists, but these ideas were greeted by larger groups and created a discourse community, where they were shared and developed. The Craze must be examined for what it teaches us about perennial fantasies and family tensions, as well as what it teaches us about the modern mental health enterprise, claiming professionalism and authority, and losing credibility, time and again.

How did this historical development come about? The history of the Satanism Craze starts with the commendable concern of medical practitioners and mental health professionals about the welfare of children, who are always vulnerable, if not defenseless. The 1962 appearance of the battered child syndrome (Kempe et al., 1962) was a milestone. In the 1970s, new forms of abuse were presented and labeled. Clinicians have realized that diagnosing child abuse is difficult and making the wrong decisions may lead to tragic consequences. In 1977, *Battered Women: A Psychosociological Study of Domestic Violence* was published (Roy, 1977). Various groups struggled to have newly recognized phenomena put on the agenda, the implication being that they had been understudied or ignored (Olivier, 2000).

In the 1980s, a three-pronged move affected the discussion of trauma among some mental health professionals in the English-speaking world. It started with the dubious idea of recovering "repressed" memories. Trauma, by definition, is something you cannot shake off. Freud's best-known treatment of trauma is *Beyond the Pleasure Principle* (Freud, 1920), where he discussed the compulsive tendency of the traumatized to reexperience the trauma, contrary to the natural reaction of avoiding pain. This challenge was one of the factors that led Freud to speculate about the human drive to masochism and the death instinct.

Over the past 50 years, some self-described trauma experts have claimed that many trauma survivors have lost their memories to dissociation or repression (for evaluations of such claims, see Alexander et al., 2005; Eisen et al., 2007; Goodman et al., 2003; Goodman, Quas, and Ogle, 2010; Loftus, 1993; Otgaar et al., 2019). This complex of ideas about trauma and memory gained a following among numerous practitioners of psychotherapy, and then led to some lawsuits by clients against their families for abuse carried out decades earlier and supposedly leading to a host of symptoms.

Psychotherapy has become trauma-oriented, and this means that the disturbed are first and foremost victims. The idea of trauma has become so central that some "therapists" now call themselves "traumatists." Something known as RMT (recovered memory therapy or repressed memory therapy), or "memory work" did come into being. The assumption was that uncovering the hidden memory of the early trauma leads to improvement, if not cure. The idea is that childhood traumas are so severe that they create an amnesia, lifted when the sufferer from amnesia is in treatment, and the memory uncovered or recovered.

The notion of trauma-induced amnesia was central to the RMT fad. Techniques used in "memory work" included hypnosis, "guided imagery," "memory enhancement," or chemical "truth serums." These were used to overcome the presumed repression of early memories. The techniques themselves are very much is dispute (Yapko, 1994) and are considered highly suggestive. The use of hypnosis, a controversial technique that leads to totally unreliable testimonies has played a central role in many Satanism reports, as well as in most cases of "recovered memory," or MPD. Many of the therapists who believed in MPD and Satanism were enthusiastic about hypnosis as an "uncovering tool" (Bliss, 1980).

You do not need a PhD in clinical psychology to understand that memories recovered through hypnosis, or any "memory enhancement" technique, could be ignored with no loss to knowledge, and only a possible financial loss to their purveyors (Orne et al., 1988).

The next step in creating the new discourse about trauma and dissociation was the even more dubious idea that the phenomenon of multiple personality is widespread, but unrecognized. What is the actual phenomenon? "Dissociative disorders are characterized by a disruption of and/or discontinuity in the normal integration of consciousness, memory, identity, emotion, perception, body representation, motor control, and behavior. Dissociative symptoms can potentially disrupt every area of psychological functioning" (*DSM-V*, 2013: 291). This description corresponds to what has been reported since the nineteenth century and will be accepted by most as phenomenologically relevant. Dissociative phenomena include such things as loss of memory (amnesia) or temporary loss of identity. In extreme cases, individuals have been described as suffering from identity fragmentation or multiple personality.

In 1957, two psychiatrists shared with the world an amazing case, in which three independent personalities were inhabiting the same body. Justifiably, *The Three Faces of Eve* became a global sensation, won mention in every introductory psychology textbook, and was turned into an Oscar-winning film. Chris Costner Sizemore, the real Eve, published three books about her life experiences. Her case and similar ones were so sensational because of their rarity, and the diagnosis has always been challenged. One psychiatrist stated, "The diagnosis of MPD represents a misdirection of effort which hinders the resolution of serious psychological problems in the lives of patients" (Merskey, 1992: 327).

The MPD epidemic of the 1980s was partially triggered by Cornelia Wilbur, a psychiatrist who claimed to have come across a patient, "Sybil," with sixteen personalities. The story of "Sybil" became a 1973 bestseller and then a 1976 film (Schreiber, 1973). The "Sybil" story has been exposed as a manufactured case, part of an unorthodox relationship between Wilbur, her patient Shirley Mason (Sybil), and Schreiber (Nathan, 2011; Rieber, 1998). Wilbur remained a major figure in the continuing discussion of MPD and its causes until her death in 1992 (Wilbur, 1984).

Following a wave of claims about memories of sexual abuse, recovered during psychotherapy, there was a meteoric rise in the number of individuals diagnosed with MPD. Whereas before 1980 the number of cases in the literature was under 100, by 1995 there were tens of thousands of such cases. By 1991, it has been claimed that the prevalence of multiple personality disorder in North America was 1 percent (Ross, 1991). The number of reported personalities in one body skyrocketed, and the record was 4,500. Hendrickson, McCarty, and Goodwin (1990) reported that some of the personalities were actually animals. Ninety-five percent of the cases were diagnosed in North America, of which 95 percent were women (Acocella, 1999; Littlewood, 2004). Thigpen and Cleckley, the psychiatrists who published the famous case of Eve in 1957, denounced the new epidemic and described the newly reported cases as fake (1984). No one listened, and dissociation diagnoses became ever more popular (Kihlstrom, 2005). It should be mentioned that individuals with MPD (later changed to Dissociative Identity Disorder or DID) diagnoses showed significant behavioral overlaps with other psychiatric syndromes, such as schizophrenia (Murray, 1994).

The International Society for the Study of Multiple Personality and Dissociation (ISSMPD) was founded in 1984 by the psychiatrist Bennet Braun, of the Rush North Shore Medical Center in Chicago. Braun was practicing psychiatry before he was board-certified and passed the oral part of the board exam in 1989 after three earlier failures (Irvine, 1999). When it came to promoting the importance of the idea of dissociation in psychiatric practice, Braun attracted a number of mental health professionals, won a reputation, and a movement was formed (Braun, 1986; Kluft, 1985; Kluft, Braun, and Sachs, 1984; Putnam et al., 1986). Soon the promotion of dissociation as a psychiatric category was not only a movement but also a cause.

The ISSMPD was also responsible for the next stage of the epidemic. The assumption was that MPD was the result of a massive childhood trauma. In 1988, Bennet Braun connected MPD with what became known as Satanic Ritual Abuse (SRA). Leaders of ISSMPD started educating the public about an underground intergenerational network of Satanists, responsible for killing thousands of children every year. Children born into Satanic families witnessed their siblings, or other children, being sacrificed and were subject to other forms of abuse. The resulting trauma then led to dissociation and MPD. The concepts of "recovered memory," SRA, and MPD became inseparable (Nathan and Snedeker, l995).

Paul McHugh describes the development of what he calls the "Mannerist Freudian" view:

> They picked up Sybil, multiple personality, and shameful buried traumas from Cornelia Wilbur. They threw in repression, symptom formation, and psychic defenses. They ended up by explaining mental disorders in a way that seemed at once fashionable and linked to tradition. (2008: 21)

Starting in the 1980s, there were thousands of allegations, reportedly based on "recovered memories" discovered during psychotherapy (and reported by therapists), about rituals that are an integral part of a secret religion that worships Satan. Bottoms and Davis (1997: 120) report that in "95% of ritual abuse cases reported to us, the allegations were first disclosed in therapy."

Young et al.'s (1991) study reports on a sample of 37 individuals, 34 women and three men, who are described as reporting ritual abuse. Among the activities supposedly reported by the patients, we find witnessing animal mutilation/killings (reported by 37 out of 37), witnessing and forced participation in human adult and infant sacrifice (reported by 31 out of 37), forced cannibalism (30 of 37), marriage to Satan (26 out of 33 females), and forced impregnation and sacrifice of their own child (20 of 33 females). The authors do not suggest that these reports are true but consider them spontaneous. The authors admit that they used hypnosis and wonder about the implications of that fact in terms of their credibility.

A survey of the US population found that 9 percent of the sample reported seeing therapists who raised the possibility of "repressed abuse," and 5 percent reported recovering memories of abuse in treatment. Those who recovered abuse memories were twenty times more likely to have seen psychotherapists who mentioned repressed memories of abuse. Recovered memories of abuse were mostly associated with those who reported starting therapy in the 1990s (Patihis and Pendergrast, 2019).

The therapists who were telling the world about dissociation, trauma, and Satanism were supposedly relying on evidence from clients who, during intensive treatment, recovered memories of childhood abuse. Braun and his colleagues argued that they uncovered connections, which had been neglected or overlooked, between childhood trauma, repressed and recovered, MPD and SRA, and this was a major breakthrough in the history of psychiatry and in the history of religion.

The religion they uncovered was alleged to exist underground, hidden from our everyday knowledge, but involving many thousands of individuals and families. Just like any religious tradition, this one purportedly had been transmitted across generations for many hundreds of years. It involves the most gruesome deeds humans can imagine as necessary components of its rituals, and so not only its adherents but also its victims number many thousands. Human sacrifice, and especially child sacrifice, is central to its practices.

The realization that a Satanic underground, which sanctifies cruelty and aims at creating a world of pure malice and pure lust, has always been with us, side by side with our respectable, visible reality, forces us to rethink and reevaluate everything we know, or claim to know, about humanity, history, and culture.

If indeed such a secret religion exists, we will be forced to revise everything we know about human history, human culture, and human behavior, as our ideas of human evil, the horrifying deeds we are ready to ascribe to fellow humans, were being challenged. This implied a radical revolution not only of all our concepts about the visible and the invisible in humanity. If there is any truth to these allegations, something must be done to stop these monstrous activities; if there is not, some judgment must be made about those who make these claims.

Beliefs about imaginary religions are just as instructive as observations of actual ones in learning about the religious imagination.

The idea of human sacrifice, especially child sacrifice, and of related cruel and repulsive practices, such as cannibalism (the eating of human flesh and the drinking of human blood), has been found quite often in all known cultures. When claims were being made, in the form of eyewitness testimonies, about the reality of such practices, we may tend to dismiss them as reflecting individual psychopathology. If such suggestions gain currency, we are faced with a transition from bizarre individual ideation to folklore and modern mass culture. The most unlikely aspect of this phenomenon was the involvement of psychotherapy practitioners, including some prominent psychiatrists. Here the stories were being used, consumed, and manipulated by supposedly reputable (and credentialed) professionals.

This was how Braun presented his work in its heyday:

> Another doctor who believes that MPD is fairly common is Bennett Braun, medical director of the dissociative-disorders program at Rush-Presbyterian-St. Luke's Medical Center in Chicago. Braun says the number of cases of MPD has risen not for faddish reasons but because therapists have become better at recognizing the symptoms.

In his twelve-bed unit at Rush North Shore Medical Center in Skokie, a branch of Rush-Presbyterian-St. Luke's Medical Center, Braun treats MPD cases, some of whom think that they are victims of SRA. When he first began to hear the Satanic stories in 1985, Braun says, he was incredulous. Now, having heard similar tales from many people from different states and countries and having treated more than 200 of them, he declares, "Yes, there is satanic-ritual abuse" (Jaroff, 1993).

When the fantasy of a Satanic religion was claimed to be a reality and this claim was made by psychiatrists, psychologists, and social workers, we were faced with a puzzle and a challenge. Such claims were being heard, since the 1980s, in Canada, the United States, Great Britain, Australia, New Zealand, the Netherlands, and Sweden. The phenomenon was international in scope, though concentrated mostly in English-speaking countries. In the spring of 1995, I had the honor of attending an informal lecture by Nobel Laurate Doris Lessing, at Keats House in London. She spoke about her life, her writings, and about modern society. About the latter, she did not neglect to mention the Satanists engaged in human sacrifice as another symptom of our collective decline.

A series of shocking testimonies appeared, some on television, first in North America and then elsewhere, seeking to acquaint us with the realities of a hidden world coexisting with ours. In that subterranean universe, rituals of cruelty on a massive scale were carried out, and ultimate evil was the goal. This world had been hidden from our view for most of human history, and while its existence was often hinted, rumored, or claimed, now, in our modern times, it was to be proven decisively.

Between 1970 and 2000, the belief in a Satanic conspiracy involving horrifying rituals, performed by parents on their children, gained a certain degree of acceptance in the United States and Britain (La Fontaine, 1994; Lotto, 1994; Mulhern, 1991, 1994; Nathan and Snedeker, 1995; Richardson, Best, and Bromley, 1991; Spanos, 1996). There is now a significant body of literature dealing with "SRA" or "Satanists" as a "mental health" issue, connected to "recovered memory" and MPD, some of which written by believers, and most of it published before 2000 (Ganaway, 1995; Jonker and Jonker-Bakker, 1991; Kelley, 1989; Lundberg-Love, 1988; Mayer, 1991; Moriarty, 1992; Raschke, 1990; Schmuttermaier and Veno, 1999; Smith, 1993; Snow and Sorensen, 1990; Young et al., 1991).

It would be wrong to suggest that belief in Satanism was universal in American society among mental health professionals at any point. There were doubting voices and determined dismissals of all claims. There was an official Federal Bureau of Investigation (FBI) report that found no evidence for (Lanning, 1992). It should be noted that some prominent mental health professionals have been critical of the Satanism Craze. One of them stated, "Despite almost a decade of sensational allegations, no independent evidence has emerged to corroborate these claims" (Putnam, 1993: 85). In both the elite and the mass media, there have been disbelief and ridicule. "Sensible people can only scoff at reports of widespread Satanic rituals in which Babbitts consume the flesh and blood of babies" (Lewontin, 1995: 24). This is how a renowned biologist at Harvard University responded, on the pages of the highbrow *New York Review of Books*.

The fact that most first-person testimonies have been formed within the framework of "recovered memory therapy" has been a major cause of skepticism. Some professionals have criticized the use of "therapy" to elicit hidden memories of early abuse (Yapko, 1994). Parents who have been damaged by accusations of child abuse on the part of adult children did fight back (Goldstein, 1992).

These fantasies of sacrifice tell us something about those who consider them true. "Only a sick mind would invent something like this," say some believers, and this may indeed be the case. A small subset of the general population is responsible for the appearance of the Satanism epidemic, because of their vulnerabilities and sensitivities. It has been suggested quite convincingly (Mulhern, 1991) that contemporary Satanism accounts resulted from a relatively small minority of highly disturbed, highly suggestible, individuals, who are in therapy with a group of unethical psychotherapists. According to Mulhern (1991), 5 to 10 percent of the clinical population, who are highly hypnotizable and suggestible, are likely to report the most bizarre testimonies, in response to the slightest suggestion. This inference is supported by the Goodman et al. (1994) report, which found that a small number of professionals were responsible for most of the cases. It seems that certain professionals become Satanism "specialists" and "uncover" many alleged cases.

In the global media, there have been allegations of "Satanic" crimes. In 1989, there were killings carried out by criminals in Matamoros, Tamaulipas, Mexico, tied to drug trafficking. Adolfo Constanzo (1962–89) a criminal who offered divination and "secret spells" to leading drug cartel operatives, who were ready to pay for his advice, was eventually charged. Constanzo performed animal sacrifices as part of his sorcery, and in the late 1980s decided that the use of human body parts would improve the effectiveness of his practices. More than 20 individuals were murdered, and some of the killings seemed ritualistic, because of victims being horribly mutilated. A rumor started about the killings being part of Satanic rituals. It turned out that the mutilations reflected Constanzo's connection to the Palo Mayombe Afro-Cuban religion. Palo Mayombe uses human remains, usually robbed from graves (Gill, Rainwater, and Adams, 2009).

As shocking as these crimes were, they could not have anything to do with the imaginary religion of Satanism, described by Braun and Hammond (Andrade and Redondo, 2019). Believers in the existence of Satanism still used sensational reports of this event as supporting evidence (Provost, 1989).

Michelle Remembers (Smith and Pazder, 1980) is the prototype of modern Satanism narratives, presented with the authoritative aura of a psychiatric case study. The book is also introduced and presented within a Roman Catholic framework and comes with an official church imprimatur. Michelle, who was diagnosed as having MPD, and enters therapy in the 1970s, recovers memories of her childhood in the 1950s. This happens with the help of hypnosis over many months. These elements of "recovered memories" and "multiple personality" are encountered in most of these testimonies. What we don't have in many other cases, but we get from Michelle Smith, is Satan visiting, in person, the rallies attended by hundreds of his followers in Victoria, British Columbia. A picture in the book shows us a rash that is a "body memory" of being touched by Satan.

The descriptions provided by Michelle Smith are shocking because sadistic acts are carried out in cold blood, sans passion:

> However bizarre and helter-skelter the rituals might have seemed ... they were in fact carefully orchestrated ... Their rituals are really formal and established ... nothing really spontaneous is allowed to happen. (Smith and Pazder, 1980: 126–7)

If we look at "Michelle" as a work of literature, it is really a fable of innocence and evil. Rituals of evil are meticulously devised to corrupt the innocence of a perfect child. It is also a religious tract, in which Roman Catholic popular devotions meet "professional" mental health practice. Dr. Lawrence Pazder, the psychiatrist, who first treated Michelle, and then became her second husband, is also Roman Catholic.

The apotheosis is a cosmic battle between the Virgin Mary and Jesus against Satan, in which good (surprise!) triumphs over evil. The story is full of holes and inconsistencies, but its several messages are clear. In addition to the idea of the massive underground organization of Satanists, the role of Michelle's parents is notable. Her father apparently deserted the family quite early on. Her mother was a Satanist, eagerly offering her child to other Satanists, to be tortured and tempted. The mother's cruelty and betrayal (forgiven by the daughter) are the subtext of the whole narrative.

What Exactly Is Satanism?

I am relying on quotations from the Sinason (1994b) book, a collection of chapters by mostly British mental health professionals. Ritual abuse is defined as

> the involvement of children in physical, psychological or sexual abuse associated with repeated activities (ritual) which purport to relate the abuse to contexts of a religious, magical, supernatural kind. (Bentovim and Tranter, 1994: 102)

SRA is described as the deliberate infliction of suffering on others as part of a prescribed ritual system, not for any sadistic gratification. What the stories emphasize is the scripted style, and the religious nature, of the activity, which is a ceremony, not a spontaneous eruption of evil impulses. Clinicians who promoted the Satanism Craze emphasized its sacrificial logic:

> Ritually abused patients have experienced concrete enactments of primitive and very violent scenarios of murder, dismemberment and cannibalism, which for other people are mere phantasies. (Mollon, 1994: 145)

> Satanic worship is manifested by the holding of ceremonies, the denigration of Christianity and the instruction of children. Satanic ceremonies, Sabbats, occur usually in the middle of the night and take place in barns, churches, churchyards, crypts, cemeteries, tunnels, caves, cellars, ruined abbeys, castles or derelict houses ... accounts are consistent regarding robes with hoods or masks being worn ... at other times the participants are naked ... Men and women ... worship Satan as their god ... In so doing they turn upside down any moral concept that comes with Christianity. They practice every sexual perversion that exists with animals, children and both sexes. They drink blood and urine and eat faeces and insects. They are involved in pornographic films and drug-dealing as a means of raising money. They are highly organized, successful in their secrecy and have a belief that through this pain and abuse they are getting closer to their god. (Sinason, 1994a: 3)

Sinason emphasized that Satan worship is going to be expressed through the worst acts she can imagine.

[Valerie Sinason was a consultant child psychotherapist at the Tavistock Clinic, and Honorary Lecturer at the Anna Freud Centre and University College London Psychology Department.]

Here is another description, written by a British psychiatrist:

> Young children, born into the cult, who were unable to walk or talk, having been kept from childhood in hanging cages, within the basement of a large house ...

they did not cry or scream ... but whimpered occasionally ... they were brought out only for abuse or experimental operations performed by the cult leader ... Some of them were sacrificed. (Coleman, 1994: 243). [Dr. Joan Coleman was Associate Specialist in Psychiatry at Heathlands Mental Health Services, Surrey.]

Please note: This is not a scene from a novel or film; it is supposed to be the reality somewhere in Britain in the 1990s. What is shocking is not the story, obviously a bizarre piece of fiction, but its seeming plausibility to those who are supposedly sophisticated and critical.

A central element in Satanism allegations was that such occurrences were far from rare, with vast numbers of children and adults involved. What is original here is the idea of the secret transmission of horrifying traditions and rituals over thousands of years, and in many countries, until now never detected, and now miraculously uncovered. The idea of a secret, underground, international religion sometimes takes the form of old claims about known groups (Masons, Mormons) only now finally exposed as part of the Satanist network.

Braun (1988) claimed,

We are working with a national–international type organization that's got a structure somewhat similar to the Communist cell structure, where it goes from local small groups to local councils, regional councils, district councils, national councils, and they have meetings at different times. (quoted in deYoung, 1996b: 240)

If such a secret organization exists, this should be brought to the attention of all world governments, and not just your local police. We should raise an army to fight these killers!

If true, this is certainly the most important discovery in the history of research on world religions. We just must wonder why this breakthrough in our knowledge of human history (totally unknown to professional historians) has occurred, and why was it made by psychotherapists and their clients. If this secret activity has been going on for such a long time, why did we discover this only in the 1980s?

If you are aware of any Satanists who are engaged in murdering children and adults as part of their rituals, you should report it to the nearest police station. Braun and his allies claimed to have uncovered an international secret religion, with a membership of hundreds of thousands, devoted to killing thousands of helpless victims, but never turned to the police. According to court documents, Braun did contact the FBI, but then became convinced that the FBI (and the Central Intelligence Agency [CIA]) were part of the Satanist conspiracy.

The narratives relating to Satanism are of three kinds:

1. General claims, without personal involvement, or stories about a conspiracy "out there," involving Satanic cults, run by dangerous "others."
2. One level of personal involvement, where allegations come from parents, who accuse their children's caretakers of abusing them as part of Satanist rituals. Children's testimonies are said to support the allegations.

    In 1990, a nursery school volunteer in a charismatic church in Southern California was charged with forty-three counts of abusing nine children, aged three to five years, under his care. The accusations against Dale Akiki included allegations of sacrificing animals (in one case an elephant and a giraffe) in front of the children and forcing them to drink blood (Granberry, 1993). He was also reported to have sacrificed a baby in front of the children.

    After two and a half years in prison and the longest trial in the history of San Diego County, Akiki, who is severely deformed because of a rare disease, and mildly retarded, was acquitted of all charges.

    In Oude Pekela, the Netherlands, an epidemic of Satanism accusations started in 1988. Hundreds of children allegedly reported being made to swallow feces and urine, being sexually abused and forced to participate in the making of pornographic movies and witnessing rituals in which babies were murdered. There was no evidence for the allegations, but Satanism crusaders still mention the case as proof.
3. Direct personal involvement testimonies. "It happened to me. My parents were Satanists" (Wright, 1994). These allegations were made by adults, who were accusing their parents. These testimonies are not Friend-of-a Friend (FOAF) stories. They are reported as personal recollections, not as secondhand accounts. The witnesses and their testimonies are at the center of the Satanism Craze, as their accusations are the most detailed and dramatic.

First-Person Accounts

Most first-person accounts of Satanism, which are usually quite detailed, were reported to appear during psychotherapy (Young et al., 1991). The individuals allege that "they are the victims of abuse involving sexual torture, human sacrifice and cannibalism by international religious cults worshipping Satan" (Putnam, 1993: 85). As will become clear, we have reason to believe that the so-called first-person accounts were suggested (or dictated) to the alleged victims by the mental health professionals supposedly charged with treating them.

What follows are more quotations from the Sinason (1994b) volume. The authors seek to persuade us that the imaginary activities are scripted and well-attended:

> Her uncle, who wore "long funny clothes," held a chicken over her and strangled it. He then cut the chicken open and collected its blood in a glass. The other men dipped long sticks into the blood and had used it to draw marks on their faces and bodies. The sticks were then inserted into Helen's vagina. (Morris, 1994: 162) [Steve Morris was a "counsellor, freelance consultant, and psychotherapist in training" (159).]

> A memory of a ceremony in which blood from a headless chicken was spilled over a plain white dress she was wearing ... her father, taking on the appearance or costume of Satan, had intercourse with her. Although adopted she came to believe that she was the product of a ritual satanic intercourse between her adoptive father and her biological mother—so that she was identified as the "devil's daughter"— she was made to go to church twice every Sunday, and she now believes that this was done to increase her value as an object of defilement. Many further scenes of horror, macabre, obscene and criminal in the extreme, have ... emerged ... the image of a baby being fed a bottle of blood. (Mollon, 1994: 143)

> From at least age 6 and probably age 3, she had been subjected to repeated intercourse, both anal and vaginal, by a large group of people and by animals. It also seemed that she had participated in, and possibly been made to be active in, some ritual mutilations and probably murders of three young children and one young man. (Cooklin and Barnes 1994: 122)

> She was still not sure how old she was—perhaps about 7 ... Somebody had arrived from a long way away who was called a warlock. A man was brought from somewhere who looked very ill (unconscious, drugged?). With some large ceremonial knife his throat was cut ... Then a woman knelt down beside him and made another cut in his neck and drained blood into a kind of bowl ... everyone was sitting around in a circle and a vessel was passed around containing blood. Helen only pretended to drink it, remembering a disgusting warm smell. (Mollon, 1994: 138)

The Common Elements of Satanism Stories

The testimonies allege that children are exposed to animal mutilations, then animal sacrifice (including pets), sometimes human mutilations (fingers, nipples, and penis), sexual abuse, impregnation, child sacrifice, baby breeding for ritual sacrifice, and incest. One psychiatrist working with dissociation cases stated that half the patients in his clinic had "vividly detailed memories of cannibalistic revels, and ... being used by cults during adolescence as serial baby breeders for ritual sacrifices," which killed 50,000 victims a year (Ganaway, 1989: 211). "Breeders" who told stories of childbirth and gruesome sacrifices they experienced directly were popular on television shows in the United States between 1988 and 1992 (deYoung, 1996a).

The unique and most striking element in the contemporary Satanism discourse is the role ascribed to the witness' own parents, who are portrayed as Satanists. Unlike other historical accusations, where outsiders (Christians, Jews, "heretics") play the role of human monsters, here parents and other relatives take the lead in torturing and even killing their own flesh and blood as part of Satanic rituals. The theme of familial, transgenerational version of this fantasy is unique to late twentieth-century culture. If such stories have been told before, they were rare, word-of-mouth legends. Since the 1980s they have become part of "mental health" literature. The typical first-person testimony is of a child born to Satanic parents.

The conscious message contained in Satanism testimonies is one of betrayal, disillusionment, and the shocking loss of innocence. Some of those promoting Satanism narratives tie the alleged child sacrifice to ancient and timeless practices.

Following are some detailed claims offered by a true believer:

> Differential infanticide (killing more girl babies) is the rule in tribes all the way back to the child sacrifice of infants to Beast-Goddesses that took place in Paleolithic caves, Jericho and Stonehenge ...
>
> The children who watched their mothers killing or eating babies suddenly avoided their parents, shrieked in their presence, or expressed unusual fear of them ... recounting dreams about animal-man beings with the faces of parents smeared with blood. (DeMause, 2009: 195). [These are DeMause's fantasies about parental cruelty.]
>
> Also, most African tribal mothers still kill at least one of their children, sometimes as a child sacrifice to the gods. (DeMause, 2009: 209)

DeMause will have us believe that killing babies is routine in many cultures.

This Is Real!

The simplest explanation for the epidemic of Satanism stories is that Satanism is a reality, but this simple explanation is not likely to be correct. Is there a chance that one day the international Satanist conspiracy will be fully exposed, and all the skeptics will be finally defeated and humiliated? One of the paradoxes of contemporary Satanism allegations is the fact that Satanism has been exposed in numerous books, articles, films, and testimonies since the 1970s, and all the while, it remains hidden from sight.

And how did it happen that this great unmasking started when it did, and not earlier or later? If we take the stories seriously, what we have here is a massive failure of the Satanists, as hundreds of victims, one by one, have escaped their clutches to tell the world what was really going on. And still, there is no evidence of anybody having been harmed by this reportedly powerful underground network.

Why should we not accept the claims for the reality of SRA?

1. Not only is the claim of human sacrifice supported by no evidence, but any case of anybody worshipping Satan, even without sacrifices, remains to be proven. Both historically and psychologically, there is no evidence for the idea of devil-worship. There has never been any case of a true religious group devoted to worshipping the devil.

    Christians and Muslims believe in the devil, but there has never been a case in which the devil has been perceived as a religious object, i.e., the source of reported communications, visions, or ecstasy. The entities populating the invisible spirit world in any religious beliefs system may include demons, but they are rarely venerated or worshipped. Most often they are acted against. Many religious groups have been accused of being in league with the Devil, but there has never been a religion in which "Satan" has been a sole, or major, deity.

So called "Satanic churches" in the United States and in Europe represent commercial ventures or countercultural theater, or both, but I still have to be convinced that any of their members believe in Satan in the same way that religious believers think about, and experience, their deities. "Satanic" scriptures seem like purely intellectual (or commercial) exercises, devoid of any religious sentiment.

The idea of worshipping Satan seems singularly unattractive to most humans. If there has ever been a religion of Satanism, it has escaped all notice. Checking out the vast literature we now have on world religions does not lead to any traces of a religion based on the worship of Satan by any name. It does reveal, however, a plethora of accusations about somebody, somewhere worshipping the Devil or committed to witchcraft. The scholarly verdict on the idea of witchcraft or

Satanism is clear and resounding; it is mere fantasy. It is significant that all experts on the history of religions are not aware of global Satanism as described by Braun et al.

2. The onus is on the believers in to prove the reality of Satanism and Satanists. In all alleged Satanism cases there is no corroborative evidence beyond the testimonies, and none of them can survive scrutiny. There are many documented cases of rape, torture, every kind of abuse imaginable and unimaginable inflicted on children within families and outside of families, but not one corroborated case of abuse, torture, or even benign rituals carried out as part of a Satanist religion.

    But how is it that these crimes are so often recalled years later, and no one was ever caught in the act? The enormity of the crimes seems to be matched by the elusiveness of the evidence for them. These allegations remind us so much of the amazing feats of mediums and various ghost stories, which the Society for Psychical Research has been looking into since 1882. All these miraculous events cannot bear a close examination, and they evaporate into thin air as soon as more critical minds get close to the scene.

Satanism, if it exists, is a crime, and as such should be uncovered, or stumbled upon, by law enforcement authorities, or by accident. These allegations are first and foremost reports of horrendous criminality, and should, in the real world, first be treated as such. This does not happen.

The lack of physical evidence is remarkable. Despite the tens of thousands of alleged Satanic acts, not one item of tangible evidence has ever been presented. A single blood stain, a single foot track, a single speck of ashes, or a single scar would go a long way toward establishing the reality of alleged activities involving thousands, tens of thousands, or millions of individuals. Such evidence is still being awaited.

This seems to be the perfect crime, as there is no physical evidence, and the perpetrators are never caught. This perfect crime is apparently committed intelligently and methodically by supermen and superwomen. Even though many of the stories include verifiable details regarding the identity of perpetrators, law enforcement authorities are only rarely called in.

The absence of any effort to find the perpetrators and punish them seems amazing, as the following quotation shows: A man who claimed to be a reformed Satanist did once consult me but, after telling me of a ritual murder of a recalcitrant member of the group, he declined to continue seeing me" (Mollon, 1994: 140). So why didn't Dr. Mollon go the authorities with this information?

Instead of such simple steps as going to the police and searching for hard evidence, we hear stories about an incredibly efficient mass conspiracy. All conspiracy theories attribute superhuman cunning to hidden perpetrators, helped by thousands of collaborators in high places.

The conspiracy delusion includes the fantasy of the paranoid pseudo-community, which consists of real and imaginary people, all united in one effort: "To complete his conceptual organization of a paranoid conspiracy, the patient also introduces imaginary persons ... helpers, dupes, stooges, go-betweens, and master-minds, of whose actual experience he becomes certain" (Cameron, 1963: 56).

There were two systematic surveys of alleged Satanism reports done in the 1990s. Both the La Fontaine report in Britain (La Fontaine, 1994) and the Goodman et al. reports in the United States (Bottoms et al., 1995; Bottoms, Shaver, and Goodman, 1996; Goodman et al., 1994) concluded that there was no evidence for SRA or a Satanic religion. The US report looked at religion-related abuse, including things such as child abuse by clergy, exorcisms, and the denial of proper medical care for religious reasons. They concluded that "there are many more children being abused in the name of God than in the name of Satan" (Goodman et al., 1994: 14; Goodman et al., 1998). The British report found three cases in which pedophile men used "Satanist" trappings to threaten children who had been molested. In all cases, they were strangers, not family members. In 2012, an academic review of cases of child abuse tied to spirit possession, witchcraft, and ritual was published in London. It concluded that very few such cases had been reported, and even if underreporting is assumed, as it should be, they represent a tiny fraction of the real maltreatment of children (Simon et al., 2012). Such reports may be dismissed, of course, by the true believers as the work of Satan or his followers.

Animal mutilation claims, which were mentioned by Young et al. (1991) as reported by all their cases, became a common topic in the US media over the years as evidence of Satanic activities. These allegations were examined by veterinarians, and turned out to be completely fictional, or in a few cases, carried out by grossly disturbed individuals (McDonough and Holoyda, 2018).

3. A third reason for not accepting Satanism stories is their obvious similarity to claims already made in other times and places. Promoters of the Great Satanism Conspiracy seem to be ignorant of similar historical phenomena, and of stories told about Jews in the Christian world, Yezidis in the Islamic world, and witches in Europe between the fourteenth and eighteenth

centuries. The Great Satanism Conspiracy reminds us too much of similar modern conspiracy theories about the Illuminati, the freemasons, the Jesuits, and the Elders of Zion.

The renowned philosopher Ian Hacking (1995) regarded the epidemic of MPD diagnoses, which started with the publication of *Sybil* in 1973, as an irreversible turning point in the way we think about identity. Even though he was aware of the connection between MPD, "recovered memory," and Satanism allegations, and of at least one lawsuit against Bennett Braun, accusing him of "finding three hundred ... personalities" (1995: 123), and of Colin Ross and his theories of the CIA's role in the creation of multiple personalities, Hacking still took the MPD phenomenon to be a reflection of advances in psychiatry. He asserted that "multiple personality is not usually 'iatrogenic' ... it might still be that many of the florid bits of multiple behavior are iatrogenic" (1995: 12). Hacking approach is naïve and uncritical, as we shall see below.

As the twenty-first century began, the epidemic seemed to fade. There were precipitous declines in the frequency of reports about recovered memories, multiple personalities, or Satanists at work. If all these phenomena are real, how can we explain such a precipitous decrease in their prevalence, and why did they disappear from public view together after 2000, just the way they had appeared in the 1980s? If recovered memories, multiple personality, and Satanists were so real and prevalent as once claimed, how could they so completely disappear? (It turned out that reports of child sexual abuse without any Satanism allegations declined at the same time, see Finkelhor and Jones, 2006.)

The end of the dissociation epidemic is especially interesting. Why has the diagnosis become so rare again? Large fluctuations in the prevalence of diagnostic labels must cause concern. Credentialed professionals were telling us in the 1980s that MPD, which later became DID manifested itself in at least 1 percent of the population. What happened to that 1 percent? Large fluctuations in the prevalence of particular diagnostic categories must raise doubts about its reality.

One reason for the dramatic decline might be the large sums of money, in tens of millions, paid out by insurance companies to former MPD–DID–Satanism psychotherapy clients, who went to court to pursue their therapists.

Bennet Braun, the person most identified with the dissociation cause, was the defendant in some of the best-known legal cases, after being sued for malpractice twelve times. The legal proceedings showed dramatically and unequivocally how the DID–Satanism enterprise victimized individuals and families.

Such is the case of Elizabeth Gale, who entered therapy with Braun in 1986 for serious depression, and during the next eleven years was hospitalized eighteen times for a total of 2,000 days. She was made to believe that she had MPD and was active in an intergenerational Satanic cult. She was also made to believe that she was a "breeder," who had bred babies for the Satanists, who were sacrificed after birth. With the approval of Bennett Braun, in 1991, at age thirty-one, she went through a tubal ligation so that she would no longer harm children. In 2004, Bennett Braun and his colleague, the psychologist Roberta Sachs, paid Elizabeth Gale $7.5 million to settle her claim that they persuaded her that she needed to be sterilized so she would have any more babies to be sacrificed to Satan. Roberta Sachs (1990) claimed that not only did Satanic groups produce babies for sacrifice through "breeders," but that they also used "selective breeding for high dissociative ability" to produce well-disciplined children. Another colleague of Bennett Braun, who was part of the team that victimized Elizabeth Gale, Dr. Corydon Hammond (of the *Greenbaum Speech* fame, discussed earlier), paid $175,000 (Dardick, 2004). Elizabeth Gale never gave birth to any babies, and never will.

Braun was involved in another case that made history, thanks to one courageous woman. Patricia Burgus began experiencing depression in 1982. In 1986, she was admitted to Rush North Shore Medical Center in Chicago and began treatment with Braun (Irvine, 1999). Burgus was frequently being told about Satanism and human sacrifice. According to the narrative she was fed, her family had been involved in Satanism since 1604, and she had often born children who were then sacrificed. Eventually, she had become a High Priestess. Her eldest son was admitted to Rush North Shore Medical Center at age five, and the younger at age four. The children were hospitalized for three years to save them from being sacrificed. Burgus was released in 1992, and in 1993 sued Braun for malpractice. She ultimately accepted a settlement of $10.6 million from Bennett Braun and his colleague Elva Poznanski (Hanson, 1998; Ofshe and Watters, 1994).

In 1999, Braun's medical license was suspended for two years to Illinois, for "dishonorable, unethical and unprofessional conduct." He moved to Montana, regained a medical license, returned to psychiatry, and was sued once again for malpractice. In January 2021, Bennett G. Braun had his medical license revoked by the State of Montana.

In 2001, the American Psychiatric Association (APA) expelled Bennet Braun from membership "after Dr. Braun was found to have provided incompetent medical treatments unsupported by usual standards of practice; violated ethical boundaries with the patients, including inappropriate sexual behavior and exploitation; a seriously breached patient confidentiality with the media" (APA, 2001).

Another ISSMPD founder, who also served as its president twice, George Greaves, had his psychologist license revoked by the State of Georgia in 1994 for, among other things, having sex with patients and having sex with patients while under hypnosis. Dr. Greaves also agreed to retire from working as a psychologist in Ohio. It turned out that Dr. Greaves has a special interest in ethics (Greaves and Faust, 1996).

The Case of Gloria Steinem: Feminism, New Age, and Satanism

Gloria Steinem (1934–) has long been celebrated as one of the world's leading feminists and seems to have always been in the public eye, with every aspect of her life scrutinized. A look at a less examined chapter in her life finds that in addition to her many efforts on behalf of women, she managed to find the time and the energy to become involved in the craziest episode in the history of modern psychiatry, which victimized thousands of women, and has been a promoter of the notion of the secret religion of Satanism. Why did members of the feminist elite embrace the Satanism fantasy, and how is Gloria Steinem involved?

Gloria Steinem met Bennet Braun in Chicago in 1986, while on a journalistic assignment, and became an instant admirer and disciple. Her attachment to Braun energized her involvement in the cause. The record shows that Steinem was not just an observer who commented on cultural developments, but an active member of the dissociation movement.

At the 1990 ISSMPD conference, there were already some skeptical voices about Satanism claims. There were at least two psychiatrists who were concerned about the reputation of the ISSMPD being harmed by Satanism stories. There were also two speakers who told the audience that any reports about Satanists were delusional nonsense. Richard Noll, a clinical psychologist and historian, was one of them. Following his talk, he was approached by Gloria Steinem, who suggested some materials he should read that would help him change his view of Satanism stories (Noll, 2013).

Steinem thanked Bennet Braun in her book *Revolution from Within* (1993). In the 1994 meeting of the ISSMPD, he received an award from Steinem, for his services to women. In 1993, *Ms.* magazine, a feminist flagship, published a cover story titled "Surviving the Unbelievable: A First-Person Account of Cult

...nted as true story by a woman who grew up in a Satanic ...ed babies and practiced cannibalism. According to the article, ...er baby sister being decapitated and eaten, and a young boy's ...s is in addition to having been raped by both men and women, ...ith crucifixes. The *Ms.* cover proclaimed, "Believe It! Cult Ritual ...ts! One Woman's Story" (Rose, 1993).

...m's writings reflect her commitment to the dissociation movement. In ...-help book, *Revolution from Within* (1993), she addressed specifically the ...y of repressed memories and multiple personalities. Here is some of what she wrote:

> Perhaps, the memory has been pushed out of our consciousness completely. But those images and feelings remain alive in our unconscious—and they can be uncovered ... (Steinem, 1993: 72)

> There are telltale signs of such buried trauma ... fear of expressing anger at all; substantial childhood periods of which you have no memory of emotions or events ... depression ... severe eating disorders ... Trust these clues—there is statistical as well as personal evidence that the conditions they point to are widespread.

> Perhaps a third of the children in the United States have been subjected to sexual and other kinds of severe abuse or neglect. ... Frequently, such memories are so painful that they don't surface fully until years after the events occurred. The more extreme and erratic these events, the younger we were when we experienced them, and the more dependent we were on the people who inflicted them, the more repressed they are likely to be. (Steinem, 1993: 162–3)

Steinem here presents none other than Freud's theory of the etiology of hysteria, which he discussed in the 1890s. According to Sigmund Freud and Josef Breuer, the problem in hysteria was not repression but incomplete repression. Steinem, who has compared Freud to Hitler, doesn't realize that she has become a Freudian. Some version of Freud's idea of repression became a feminist battle cry.

Things get curiouser and curioser as we read on. *Revolution from Within* contains a bizarre section that praises MPD as increasing individual potential and talents:

> Suppose, for instance, that ... you could:
>
> — change your brain's right- or left-hemisphere dominance to the opposite side—and back again—regardless of your biological sex ...

- raise or lower your pulse rate, blood pressure, temperature, level of oxygen need, and thresholds of pain and pleasure;
- eliminate an allergic reaction ... or create an allergic reaction ...; ... reexperience your mind's stored memories of the past as if they were happening in the present;
- call up your body's somatic memory of everything that has happened to it with such clarity that "ghosts" of past wounds and bruises reappear on your skin in minutes, and then slowly disappear as you leave the memory;
- activate visions of a past or future state of health so powerful that they can speed the healing of current wounds, measurably strengthen the immune system, and give you access at any time to the superhuman abilities usually reserved for emergencies;
- change voice depth and timbre ... body language ... darken the color of your eyes—so totally that an unwitting observer would assume you to be of a different ethnicity, age, race, class, or gender from one moment to the next;
- change your response to medication—or achieve that medication's result without taking it—and thus have all the benefits of a tranquilizer, sleeping pill, "upper," or anesthetic, but none of the side effects;
- heighten or lessen sexual desire, and widen or narrow the range of those people for whom you feel it;
- adjust your body's response to lunar and diurnal cycles;
- bring into one true self the strengths of all the selves you have ever been in every setting and situation from infancy to now.

All of these abilities have been demonstrated—and verified through a wide variety of double-blind tests, brain scanning, and other objective techniques—in people who have what is called "multiple personality disorder," or MPD ...

People in different alters can change every body movement, perfect a musical or linguistic talent that is concealed to the host personality, have two or even three menstrual cycles in the same body and handle social and physical tasks of which they literally do not think themselves capable ... What the future could hold, and what each of us could become, is limited mainly by what we believe. (Steinem, 1993: 316–19)

In the delusional statements above, Steinem tells us not only that woman with MPD can have "two or even three menstrual cycles in the same body," but also that they develop unimaginable abilities, including having all the benefits of "a tranquilizer, sleeping pill, 'upper,' or anesthetic," without taking them. In this insane portrayal, MPD is no longer a pathology, but the royal road to humanity's future. So now the pathology of multiple personality has become a gift, making individuals into "accidental prophets," in an incredible display of New Age psychobabble. This utopian nonsense is just as ridiculous as the stories about parents sacrificing their children to Satan. It is not the only bizarre claim in the book, which is really a New Age product with the usual advice on "spirituality" and meditation.

Revolution from Within: A Book of Self-Esteem has been sold by the millions and is still selling. Not a word has been changed since 1993, and we can assume that Steinem still holds the same views on repression and multiple personality. Most accounts of her life you may run into do not mention her commitment to Bennet Braun and the dissociation movement. In 2015, Steinem published an autobiography (*My Life on the Road*), which is naturally selective and unreliable, as such works are. It does not mention her involvement with Braun, but the book ends with an "About the Author" section, and there we find the following sentence: "In 1993, her concern with child abuse led her to co-produce an Emmy Award-winning TV documentary for HBO, *Multiple Personalities: The Search for Deadly Memories.*" Steinem was indeed co-producer and co-narrator (with Michael Mierendorf) of this HBO film.

Gloria Steinem aided and abetted the credentialed professionals who inflicted horrific suffering on many thousands of parents and children. Some may suggest an application of the sincerity test. Steinem was not going to profit and was sincere in her concern for victimized women. She failed to recognize the reality in which these women were victimized not by any Satanists, but by Dr. Braun and his partners.

As a major public opinion leader, political activist, and an icon of feminism, it is sad to realize that she could be so gullible and unthinking. Our wish to help those suffering abuse should not extinguish a basic level of critical thinking.

Catharine MacKinnon, another well-known feminist, joined the Satanism bandwagon in 1988. Later, she compared the victims of rape in Croatia to the survivors of ritual abuse in the United States (Nathan, 1994).

Joan Baez may be better known than both Gloria Steinem and Catharine MacKinnon. She has devoted her career to giving voice to the victims, and presented her song "Play Me Backwards" (1991) as dealing with "ritualistic child abuse," one among many ways in which children were being victimized (Baez, 1991).

This is another indication of how Satanism discourse was viewed as part and parcel of the struggle against oppression and injustice.

Victims of the Satanism Craze

The celebrated *Ingram* case in the United States (Wright, 1994) has been presented as paradigmatic of the epidemic, but on closer examination turns out to be atypical. In this case, which appeared in 1988 in Olympia, Washington, Paul Ingram, then forty-three years old, was accused of Satanic crimes. Ingram was a pillar of the community, chief deputy of the Thurston County sheriff's department and chairman of the county Republican Party. Ingram was a former Roman Catholic, who with his family became a Fundamentalist Protestant. They joined the Church of Living Water. Sandy Ingram, his wife, ran a day care center at their home.

Paul Ingram's two daughters, Ericka, twenty-two, and Julie, eighteen, accused him of assorted crimes, and he was arrested by his colleagues in the sheriff's department. The accusations first appeared three months before the arrest, at a church retreat, where a self-styled healer told a group of sixty girls that, according to a vision she had, somebody in the audience had been molested by a relative. Ericka Ingram responded by claiming to have been abused by her own father. Later Julie Ingram joined her sister in accusing their father, their brothers, and numerous others. Their mother, Sandy Ingram, also related accusations of rape and Satanic rituals.

The two daughters reported being molested and raped by their father, and by family friends, including police officers conducting the investigation, judges, physicians, lawyers, as well as having sex with their brother, and being raped by a dog. They also reported witnessing child sacrifice as part of Satanic rituals. One daughter reported having an abortion at age sixteen while being five months pregnant. The fetus was still alive when taken out, according to her story. It was then cut up and eaten by members of the Satanic group involved. Ericka claimed to have participated in 850 ritual sessions and witnessing twenty-five babies being sacrificed. The daughters' testimonies led to the conviction of their father, who was then serving a twenty-year sentence for acts of "gross indecency." The Satanism allegations were not cited by the prosecution, and he was only accused of six cases of rape (Wright, 1994). He was released in 2003.

Despite the scores of books and articles totally exonerating Ingram, there have been some doubters. Lanning (1996), based on his thirty years' experience with the FBI, advocates looking at each case and separating delusional allegations about Satanism from common crimes such as child abuse.

In addition to Paul Ingram, others have been imprisoned, most of them day care workers, who were unjustly accused of "ritual abuse" (De Young, 2004; Finkelhor and Williams, 1988). Some spent decades in prison. There was also the notorious case of three young men in Arkansas, who were convicted of murder "as part of a Satanic ritual" and were freed after serving eighteen years (Laycock, 2014).

While the debates about alleged perpetrators were raging, not enough attention was paid to the client-victims, the women described as the supposed bearers of revelations about childhoods spent in a Satanic family, and their real families. A few, such as Elizabeth Gale and Patricia Burgus, were recognized and compensated. Countless others were not.

A few shocking reports on women victimized by therapy did appear (Gangelhoff, 1995). The professionals involved were evil in the worst case, or sincere and deluded in the best case. Their treatment of the victimized women was cruel and sadistic. Is it possible that the Satanism epidemic was a cynical way of producing lavish profits?

Court cases made it clear that the stories about Satanist rituals were invented by therapists and fed (often forcefully) to their clients. This is how Ewing Werlein Jr., US District Judge for the Southern District of Texas, described the actions of MPD–Satanism therapists in 1999 after listening to weeks of detailed testimony:

> Numerous psychiatric patients who had generous, high dollar mental health insurance plans, who had been treated by various of Defendants over extremely long periods of time (one to two years and longer) while they were hospitalized at Spring Shadows Glen Psychiatric Hospital, and who demonstrated virtually no mental improvement (the reverse seemed to be typical) throughout their treatments, but who soon recovered once their insurance benefits had been exhausted or terminated and the patients were discharged and freed from the ostensible psychiatric and psychological care provided by Defendants.

> These Defendants diagnosed and/or treated various of these patients as members and/or victims of clandestine "Satanic cults" that committed horrendous crimes (e.g., murder, rape, cannibalism, etc.) upon their own members and their children. The evidence consistently revealed, however, that while these Defendants in different ways regularly encouraged their patients to divulge tales of such brutal crimes, which thereby perpetuated their insurance-paid "treatments," Defendants never reported any of these supposed crimes to the police for investigation. (Werlein, 1999). [The facility in Texas that Judge Werlein was discussing in the quotation above happened to be the location where the 1993 film on multiple personality, that Gloria Steinem was so proud of, had been produced.]

What Judge Werlein described was indeed a diabolical conspiracy, perpetrated and perpetuated by mental health professionals. With hindsight, it is obvious that these professionals might have been sincere but deluded. A classical delusional complex was created by the persuasive Dr. Braun. Even if we blame Braun for promoting "repressed memory," MPD, and Satanism, and even if he was remarkably persuasive, it was the support and involvement of other people that made the epidemic possible. The real casualties were the women manipulated by psychotherapy practitioners. These women, undoubtedly abused by the world around them, were desperately seeking a sense of worth and falling victim again to cynics. The trauma/dissociation model was a way of exploiting, oppressing, and humiliating women (Haaken, 1996).

In the twenty-first century, the Satanism Craze is being kept alive by a persistent camp of true believers. A survey in Germany found reports of groups teaching Satanic worship (Schröder et al., 2020). One can find a case study about a well-functioning man, a victim of Satanic abuse, who suffers from DID (Precin, 2011).

Richard Kluft remained a believer. In 2014, he stated, "I remain troubled about the matter of transgenerational satanic cults" (12) and advocated moderation:

> There is every reason to argue that many reports of satanic ritual abuse were ill founded, and to doubt the extent of what these reports alleged. There is also good reason to avoid going to the extreme of dismissing them completely. (Kluft, 2014: 9)

Colin Ross has been a major proponent of the MPD–DID–SRA connection. In addition to believing in the Satanist conspiracy, he also claims that the CIA creates multiple personalities and organizes the criticism of Satanism claims. While the CIA realized a long time ago that its various "mind control" programs were a joke, Ross did not. Like Corydon Hammond, he believes that Manchurian candidates, programmed with the required multiple personalities, are roaming the earth ready to carry out their secret missions. The technology utilized to create these agents remains just as much a secret (or a fantasy) as it ever was. Actually, Ross believes that

> in the interest of national security, it is important that the CIA and military intelligence agencies have mind control programs in place. This is true, for one reason, because mind control methods are being used by leaders of destructive cults, dictators and terrorists ... The problem is the conflict between the National Security Act and the Hippocratic Oath. (Ross, 2000: 266)

A number of suits for malpractice have marked Ross's career in Canada and then in the United States. According to court documents, he persuaded his patient Roma E. Hart that she was a member of a Satanic family, causing here to give up custody of her daughter to save her from the family legacy. She also became estranged from her parents because of that. In addition, Ms. Hart was persuaded that she gave birth to a hybrid alien–human baby, in the course of alien abduction (Ross, 1998).

Books and articles offering information on how to treat Satanism victims are still being published in the twenty-first century (e.g., Badouk-Epstein, Schwartz, and Schwartz, 2011, 2018; Matthew and Barron, 2015; Miller, 2018; Ross, 2017). The books by Badouk-Epstein, Schwartz, and Schwartz and by Miller deal not only with ritual abuse, but with victims of "Mind Control."

Valerie Sinason, a major figure in the Satanism Craze of the 1990s in Britain (Sinason, 1994b), has continued to speak out in the media and to author more publications (Frankish and Sinason, 2018; Sinason, 2011a, b; Sinason, Galton, and Leevers, 2008).

And here is some of what she had to tell a journalist in 2011:

> Sinason talks of a popular ritual in which a child is stitched inside the belly of a dying animal before being "reborn to Satan." During other celebrations, "people eat faeces, menstrual blood, semen, urine. There's cannibalism." Some groups have doctors performing abortions. "They give the foetus to the mother and she's made to kill the baby." "And the cannibalism—that's foetuses?" I clarify." Foetuses and bits of bodies." "Raw or cooked?" "The foetuses are raw." "Not even a bit of salt and pepper?" I ask. "Raw. And handed round like communion. On one major festival, the babies are barbecued. I can still remember one survivor saying how easy it is to pull apart the ribs on a baby. But adults are tougher to eat." (Storr, 2011)

What are we to make of Sinason's wild fantasies? There is an obvious desire to shock, but the moral of the story is that, as usual, the believers in Satanism tell us more than we want to hear about their hidden thoughts. We are indeed shocked, especially by what seems like the enjoyment in delving into details of the imagined scene.

In 2012, another autobiography of a Satanism survivor, including MPD–DID and recovered memory was published, written by her therapist, with a foreword by Colin Ross (Byington, 2012). The book contains all the ingredients we are familiar with, including the monstrous Dr. Green (Greenbaum). The heroine, Jenny Hill, and the therapist-author, Judy Byington, gained an appearance on the Dr. Phil show, which demonstrated the blatant exploitation of s seriously troubled woman on trash TV. It turned out that Ms. Byington is also a QAnon activist.

At least two organizations, the International Society for the Study of Trauma and Dissociation (ISSTD) and Stop Mind Control and Ritual Abuse Today (S.M.A.R.T.) still hold annual meetings, and some of the believers still produce publications that proclaim advances in theory (Dorahy, 2017). Still, in the absence of media attention, the movement is marginal, and only a small number of professionals take the Satanism message seriously.

One group of self-declared Satanists has recently attracted global media attention. The Satanic Temple is a group of atheists in the United States that has challenged the political establishment by inserting itself into any public display of religion. If a city allows the erection of the Ten Commandments in a public square, The Satanic Temple will demand the right to set up a statue of the "Satanic god Baphomet" next to it. In this way, the group has gained much attention and admiration for its creativity in ridiculing religion.

Following a totally different course, in 2015 The Satanic Temple formed a Grey Faction, which decided to publicly attack the ISSTD and S.M.A.R.T., as well as specific members of these organizations. We may consider anybody promoting ideas about recovered memory, dissociation, MPD–DID, or Satanism, to be in a pathetic and marginalized situation, but the Grey Faction, correctly, suggests that the damage caused by such mental health professionals, labeled by the Faction "conspiracy therapists" is sufficient to warrant acts of public shaming.

Real, horrifying crimes against children are being committed every day by family members and strangers all over the world (Richter, Dawes, and Higson-Smith, 2004). Child abuse is real, sexual abuse is real, incest is real, MPD may be real in extremely rare cases. Claims about Satanic rituals are different, because they are delusions, without any basis. If recovered memories include accounts of incest or torture, we know that in principle they could be about real events. If a psychiatrist claims an MPD diagnosis, we should be skeptical. If anybody claims to have uncovered an underground religion whose followers sacrifices their babies to Satan, we know that it is a crazy fantasy.

What he calls a "personal note," the philosopher Ian Hacking presented is a statement of faith in the reality of Satanism:

> I think it is possible that there have been and will be ongoing satanic rituals by organized sects in which children are viciously abused. I know that in my hometown, which has an undeserved reputation for being the most decent, safe,

urbane and dull large city in North America, goats are sacrificed to Satan on the roofs of warehouses only a few streets from my home. I fear that once any idea, no matter how depraved, is in general circulation, then someone will act it out. Even if a decade ago no goat-sacrificing Satanists tortured children, my lack of faith in human nature leads me to think it possible that some do so now. When vile stories are rampant, minds that are sufficiently confused, angry, and cruel will try to turn fiction into fact. It is possible that some local secret society, with loose relationship to other groups in other places, has gone completely off the deep end. Perhaps somebody, somewhere, has used an adolescent to breed a baby for human sacrifice. I sadly do not think it impossible for such things to happen—or even terribly unlikely. Hence in my view a person could in principle have rather accurate memories of such events. (Hacking, 1995: 284)

Hacking's fantasies and arguments are interesting. He makes two psychological arguments: First, that human beings are basically evil, and second, that any fantasy will be acted out by some humans, given the first assumption. The prediction about the acting out of vile fantasies is obviously wrong, and Hacking's claims about Satanic rituals are totally delusional.

We sometimes, but not too often, hear about abominable, shocking acts, which fit any and every definition of evil. In a well-documented case uncovered in the mid-1990s, Rosemary and Fred West committed a series of horrifying murders, preceded by sexual violence, in which they have killed at least ten young women, The victims included their own daughter, and Fred West's daughter by a previous marriage. The victims' bodies were all buried under their home in 25 Cromwell St., Winchester, England. The remains of the victims were uncovered in 1994, and in November 1995, Rosemary West, age forty-two, was sentenced to ten life sentences. Her husband Fred committed suicide at age fifty-three on January 1, 1995, in his prison cell. This story of depredation and perversion makes us shudder in disbelief (West and Hill, 1995; Woodrow, 2011). What were the motives of these human monsters? How did it happen that they apparently obtained sexual gratification through these indescribable acts of cruelty? Does this narrative inspire us to commit similar acts? As we know, very few people are inspired by such reports and commit such evil acts.

Is this related to Satanism allegations? No, it is not. Bizarre and horrible crimes do occur but their (well-documented) circumstances and their motives are totally unrelated to Satanism allegations (or to any other religion or tradition). They do not fit the presumed pattern of a secret religion or ritual.

They do not serve to achieve other ends, as ritual acts do, and do not follow any prescribed scripts. Sadistic humans do not need any religious scripts.

The Satanism Craze was marginal in terms of history, but many lives were still destroyed. Unimaginable suffering was meted out on thousands of women and their families by mental health professionals. Many of the victims were highly disturbed women who had experienced terrible personal histories before meeting the therapists who inflicted on them the narratives of Satanism and multiple personality.

Some Satanism claims enjoyed a significant and surprising revival, tied to the political rise of Donald Trump and the political movement he created. By 2020, many Americans were aware of a belief complex known as QAnon.

> QAnon is the umbrella term for a set of internet conspiracy theories that allege, falsely, that the world is run by a cabal of Satan-worshiping pedophiles.
>
> QAnon followers believe that this cabal includes top Democrats like President Joseph R. Biden Jr., Hillary Clinton, Barack Obama and George Soros, as well as a number of entertainers and Hollywood celebrities like Oprah Winfrey, Tom Hanks and Ellen DeGeneres and religious figures including Pope Francis and the Dalai Lama. Many of them also believe that, in addition to molesting children, members of this group kill and eat their victims to extract a life-extending chemical called adrenochrome. (Roose, 2020: B4)

What are we to make of this dramatic revival of Satanism fantasies, complete with child sacrifice and cannibalism? Is it related to the epidemic of the late twentieth century? There is a clear overlap in narrative between the two cultural phenomena, but there are significant differences.

QAnon seeks to attack the political elite, while the earlier delusional system described Satanists as our next-door neighbors. The psychiatrists and psychologists who started the Satanism Craze never mentioned politics, while trying to undermine parental authority.

4

Proximal Explanations for the Satanism Craze: Social Context

It is a truism to describe the Satanism Craze of the late twentieth century as a symptom of the times and social conditions. More needs to be said about specific conditions and actors that made the Satanism Craze possible.

The Satanism Craze was not a major social movement. It was a marginal phenomenon, not even officially defined as a "social problem," despite all the efforts to make it that. It has been classified by some as a "moral panic."

A moral panic, as described in the literature, started with a real event that has been exaggerated. In the case of Satanism, we are looking at fictions followed by other fictions and promoted by psychiatrists, first Cornelia Wilbur and then Bennett Braun, and other mental health professionals.

Smelser (1962) suggested that different kinds of stresses evoke anxieties and arouse beliefs of hysterical, wish fulfillment, and hostile types, with the consequences being social panics, crazes, and riots. Trying to account for the appearance of the Satanism Craze, we can look at research on related phenomena from other cultures.

Satanism stories could be also classified as rumors (a fantasy where hostility is "caught" and projected). Rumors are produced when humans suffer anxiety, insecurity, and helplessness, which occur often enough. In many cultures, we can find rumors about children and adults being kidnapped by headhunters (an old story), to be used in construction sacrifice (an old story), or by organ thieves (new story). Research in Indonesia has shown that such rumors become more common with growing social dislocations. They have had tragic consequences, as innocent strangers were killed after being suspected of these imaginary crimes (Barnes, 1993; Bubandt, 2017).

The relevance of religious traditions and myths is clear. In Satanism stories, the prevalent elements of infanticide and human sacrifice fantasies, presented in ancient religious traditions, have been attached to a supposedly secret, evil, network of human monsters. We need to remind ourselves that ideas, and rituals, of human sacrifice and blood drinking appear in religious texts, and, far from being hidden, literally stare us in the face.

Those exposing the great Satanic Conspiracy may see themselves as a modern incarnation of the great mythological heroes who had the courage to overcome great monsters in stories told everywhere. These heroes may face serious obstacles but manage to overcome those and save their tribe or the whole world.

The anxieties and dislocations that have given rise to the surge of Satanism rumors could be explored. Was there an overall cultural climate or specific triggers that had made it possible? This is the first question to be raised. Why did the Satanism Craze (together with MPD–DID and recovered memory therapy) erupt after 1970?

An interesting issue, mentioned above, is that of the group targeted for accusation. In this case, it is imaginary Satanists who are busy carrying out horrifying crimes. We realize that a nonexistent group may serve as a target.

The accused in most historical child sacrifice allegations are usually outsiders or enemy groups, starting with the Hebrew Bible. Some individuals, even today, are ready to believe that "outsider" religious groups engage in ritual murder. I can report a conversation with a retired psychiatrist, who, when Jehovah's Witnesses were mentioned, said, "They are nasty; they engage in human sacrifice."

In 1993, David Koresh, of the Waco Branch Davidians, was being accused of planning to perform child sacrifice (Urban, 2015). He might have been guilty of many crimes, but not of that.

How easy it is to develop suspicions, which turn into accusations, and then may turn into conspiracies and persecution, when you live next to people who do not share your beliefs, identity, or looks. Paranoia, which is about personal fear, may develop into generalizations and actions. Frankfurter (2020) provides a fascinating example from late antiquity on the dynamics of spiraling suspicions between Christians and pagans in Egypt, which turn into atrocity fantasies.

The Jew is the prototypical Foreigner in Western culture, and thus attracts the projection of repressed impulses on the part of the majority (Fenichel, 1946). Jews used to be the Other, the terrible Other, capable of drinking blood, but who is the Other now?

Some of the recent Satanism testimonials also refer to known outsiders, but this is rare. Here is one example, involving the Masons:

> There was a group of freemasons who used to use the boys in ceremonies. They used to worship a boy God and they needed a boy to take on the role of the boy

God in the ceremonies. I became the boy God. Before the ceremony started, they would give me high tea with the doctor. He was one of lodge members and part of the tea consisted of those cakes with sugar rice characters ... those sugar rice characters were acid tabs. That makes sense of the visions I was having. As Head Boy I was given a pendulum, a pendulum of protection ... I would be wearing a red robe with nothing underneath. There was a big bed in the middle of a circle with a five-forked star ... On each of the points of the star was a black candle. I was tied to the bed. The person would come into the room, and he would walk around the room anti-clockwise once and then he would untie me ... He would fuck me then, being watched by all the others. Then he would come over my face. While he was doing that, they would take photographs which were kept so he could never break from the lodge ... During the sacrifice they would bring out what they said was a young child's heart and put it in front of me. They said they had sacrificed a child for me so I would be pleased with them. It was difficult to know what was real and what wasn't, especially when the room was going round and you see flashes of light around you and you have just been fucked. (Charleson and Corbett, 1994: 165–7)

We are presented here with an additional question. Not only do we have to account for the meaning of the actions described in the narratives under discussion, but we have an accusation targeting a group that does not exist. But we actually have other conspiracy theories blaming groups hidden from sight, which proves, of course, their existence. This modern cultural phenomenon was noted in the classical social psychological research on authoritarianism, carried out in the United States in the 1940s. The F Scale questionnaire contains the following item:

The wild sex life of the old Greeks and Romans was tame compared to some of the goings-on in this country, even in places where people might less expect it. (Adorno et al., 1950: 250) [This item exemplifies the concept of projectivity, introduced by the researchers, and reflected in ideas of secret orgies, conspiracies, and the general mistrust of authority.]

The American tradition of individualism and suspicion of a strong government has been tied to popular suspicions and a readiness to believe in conspiracy theories. The idea that one cannot trust the government or the mass media and that there may be huge conspiracies threatening all of us and hiding things from us is commonly expressed. Belief in conspiracies is clearly an expression of mistrust in authority and parents.

Objective Stress

Bromley (1991) and Victor (1993) emphasized the importance of economic stresses in the United States since 1970. That period has been characterized by stagnation and income decline for most workers. The lower 80 percent of salaried workers in the United States saw their average weekly earnings fall (in real terms, i.e., adjusted for inflation) between 1973 and 1995 by 18 percent, from $315 per week to $258 per week (Mishel and Bernstein, 1994). Such stresses might have led to the prevalence of Satanism stories among "unskilled, poorly educated, working class" (Victor, 1993: 233) populations in the United States.

This family crisis is undoubtedly related to economic insecurity. According to the US government data, births to unwed mothers grew by 70 percent between 1983 and 1993, the number of unmarried adults doubled between 1970 and 1993, and 58 percent of those have never married. This is while marriage and an intact family remain a cultural ideal. The reality is much different. In both Europe and the United States, the connection between parenting and heterosexual coupling has been eroded, if not severed completely. In the United States in 1993, twenty-seven percent of the children under eighteen years were living with a single, never-married parent, double the figure in 1983 (Census Bureau, 1994). Single parenting, which in reality means parenting by a single mother, has become an intergenerational pattern. And if the majority of families were still headed by a heterosexual couple, there was still instability involved. In 1995, 33 percent of children in the United States were expected to live in a stepfamily (meaning, having one stepparent) before they reach the age of eighteen (Martin, 1995).

The Satanism epidemic may be judged to be a symptom of a moral crisis, but one can point to a real historical crisis of the Western family, true decline and disintegration, reflected in the data on high rates of divorce, single-parent families, more working mothers, and a variety of new family-living constellations (Berger and Berger, 1984; Popenoe, 1988; Stacey, 1998). This reality, in evidence toward the end of the twentieth century, might have created a certain openness to stories about the Satanic conspiracy. The conditions that created the crisis have not disappeared.

Parental Insecurity

In Satanism narratives, the modern terminology and the modern awareness, of real and imagined tensions within the family haven, are rejected in favor of a wild outcry against parenthood.

Is this outcry really that new and that modern? We find countless historical examples where children make the same claims about (and against) their parents.

One possible factor creating these ideas is the growing feeling of insecurity among parents as they doubt their own adequacy. From the adult's, and the parent's, point of view, the child is obviously an object of ambivalence. Consciously, we respond to children with love and protectiveness, as well as annoyance, envy, and resentment.

Modern culture deals more openly with negative impulses and ambivalence in intimate relations. In Satanism stories, this awareness, and the universal insecurity it evokes, is turned into the ultimate accusations against parents,

The anxieties and fantasies were there even when the family was seemingly strong. Parental and paternal insecurities have always been there. It may be that the same conflicts get worse in a family that is smaller, truly more nuclear, and under more pressures.

The Media

The special power and the special impact of the modern media is universally recognized, and never underestimated. We sometimes hear the mass media being blamed for many "social problems," including the hysteria around Satanism allegations. The media undoubtedly play a role in transmitting these stories, but the response on the part of audiences is the significant fact here and raises further psychological questions (Ellis, 2014).

In the late 1980s, television audiences in the United States were presented with shocking evidence for the reality of Satanism, especially in the form of first-person testimonies. Geraldo Rivera was one TV star associated with the phenomenon, with an audience that was eager and responsive. Those appearing on Rivera's shows were not only self-described Satanism victims but also psychotherapists who were there to support their clients and the Satanism fantasy.

In October 1988, Rivera did a show about Satanists that included interviews with parents of alleged victims. "Estimates are that there are over 1 million Satanists in this country" is the best-remembered statement from the show. It was seen in about 19.8 million homes, one-third of the number that were watching TV between 8 and 10 p.m.

Devil Worship: Exposing Satan's Underground (Rivera, 1988) attracted criticism, despite its success with the audience (Boyer, 1988). Today, the show is remembered as a low point in television history (Matthews, 2015). Rivera also hosted Satanism-themed shows in 1991 and 1995. To his great credit, in December, 1995, he apologized for his Satanism coverage, blamed the psychotherapists involved for misleading him, and explicitly criticized the recovered memory idea (deYoung, 2004).

If Geraldo Rivera is a star, Oprah Winfrey has become an American superstar, a major cultural export, and a "spiritual"/New Age/self-help super-guru with an optimistic message about "the Universe" (Decker, 1997; Harrison, 1989; Illouz, 2003; Travis, 2009).

The *Oprah Winfrey Show* was started on September 8, 1986. In the late 1980s, Oprah gave her imprimatur to the Satanism Craze, and hosted some leading figures.

Satan's Underground: The Extraordinary Story of One Woman's Escape was a 1988 book in which the author, calling herself Lauren Stratford (real name Laurel Rose Willson, 1941–2002) described her experiences of baby sacrifice, torture, and rape. She also claimed to having been a breeder, producing babies who were sacrificed by Satanists. In the 1990s, Stratford assumed the identity of "Laura Grabowski," a survivor of the Auschwitz-Birkenau death camp. As "Laura Grabowski," she supported the claims of the Swiss hoaxer Bruno Dössekker, who called himself Binjamin Wilkomirski, and presented himself as a Holocaust victim (Wilkomirski, 1996). *Satan's Underground: The Extraordinary Story of One Woman's Escape* is still in print, and we can imagine that its audience is made up mostly of devout Christians.

In 1989, Oprah Winfrey featured Michelle Smith (of *Michelle Remembers* fame), as a guest on her show together with Laurel Rose Willson. Winfrey presented both women as reporting factual histories, even though it was easy to see that their books were totally fictitious.

In May 1989, a woman named "Rachel" (real name Vicki Polin), supposedly suffering from MPD, told of her childhood in a Satanic family. Here is some of the dialogue:

"Rachel," Winfrey said, "participated in human sacrifice rituals and cannibalism." Rachel: "My family has an extensive family tree, and they keep track of who's been involved ... and it's gone back to like 1700." Winfrey: ... "Does everyone else think it's a nice Jewish family? From the outside you appear to be a nice Jewish girl. ... And you all are worshipping the Devil inside the home?" (Gerard, 1989) [The show can be seen at https://www.youtube.com/watch?v=n7QXz6hDtxI. The predictable protest from Jewish groups led to a clarifying statement, but no apology, from Winfrey.]

Against the background of trash TV programs, with Geraldo Rivera, Oprah Winfrey, and others, and audiences of many millions swallowing whole the Satanism epidemic message, a serious analysis was offered on *Frontline*, the leading PBS program. One producer, Ofra Bikel, single-handedly ridiculed so-called mental health professionals and exposed their incompetence, or worse. In *Innocence Lost* (1991), *Innocence Lost: The Verdict* (1993), *Innocence Lost: The Plea* (1997), *Divided Memories* (1994), and *The Search for Satan* (1995), she preserved for posterity the record of late twentieth-century madness, created by those charged with offering psychological help.

What role did the media play in inducting women to embrace first-person testimonies?

When Oprah Winfrey and Geraldo Rivera were hosting the superstars of the Craze, women who shared with the world their horrifying (and fictional) childhood histories and the resulting symptoms that proved the original traumas, every member of the audience was learning a script. Not all members of the huge audience of many millions embraced the script, but some did. Every appearance of a Satanism victim in the media created a few women who became capable of presenting a similar story. Not necessarily on television, but some women were learning a role that with the help of additional teaching aids, such as books, they could almost master. When a therapist enters the scene, the script is complete.

The media offer us plenty of information about unusual roles and symptoms. Let's look at Near-Death Experiences (NDEs) or alien abduction. Cases of NDE have been reported in great detail since the 1970s. It seems that only those hiding in a cave don't already know what to experience when the time comes, and they are having an NDE. What struck me was the state of bliss described, which is identical to what I have heard from spiritualist mediums.

Media influence was evident outside the United States also. After the British Channel 4 broadcast a program on Satanism on February 19, 1992, a special phone line was set up. Reportedly, 94 out of 194 phone calls dealt with "ritual abuse," including "rape, torture, mutilation, sleep deprivation, hypnosis, ritual murder, abortion and cannibalism" (Scott and Snelling, 1994: 178). The authors of the report state that "perhaps the most striking element of this helpline was the similarity of the testimonies of torture and abuse from callers throughout the UK" (Snelling and Scott, 1994: 179). It has never occurred to them that callers might have gotten the exact ideas from the broadcast itself!

The fact of the similarity, or virtual identity, of testimonies coming from numerous sources is no proof of veracity or reliability. Just the opposite is the case. The phenomenon is well known from research in folklore and mythology. Identical stories claimed to be true are often recorded all over the globe, and they make up the material of folklore and comparative mythology. Stories of a virgin birth have been told, and believed, all over the world. Should we take them seriously because of their popularity? Identical mystical experiences, as well as psychotic delusions, are often reported, and are claimed to represent a higher truth. Does their prevalence support any claims of validity?

We have had reports all over the world of teenage groups acting out "Satanism" fantasies in response to media portrayals and their own suggestibility. Their acts included such things as the desecration of cemeteries and the killing of cats, but no acts of violence against humans (Lowney, 1995).

Religious Beliefs and Satanism Fantasies

"In your opinion, does each of the following exist? The Devil/Satan," the question was asked in the Baylor Religion Survey, 2007. In a representative sample of 1,598 Americans, the results were as follows: not: 12 percent, probably not: 15 percent, probably: 19.5 percent, and absolutely: 53.6 percent. So, in this sample, 73.1 percent believed in the existence of Satan. The prevalence of this beliefs must have an effect in any conversation about Satanism (Bader, Mencken, and Froese, 2007).

Research has shown (Goodman et al., 1994) that ideas about Satan and Satanism are acquired during mainstream religious socialization, which is still active despite secularization. Satan is conceived as the great opponent, the Other Side, and so even children naturally imagine that he is tied to everything that is forbidden and evil in terms of mainstream morality.

The belief in the Satanism conspiracy and the circulation of Satanism legends in the United States might have been more acceptable in a particular American subculture, characterized by strong Christian faith and lower levels of education and income.

It has been suggested that for some religious individuals, proving the existence of Satan, which is part of their belief system, is a major concern. This indeed explains the involvement of fundamentalist Christian groups in the Satanism campaign. Evidence for the strength of belief in the Devil in some Christian groups is not hard to find.

Pope Francis (Jorge Mario Bergoglio, 1936–) who started his pontificate in 2013, has often spoken about the Devil and his influence.

In 2013, he stated,

> The devil also exists in the 21st century, and we need to learn from the Gospel how to battle against him ... The demon is shrewd: he is never cast out forever, this will only happen on the last day ... The devil is on the first page of the Bible and he is still there on the last, when God has his final victory. (Pope Francis, 2013)

In 2015, in an address to children and young people in Turin, Italy, Francis mentioned both Freemasons and Satanists in the same sentence:

> At the end of the 19th century there were the worst conditions for young people's development: freemasonry was in full swing, not even the Church could do anything, there were priest haters, there were also Satanists. (Pope Francis, 2015)

Francis has been described as obsessed with Satan, and this has been reported approvingly by his admirers (Rosica, 2015). In 2021, referring to the Covid-19 pandemic, the pope stated, "The Devil is taking advantage of the crisis to sow distrust, desperation and discord," adding that the pandemic had brought physical, psychological, and spiritual suffering (Pullella, 2021). We also know of officially sanctioned exorcisms in the Roman Catholic Church, and in 1992 I myself listened to a presentation by the diocesan exorcist in Lyon, France, reporting on his work, and emphasizing his ability to diagnose mental illness as opposed to possession states.

There are tragic cases, when insane individuals believe that they are possessed by the Devil, and as a result commit horrible crime. This is done in the context of a religious community, which believes in the reality of Satan. Joy Senior (1967–95), who had been brought up in the Seventh-day Adventist Church in Britain, killed her three children and then herself in May 1995, after believing that the house she was living in, and then she herself, was possessed (Mullin, 1995). A week before her death she asked a Seventh-day Adventist minister to bless her home. While it is obvious that Ms. Senior was psychotic, and represented a tiny minority of believers, one may ask about the normative perception of the Devil among Christians, Moslems, and followers of many other religions. The notion of Satan is indeed part of the dogma, and so may add to the plausibility of Satanism stories.

The Satanism coalitions in the United States and elsewhere have often included an alliance between religious conservatives and so-called mental health professionals. Fundamentalist preachers are happy to describe Satanism allegations as part of an ongoing spiritual warfare, the battle with Satan. *Satan Is Alive and Well on Planet Earth* is the title of a US best seller produced by Hal Lindsey, the leading author of pop eschatology. If this is a rearguard action in the defense of religion, then it is likely to succeed with those already convinced.

We may speak of two versions to the Satanism narrative. The religious sector of the Satanism Craze is made up of individuals who believe that the Devil does exist, as do his followers. The secular view sees only the worshippers in this world, but not a supernatural Devil. Most of the better-known Satanism claims came from the "helping professions," whose practitioners believed in Satanists, but never in Satan.

Individualism and Secularization

When we look at the parallel, but minor, epidemics in Britain and other European nations, we must consider social processes common to all modern societies, as well as differences and unique historical factors.

Western culture has clearly become more individualistic over the past 300 years, to the detriment of family, community, and religion. One of the phenomena exemplifying this process in recent years in the United States is the victim autobiographical narrative. In such a text, or an oral narrative, a litany of past traumas, inflicted by cruel and uncaring parents, is detailed. Ritual abuse narratives represent their culmination.

Despite global secularization, US culture is unique in the First World because of the relative salience of religious and para-religious beliefs. Americans are believers. According to surveys, the vast majority of Americans believe in God, the Devil, astrology, and the Abominable Snowman. Most Unidentified Flying Object (UFO) sightings as well as 100 percent of UFO abductions have been reported in the United States. Some observers, such as H. L. Mencken, simply suggested that Americans are gullible and ignorant by nature, but we must go further than that (Nathan and Mencken, 1921).

Therapists and Testimonies

The role of modern psychotherapists and psychotherapy in connection with Satanism allegations is central.

Behind, and in front of, every individual who claimed to be a victim of Satanism there was somebody who claimed to be a psychotherapist.

It seems that certain professionals became Satanism "specialists," and "uncovered" a large number of alleged cases, while others never encountered such cases. In a systematic survey in the United States, there were about twenty clinicians who had reported encountering more than 100 cases of Satanism each (Goodman et al., 1994).

Why are some professionals ready to adopt the Satanism allegations as reality? After suggesting that some "psychotherapists" are cynical or incompetent, let us look at the sincere, noncynical, motivations possibly involved.

As we read the literature dealing with recovered memories (of all kinds, and not just Satanism), we realize that within it there is a quasi-political stance of complete identification with the alleged victims. The technique of modern psychotherapy, and the contract with its client, is based first and foremost on nonjudgmental listening and acceptance of clients (Parsons, 1951).

While some professionals were promoting Satanism narratives, others in the United States were involved in treating alleged victims of alien abduction (Jacobs, 1992; Mack, 1994; Matheson, 1998).

First-person testimonies about encounters with aliens start with purveyors and entrepreneurs. George Adamski, whose name I first encountered in 1954, was a successful purveyor of stories about encounters with aliens in the 1950s. He started his career as a salvation entrepreneur in the 1920s, when he founded the "Royal Order of Tibet," which sold legal "religious wine" during prohibition, but was able to earn much more by selling stories about "Nordic," blond, kind aliens that took him to the moon (Leslie and Adamski, 1953).

If we follow alien-encounter narratives in the United States in later decades, an interesting question comes up: Why did the benevolent blonds of the 1950s become dark sexual torturers, like Satanists, in the 1980s (Bader, 1995; Strieber, 1987)? Fortunately, we have an answer. The population of "abductees" in the late twentieth century was found to be struggling with serious medical problems and serious psychological issues, such as sexual dysfunction and masochistic fantasies (Jacobs, 1992). That is why so much malevolence was projected on "aliens." It is clear that similar individuals, with significant mental health problems, end up as "abductees" or as alleged victims of Satanism.

Who were the originators of Satanism stories? What we know now is that Satanism testimonies were not spontaneous reports. They were a classic case of iatrogenesis, manufactured by mental health professionals and imposed on the clients. Court records from the cases of Pat Burgus, Elizabeth Gale, and others prove that. What Judge Werlein wrote so clearly in his opinion quoted above leaves few doubts. When a therapist has their mind made up, an imagined template of events may be imposed on clients. This may not be an unusual occurrence and might have happened more than once during famous turning points in the history of psychotherapy. It has been convincingly argued that Sigmund Freud might have been implicated in the same practice (Esterson, 2001).

I have presented above the evidence about the therapists who promoted Satanism allegations and admitted to the use of "recovered memory therapy." Bennet G. Braun was one of them, using hypnosis to produce first-person testimonies (Young et al., 1991).

A significant element in the ideology of current psychotherapy seems to be an antiparent ethos. Psychotherapists see themselves often as having to repair the damage done by parents. When reading published accounts of psychotherapy, both by popular authors and by professionals, one gets the feeling that all parenting is pathogenic, and psychotherapists are destined to properly nurture the victims of evil mothers (deMause, 2009). This ethos has been there long before the Satanism epidemic and constitutes a true psychotherapy tradition. A negative view of parenting is common in all mythologies, and its modern version is part of mental health culture.

Why have the total identification with the victimized child and the feeling that we have been betrayed by our parents become so central to modern psychotherapy? The answer probably has to do with the crisis of family and parental authority in modern times, out of which psychotherapy itself has grown. The perception of all authority as suspect, and of all parents as damaging to children, may also have to do with the psychodynamics of becoming a psychotherapist. By identifying with their clients, psychotherapists are involved in a process of self-healing, finding redress for their own (real or imagined) childhood deprivations.

Frieda Fromm-Reichmann, who is considered one of the founding mothers of modern psychotherapy, and a pioneer of psychoanalysis with psychotics (with no evidence of success), originated the term "schizophrenogenic mother," implying that mothers were to blame for this terrible disease (Fromm-Reichman, 1948). Other leading lights in psychiatry and related fields have offered similar ideas, which were highly popular for decades (Bateson et al., 1956; Lidz et al., 1957). Mothers of autistic children were similarly blamed, and described as "refrigerator mothers," beginning with Kanner (1943), and continuing with Bettelheim (1967). Not the family was blamed, nor the parents, but the mother.

Such blame has diminished over time, as the view that schizophrenia and autism are organically caused has gained dominance (Dolnick, 1998). The reports about problem behavior in mothers can be reconciled with an organic approach. These mothers may carry certain tendencies that are inherited by the children and are not at fault.

We may apply the sincerity test to the believers in Satanism. If you believe in an underground religion worshipping Satan, without one shred of evidence ever been found, then something is terribly wrong with your reality testing. Letting Dr. Braun and his colleagues treat troubled individuals demonstrates severe negligence, minimally rectified when his license was suspended for two years in 1999. Of course, the problem was not with any individual professional. It was that of psychotherapy as a cultural institution maintained by credentialed professionals, but with no real standards for care. One lesson from this incredibly tragic episode is that contemporary psychotherapy lacks professional standards and is not really a profession.

Modern Satanism stories were invented by a small group of psychiatrists, such as Cornelia Wilbur and Bennett Braun, but there was an audience for such fictions, just like there has been one for political conspiracies.

5

Possible Genealogies of Recent Satanism Narratives

It was Sigmund Freud, back in 1897, who pointed out the resemblance between the reports by witches about their contacts with the devil, and modern testimonials of psychic suffering, and asked, "Why do the confessions extorted by torture have so much similarity to my patients' narratives during psychological treatment?" (Freud, 1897a/1985: 242). My answer to Freud's question would be that the individuals involved in conducting the witchcraft interrogations on the one hand, and those administering psychological treatment on the other, shared impulses and fantasies, which they regarded consciously as the impulses and fantasies of others.

At the same time, it was Freud, in a curious and stunning show of credulity, who was ready to entertain ideas of a "Devil religion."

> I have an idea ... that in the perversions ... we may have before us a residue of a primaeval sexual cult which, in the Semitic East (Moloch, Astrate), was once, perhaps still is, a religion ... I dream, therefore, of a primaeval Devil religion whose rites are carried on secretly, and I understand the severe therapy of the witches' judges. (Freud, 1897b/1985: 243)

We find Freud entertaining the idea of an ancient Satanic religion, whose residues (and possibly more than that) are still with us in the modern world. The Freud statements I am quoting were written before the idea of psychoanalysis was introduced to the world, but its beginnings were there, as a secular theory designed to demystify once and for all ideas about demons and their human allies. Who would have believed that at the end of the nineteenth century, Freud's patients' verbalizations sounded to him like confessions produced by accused witches in early modern Europe? Who would have believed that at the end of the twentieth century ideas about Satanism and testimonies of direct contacts (including sexual ones) with the Prince of Darkness would become popular again, and among credentialed "mental health" professionals?

If we are shocked by Freud's fantasies, we also know that the image of the Moloch captivated Karl Marx, among others, even though most scholars are now convinced that the term Moloch referred to a form of sacrifice and not to any god (Newman, 1994). Still, Moloch has become part of Western vocabulary. Rudyard Kipling, whose son was killed in the First World War, lived with a sense of terrible guilt. "In 1935, not so long before his death, [Rudyard Kipling] … confessed that the British have 'passed their children through fire to Moloch in order to win credit with their Gods'" (Peterson, 2015: 40).

We discovered that in the late twentieth century some individuals in the United States, Britain, and elsewhere were eager to believe stories of parents sacrificing their children to Satan. The story was not about just parents murdering their children, which we would regard as either criminal or insane, but killing in a religious ritual. It was not a result of parental hostility, but explicitly an act done to fulfill a religious obligation. This may or may not bring to mind a paramount image of religious devotion, in which a father lifts up a knife to kill his son in response to a command from YHWH but is intercepted at the last minute by an angel sent from heaven.

Humans seem to enjoy stories of parental hostility and cruelty, especially with a happy ending, or at least they like to tell them repeatedly. When it comes to child sacrifice, there are two kinds of stories. One in which the father is about to kill his offspring and a miracle saves the child at the last minute, and the other in which no miracle takes place. Satanism stories offer no miracle, just the claim that thousands of children are being murdered. In many mythological stories, we find a clear *do ut des*, a deal with YHWH, Zeus, Poseidon, and other divine powers, with a child being killed and a parent rewarded.

Is it possible that fantasies about Satanic child sacrifice are related to the legacy of human sacrifice (or child sacrifice) practices and fantasies in mainstream religious traditions?

The modern Satanism epidemic was related to a long chain of fantasies and practices, starting in antiquity. For a historical or comparative perspective on the recent Satanism Craze, we need to consider similar cases.

Satanism and Witchcraft

The belief in witches is a religious idea, based on the notions of evil spirits and evil humans. The anthropologist Raymond Firth stated that concepts of evil principles, of sorcery and witchcraft, of demons, provide more acceptable explanations of social failures than does the notion of human inadequacy. Reinforced by ideas of sacrifice and scapegoat, of the devil and of hell, they provide outlets for aggressive impulses which need not react physically on other members of the society. (Firth, 2004: 221)

In the twenty-first century, witchcraft accusations directed at individuals are still made all over the world, leading to thousands of individuals (mostly women) being killed every year, most of them in Africa, India, and Papua New Guinea (Ashforth, 2018).

The witchcraft idea is universal, and seems totally natural and intuitive (Parren, 2017). Local practices of identifying and killing witches or sorcerers are accepted and embraced. They override the basic norms of kinship solidarity. Knauft (1987) showed that 80 percent of the killings among the Gebusi of New Guinea were of accused sorcerers, determined to have caused illness or death. Only 4 percent led to a revenge killing, which demonstrates the almost unquestioned legitimacy of sorcerer killing.

Barstow (1994) reported that during the great European witch craze, eighty-five percent of the accused were women, often older women of some standing in the community. The accusers were often younger women, projecting grudges and greed on the victims.

Witch killing, which seems incomprehensible, is sometimes a scapegoating ritual in response to economic insecurity. Miguel (2005) demonstrated that in rural Tanzania, the frequency of witch killings, but not of other murders, rises with the incidence of extreme rainfall, which threatens agriculture. The "witches" are described as elderly women killed by relatives.

The idea of the witch, and similar ones, such as that of the legendary stepmother, is a projection of the bad maternal object (Prince, 1961). The bad mother comes back to life as she collaborates with torturers, fornicates with the devil, and devours her own children. The projected accusation of the great European witch hunt, which had witches feast on babies, came back to life at the end of the twentieth century.

The Middle Ages were filled with accusation of sexual perversions and devil worship, directed at real and imagined heretics. While the Blood Libel was a relatively popular notion in the Middle Ages, rarely adopted by the Church authorities, the myth of Satan and his servants was promoted by the Church as long as it had the power to persecute and punish dissidents or suspected dissidents. The dissident Cathars (who were avowed vegetarians) and the Knight Templars were among the targets of such stories.

In 1233, Pope Gregory IX accused German heretics of worshipping the devil by kissing the posterior of their leader and taking part in bisexual orgies. In the fifteenth century, Gilles de Rais, one of France's great marshals and a companion of Joan of Arc, was accused of child murder and cannibalism, and was executed for these crimes. He was accused not only of raping and murdering children but also of torturing them in the most heinous way as they were near death.

There is an interesting connection between Christian practices and Satanism accusations. In European history, witches were accused of desecrating the Christian host, and inverting whatever was holy to Christianity. This imagined reversal leads to the fantasy of the Black Mass, "a blasphemous and erotic parody of the Roman Catholic service" (Hutton, 1999: 258). The Black Mass fantasy is enacted sometimes for the benefit of gullible tourists.

Here is a modern description of the Black Mass as an imagined reversal of sacred rites, part of the recent Satanism Craze, and coming from a mental health professional:

> Much witchcraft is a celebration of the anti-Christ. Many Christian festivals are celebrated in covens in an inverse way. Evil replaces goodness and imperfection perfection. Sadistic and selfish impulses take the place of care and concern. Even the crucifix is placed upside down. (Bicknell, 1994: 151) [Professor Jean Bicknell was Professor Emeritus in the Psychiatry of Learning Disability, St. George's Hospital Medical School, University of London.]

In European history, the Witch Craze was another occasion for accusations of devil worship and ritual child sacrifice and cannibalism (Klaits, 1985). It is important to point out that we refer to this phenomenon as the witch craze because we know that the idea of a secret network of witches and even of individual witches engaged in Satanic practices was a complete delusion. Stories of the Black Mass or the Witches Sabbath have been taken as actual accounts, but there has been no proof of either one as institutionalized practice. Confessions by witches also included the reports of sexual seduction by the Devil and his representatives and claims of a secret cult. But such an organization of witches, or an underground cult, has never been in existence the way it has been claimed since medieval times. We find here some similarity to the recent Satanism Craze. The allegations are purely fictional, and innocent individuals are targeted.

Historical witchcraft allegations included reports of orgies, cannibalism, blood drinking, the sacrifice of babies or animals, and the appearances of Satan himself (Levack, 2015). We can observe the similarity to allegations reported between 1970 and 2000.

Cannibalism, human sacrifice, and child sacrifice are naturally considered proofs of human monstrosity. The witch is the person who embodies and expresses them. In every culture, there are beliefs about humans who are really monsters. Often, such beliefs are expressed through witchcraft accusations. Because

> to accuse of witchcraft is to accuse of evil practices on a cosmic scale. The witch is no ordinary thief or adulterer, or even a common traitor. He is accused of a perverted nature, or of alliance with the enemies of humankind, in Europe with the devil, in other continents with carnivorous predators … Above all, he is a deceiver, someone whose external appearance does not automatically betray his interior nature. (Douglas, 1963: 138)

Blood drinking is reported and confessed to in recent times on the part of witches in both the United States and South Africa (Badstuebner, 2003; Rowe and Cavender, 1991). In South Africa, young women have confessed, during church services to horrifying acts. The police, however, are never notified.

Contemporary Satanism narratives follow the idea of defining some humans as both inhuman and superhuman. They have "special powers." They are inhuman in their cruelty and devotion to evil, and superhuman in their abilities. Most Satanism narratives emphasize their inhuman quality. Claims about "programming" and "mind control," as well as the stories about the Satanists' success in eliminating all evidence of their crimes, express the other aspect. Both versions agree that the putative Satanists are not like the rest of us, mere mortals. Their "special powers" may connect them to the spirit world.

Psychologically, this brings us back to the notion of the projected *imagos* of parental figures. The parent is experienced as omnipotent and omniscient, both good and evil. These experiences are then projected.

How does the epidemic of claims about Satanism compare to witch crazes of other times and other cultures? The Satanism Craze recalls scapegoating situations, such as witchcraft accusations, or the Blood Libel. It may be a modern version of witchcraft accusations, whispering (or yelling loudly): "There is a class of individuals, cunning and evil who in secret cause death and misfortune." This is indeed the essence of the recent accusations, and if there are such creatures in our midst, killing them may be the only option. It was like any witch craze in the sense of promoting delusions about human evil, but not in the way families were described as the crucible and victimization presented as an intrafamily reality. But just like any witchcraft accusation, women ended up being the victims.

The ultimate accusation expressed by Satanism legends is made against mothers (Fister, 2003). If not active Satanists themselves, as they are in most accounts, mothers stand by and watch their children being tortured and sometimes sacrificed. The witches throughout history have been our mothers, transmogrified through the split in the maternal image between a demon and an idealized good mother. But nowadays it seems that there is no more need for legendary witches or stepmothers, as mother herself, without any guises, is the monster.

The witch craze did not represent such a complete revolt against authority. Presumed witches were identified and often punished, and this might have served to bolster authority, coherence, and cohesion. The deviants were ejected, and society was stronger. Individuals might have felt better.

False accusations directed at out-groups have a long history and are regarded as the almost normal underside of identity. "Normal" prejudice has turned into claims about cannibalism, but this does not always lead to actual violence. In the case of Satanism, we have accusations against a group that doesn't exist.

In the case of witches anywhere, the accusations are directed at a nonexistent group that is being created and assembled by accusations, investigations, and executions by the thousand. The recent Satanism Craze is similar (or identical) in the accusations, but a visible group of Satanists was never assembled.

The most important psychological difference between the witch craze of 1500–1800 and the Satanism Craze of 1970–2000 was in those targeted as the evil ones. In the Satanism Craze, the accused were mainly parents, guilty of sacrificing their children to Satan, or exposing them to horrifying abuse, as part of secret rituals. Witches are always at causing misfortune, illness, and death among nonkin, or other than close relatives.

The most important difference between the two historical phenomena is in human lives. It is estimated that 60,000 women were executed in the European witch craze (some estimates are much higher), and thousands of women are still being killed every year. No one was executed for Satanism, although some innocent people were imprisoned for committing "ritual abuse."

Tylor (1871: 416) stated that myth reflected "the history of its authors, not of its subjects," and this is clearly true. The psychological history of those who have authored mythologies seems to contain a limited number of repeated themes that appear across time and space. The aquifer hypothesis, usually not spelled out, suggests that there is a perennial reservoir of themes, which are likely to take the form of myth, art, or dreams. The theme of intrafamily conflict is universal. We may observe a complete continuity in myth and folklore throughout history in the portrayal of hostility and cruelty on the part of parents toward their children. The question before us is to explain eruptions or epidemics, such as the Satanism Craze.

As we examine historical eruptions, such as the Blood Libel, or witch crazes, we search for psychological and social-psychological dynamics, not just the transmission of ideas over time.

The phenomenon of scapegoating, which is really the basic psychological mechanism of displacement, seems to appear in any human group, at various levels. In any human group, even a group of three that met for coffee two minutes ago, an outsider seeking to join will be just that, an outsider. In this book we deal with lethal violence, mostly imaginary, but throughout history, scapegoating meant killing, sometimes by a mob, such as lynching and at other times it took the form of formal ritual.

Whether scapegoating is the beginning of all sacrifices is unclear, but it has been found in many cultures. Scapegoating may be transformative, reducing tensions in group and individuals. It is clear, however, that scapegoating is not some kind of real cure or a real reduction in tensions, because it needs to be repeated. This supports the notion of aggressive impulses as a permanent issue in human behavior, or the idea of social conflicts as part of social structure.

Among the Greeks, a human scapegoat, either by expulsion or ritualistic sacrifice, was called pharmakos, and the ritual was known all around the Eastern Mediterranean and West Asia as early as 2500 BCE (Bremmer, 2001; Zatelli, 1998).

La Fontaine (1998) stated that the modern Satanism Craze is a specific case of the scapegoating dynamics. Both the execution of witches and the imprisonment of some individuals accused of SRA are forms of scapegoating, satisfying the fantasy of eliminating or at list punishing the monsters in our midst.

"The Lottery," a short story by Shirley Jackson, published on June 18, 1948, in the *New Yorker* (Jackson, 1948) tells the readers about a ritual killing that takes place once a year in a small village where everybody knows everybody else. There is nothing religious about this ritual, supported by the whole community. The greatness in this work of art is the author's ability to depict normal tensions that exist in any community, and how they lead to an annual execution, which serves the collective so well until it's needed again. Shirley Jackson teaches us all we need to know about the renewable benefits of scapegoating.

Satanism and the Blood Libel

Fantasies of human sacrifice, child sacrifice, cannibalism, and the drinking of blood, appearing in stories about Satanists are reminiscent of fantasies about ritual murder, directed at Jews.

How similar is the Satanism Craze to the perennial Blood Libel against Jews? The question has been raised, and I will try to offer an answer (Lavin, 2020). The phenomenon of the Blood Libel, which started in antiquity and is still alive today, seems to bear some similarities to the recent Satanism accusations. The long history of the ritual murder accusation has been explored by historians and should be well-known, but its persistence makes it a permanent challenge (Bemporad, 2019; Teter, 2020).

The basic formula of ritual-murder accusation might have appeared first in 40 BCE, when Apion accused the Jews of Alexandria of slaughtering a Greek man, for the purposes of ritual cannibalism (Trachtenberg, 1966). Later, it was the first Christians who were accused of child sacrifice, as well as of incestuous orgies and cannibalism. As Schultz (1991: 289) points out,

> The case in Rome against Christians, just as absurd as the one in Germany against Jews, nonetheless rested on slightly more understandable associations for spreading malicious rumors. Christians were known to believe in their redemption through the blood of a man they regarded as their God and savior.

Frankfurter (2006) pointed to the similarity between the modern Satanism Craze and the rumors about early Christians. In 177 CE, Christians in Lyon were accused of the ritual sacrifice of infants, their slaves confessed to the truth of the allegations, and the entire community was massacred (Cohn, 1975; Rives, 1995). Tertullian wrote around 200 CE: "We [Christians] are said to be the most criminal of men, on the score of our sacramental baby-killing and the baby-eating that goes with it" (quoted in Ellis, 1983: 202).

Once they were in positions of power, Christians were quick to direct the same allegations at Pagans, lepers, Jews, Moslems, and witches. It was the "Other," who was believed to commit all conceivable (and inconceivable) horrors. In the nineteenth century, such stories were told in the United States about Roman Catholics, but the most common and most powerful version of the legend was directed at Jews, part of an ideology of demonological anti-Semitism.

Despite the explicit prohibition in Judaism of the consumption of blood in any form, non-Jews have described ritual murders of children whose blood was used for ritual purposes. The blood was supposedly used either for baking or for wine. In 1150, Thomas of Monmouth, an English monk, heard about a murder of twelve-year-old boy, William, in Norwich in 1144, which was attributed to the Jews, and concluded that William had been crucified. William's remains were moved to the cathedral in Norwich, and his tomb became a site of pilgrimage and reported miracles (Langmuir, 1990).

The Gospels' anti-Judaism started a tradition that is still with us. For most of humanity, the images of the Jew and of Judaism are affected by Christianity or Islam. The resultant images of Jews in both Western and Islamic consciousness play a special role in collective discourse and imagination. Today, using the term the Jewish people brings to mind 2000 years of competition and hostility. For Christians, connecting the diabolical Jews of the New Testament with Jews living in their midst has always been natural.

Yuval (2008) argued that it was Jewish behavior in Europe that affected the creation of the Blood Libel in the twelfth century. In 1096, gangs of Crusaders attacked Jewish communities in the Rhine Valley. In addition to pillage, they forced Jews to face a choice between conversion to Christianity and death. Some Jews, and we don't know how many, chose not only suicide but also filicide, and killed their children to save them from facing the choice or growing up as Christians. Yuval suggested that Christians who were aware of these acts of martyrdom concluded that if Jews were capable of filicide, they could surely kill Christian children. Even though the events of 1096 became memorialized in Judaic writings and modern literature, it is unclear how many medieval Christians were aware of them.

In 1235, thirty-four Jews were murdered in Fulda, northwestern Germany, charged with having killed three Christian boys on Christmas Day, in order to use their blood (Langmuir, 1990). In 1246, several Jews were burned at the stake in Valréas, France, for the same crime. The thirteenth century saw the Blood Libel denounced by Roman Emperor Frederick II and Pope Innocent IV. This did not eliminate its power.

Ritual murder discourse received its prototypical formulation in Luther's 1543 tract, *On the Jews and Their Lies*. In the context of an account of the allegedly bloodthirsty character of Jews in general, Luther mentions a notorious incident that occurred in the northern Italian city of Trent in 1475 (Luther, 1971). Some of the alleged victims (the best known are William of Norwich, 1144; Hugh of Lincoln, 1255; and Simon of Trent in 1475) have been canonized as saints (Hsia, 1992).

In 1669, Raphael Levi was buried alive in Metz, the capital of Lorraine, for the ritual murder of a Christian boy. Later on, all Jews were expelled from the city.

Jacob Frank (1725–1791), who led an antinomian, messianic movement among Polish Jews, claimed that the Blood Libel was indeed true, after his conversion to Catholicism in 1759. This was a major issue in a public debate held between July 17 and September 10, 1760, in Lvov. The public statements by Frank and some of his followers about the Talmudic prescriptions for the use of Christian blood were considered by the Polish Roman Catholic church a major achievement.

Accusations of Satan worship were central in traditional Western anti-Semitism from medieval times on (Raphael, 1972). The connection between Jews and the Devil is still part of Western culture (Trachtenberg, 1966). The connection between Jews as Satan's worldly representatives and the eating of children on Passover was well established in England in the eighteenth century, and even in the nineteenth century, where expressions such as "Baron roast-child" were found (Felsenstein, 1995).

In 1840 came the Damascus Affair, when the disappearance of a Capuchin monk led to allegations against Jews by the French consul (Florence, 2004; Frankel, 1997). Rose has portrayed the Damascus Affair, and the accompanying revival of the Blood Libel against Jews, as "a turning point in the histories of Jewish emancipation and European antisemitism alike" (Rose, 1990: 20).

The first attempt to provide an academic account of ritual murder was Johannis Selden's De Dis Syris (1617), which connected this practice in the Molek cult of antiquity (Heider, 1985). By the end of the eighteenth century, there was a consensus among European scholars about the reality of child sacrifice among ancient Hebrews (Heider, 1985). In the early 1840s, three books on ritual murder appeared within a year of each other in Germany: F. C. Movers's *Die Phoenizier* (1841), Georg Friedrich Daumer's *Der Feuer- und Molochdienst der alten Hebräer* (1842), and F. W. Ghillany's *Die Menschenopfer der alten Hebräer* (1842). All three claimed that human sacrifice was a regular part of the ancient Judaic ritual, and the god worshipped was Molek, not YHWH. Ghillany claimed that the sons of Abraham, Moses, and Aaron had been sacrificed. Daumer claimed that ritual murder was being practiced by contemporary Jews and cited the Damascus Affair as evidence. In an 1842 letter to Ludwig Feuerbach, he alleges that Jews were murdering their own children as well, and sometimes even their rabbis.

Dostoevsky mentions the Blood Libel in *The Brothers Karamazov* (published in 1880): "Alyosha, is it true that at Passover the Yids steal and slaughter children?" "I don't know" (Dostoevsky, 1993: 672). For attributing this reply to Alyosha, Dostoevsky has been criticized by Maxim Gorky, among others (Goldstein, 1983).

The second half of the nineteenth century and the advent of modern, supposedly secular, anti-Semitism coincided with a resurgence of the Blood Libel, a throwback to the Middle Ages. The Blood Libel lived on in times of secularization and emancipation. In 1882, there was a case of Blood Libel in Tisza Eszlar, Hungary, which was followed by scores of similar cases all over Central and Eastern Europe, well into the twentieth century.

Some modern cases stand out. In the spring of 1903, a pogrom took place in the then Russian city of Kishinev (now the capital of Moldova), following a Blood Libel. During the two days of the pogrom, April 6–8, forty-nine Jews were killed, hundreds wounded and raped, with incalculable damage to property.

In 1911, Mendel Beilis was accused of ritual murder in Kiev, and the government of Czarist Russia put its full weight behind the prosecution. He was acquitted in 1913, after the case had attracted international attention.

In the twentieth century, the Blood Libel traveled across the Atlantic Ocean and reached the New World. On September 22, 1928, in a small town in upstate New York, a four-year-old girl failed to come home, and a search proved fruitless. The next step was for the police to call in the rabbi of the tiny Jewish community, to be interrogated about ritual murder. The girl was found on the next day, and the story ended (Friedman, 1978).

In recent memory, the pogrom in Kielce, Poland, on July 4, 1946, stands out. At least forty-two Jews, and possibly more, were massacred only fourteen months after the end of the Second World War, with a mob of men and women, including soldiers and police, busy beating, stoning, hacking, and stabbing scores of Jewish victims. This outburst of cruelty and hate was started by a little boy, who ran away from home, and whose father decided that he must have been abducted by Jews. Soon the town was filled with the cries of "The Jews are killing our children." Kielce was not the only place where the Blood Libel was alive in Poland at the time.

"Several organized pogroms, which always seemed to begin with blood-libel accusations, also took place ... The victims were all Holocaust survivors. They were brutally murdered not by stereotypical Nazis but by ordinary Poles" (Schatz, 1991: 207). According to witnesses, children were thrown out of balconies, and babies' skulls were crushed against walls. Two Poles, thought to be Jewish, were also among the dead. After 1945, there were violent outbursts related to Blood Libel rumors in Hungary as well (Peto, 2009).

Another crime of which Jews had been accused, today almost forgotten, is that of the desecration of the Christian host, something attributed also to witches.

These accusations often led to the extermination of whole Jewish communities. The first case was reported in 1243 in Berlitz, near Berlin, where all Jews were burned alive. This was followed by a case of such accusations in 1290 in Paris. In 1370 in Brussels, another mass extermination took place. In 1337, a case in Deggendorf, Bavaria, which is still celebrated locally, led to a series of massacres. The case in 1410, in Segovia, Spain, is also still celebrated as the feast of Corpus Christi. There were scores of other cases across Europe, with the last one in 1631, ending with a public execution in Poland.

It is interesting to note that no other than Sir James George Frazer stated that the Blood Libel stems from "isolated instances of reversion to an old and barbarous ritual which once flourished commonly enough among the ancestors both of Jews and Gentiles" (Frazer, 1913: 395). Lord Alfred Douglas, who had been once Oscar Wilde's lover, converted to Catholicism at age forty-one and took a public stand against homosexuality and Jews. He was also responsible for claims about "human sacrifice among the Jews" (Toczek, 2015).

In the twenty-first century, we find evidence for the survival of the Blood Libel in Eastern Europe, as folklore, and in West Asia as political propaganda.

Fanned by the Palestine War, the pronouncements that come from Arab sources are hard to believe. They should appear quite believable when we recall that the Arab world, unlike Europe, has not undergone a secularization and remains impervious to Enlightenment ideas because of the dominant position of Islam. In addition, since the coming of Zionism Jews are seen in West Asia as unwanted invaders and a permanent threat.

In the Moslem world, there were more than thirty cases of Blood Libel during the nineteenth century (Lewis, 1984). In all cases, the allegations came from Christians living among Moslems. The best-known case, mentioned above, occurred in Damascus in 1840.

Saudi Arabia, a medieval monarchy dominated by Islamic tradition, plays a major role in promoting the Blood Libel, with Saudi representatives distinguishing themselves by repeating the oldest and craziest anti-Semitic accusations about Jews having to drink the blood of non-Jews. Ma'aruf Al-Dawalibi, counselor to the royal court in Riyadh, declared at a UN meeting on human rights in 1984 that Talmudic teachings oblige Jews to drink non-Jewish blood at least once a year (Rabi, 1985).

Dr. Umaya Jalahma, professor of Islamic Studies at Saudi Arabia's King Feysal University, published an article in the Saudi daily Al-Riyad, on March 12, 2002, claiming that the Jews use human blood to make pastries for the Purim holiday.

They vampirized their victims. To this end, they use a container with an opening. The container is the size of a human being. It is inlaid with needles on all sides. These needles stab the human body from the moment it is placed inside. These needles do the job and the human blood flows out slowly. The victim suffers terrible death agonies, a torture that gives the vampiric Jews great pleasure as they oversee every feature of the blood-letting with pleasure and love. (Jalahma, 2002)

The Blood Libel is alive among ordinary people as well. A colleague of mine in Israel told me that he had discovered that his car mechanic, who happens to be a Christian Arab, does believe in the Blood Libel. The mechanic likes Jews all the same; he just thinks they follow strange customs.

Mustafa Tlass, who served as Chief of Staff of the Syrian Army (1968–72) and Syria's Defense Minister (1972–2006), published in 1983 a book titled *The Matza of Zion* in which he retells the story of the 1840 Damascus Blood Libel. Two men were murdered in Damascus in May 1840, and sixteen Jews were accused of murdering them for ritual purposes. According to General Tlass, this was no libel. The men were murdered because their blood was needed for the Yom Kippur matza. One must admit a certain degree of originality here, because Yom Kippur is a day of fasting, and the classical Blood Libel story is about Passover, when the unleavened bread is indeed eaten. General Tlass refers to the matza as "Zionist bread" and ties Jewish religious practices to Zionist policies. Only by studying the history of Judaism, according to the soldier-scholar, can we understand present-day Israel.

Psychological Origins

Accusations of cannibalism have often been used to express hostility against out-groups. Europeans tell stories of African cannibalism, while in Africa stories circulate about how Europeans kidnap Africans and supply their flesh to hotels in Europe, and that is why there is plenty of meat at European hotels!

How did this particular cultural complex, directed at Jews, develop? Simmel (1946) argued that the anti-Semitic Christian accuses the Jew of the crime that he unconsciously commits when he eats the holy wafer.

Dundes (1991) also described the Christian Blood Libel as a projective inversion of the Christian communion. The accusation that Jews use the blood of Christian children in baking unleavened bread for the Passover holiday has been interpreted as growing out of the Eucharist, where Christians used unleavened holy wafers. Christians who acted out ritualized cannibalism in the communion, selected Jews as their scapegoat, a sacrificial victim. We can speak of the Eucharist projection hypothesis, which can be relevant even today.

There is indeed an empirical correlation between the prevalence of the communion and the presence of the Blood Libel in a population. As reported above, the Eucharist gave rise to rumors and accusations of child sacrifice and cannibalism in the early days of Christianity (McGowan, 1994; Schultz, 1991).

Several psychoanalytic authors have suggested a connection between circumcision and the Blood Libel. In the European imagination, circumcision is forever bound up with Judaism. According to the presumed fantasy connecting the two, Jews, viewed as castrated or half-castrated, may want to take revenge by killing children.

Christians in the Middle Ages might have projected on the Jews in their midst their own guilt and confusion about taking part in the Eucharist. And indeed, the Eucharist was a unifying act of sacrifice for the community in medieval Europe. This was no longer the case in the late twentieth century in the United States or Britain, where Christianity was in decline. Even if we cannot claim that Satanism delusions are projections of concrete rituals, Christian imagery was still dominant, and very few were not familiar with the image of Jesus on the Cross. So, this foundational Christian image of human sacrifice is never far away, despite secularization.

These fantasies of human sacrifice, child sacrifice, cannibalism, and the drinking of blood, as alleged in stories about Satanists are reminiscent of fantasies about ritual murder, directed at Jews. Ritualized cannibalism is still practiced in the twenty-first century, and related fantasies may be projected as well. If stories about blood-drinking Satanists are told by Christians who believe that they engage in theophagy, then we may observe a clear case of projection.

One characteristic common to various conspiracy beliefs is the imagined persistence of an evil that cannot be stopped or changed. Thus, in the case of Satanism, despite all the discoveries about the global underground religion, made in the 1980s by Bennet Braun, Richard Kluft, and others, this large organization, according to believers, remains untouched and unmolested. The true believers are still calling upon us to mobilize and fight Satanism.

Similarly, despite all the thousands of witches that are still being killed, we are being told that witches are still active causing disease, death, and misfortune to no end. We are called upon to be always vigilant and expose the guilty. The reality of fighting against persistent and unending evil is frustrating, but those involved do not seem discouraged. There must be a special kind of moral satisfaction in this fight.

The message from those who believe in the Blood Libel are identical: despite all the cases where Jews have been caught and punished because they killed Christian boys, they will never stop, because Christian blood is a necessary ingredient in the unleavened bread they prepare every year for Yom Kippur, Purim, or Passover, or possibly all three.

Looking again at the comparison between the Satanism conspiracy and the Blood Libel, let me point out the significant differences between the two belief complexes. The Blood Libel is about a well-known group of outsiders attacking the children of the in-group. The Satanism fantasy is about insiders attacking their own children. The Blood Libel is a story about real people, while Satanists do not exist.

I may suggest that these belief complexes are equally absurd. Last, but not the least, the cost in lives of the Blood Libel throughout history has been great, unlike Satanism.

Going Back to Antiquity

We have to travel back over millennia, because sometimes the Satanism stories seem like a parody on the foundational child sacrifice stories of Judaism, Christianity, and Islam. But there is no parody in Satanism narratives. What we find is unintentional.

The conspiracy theory of Satanism tells us that the enemy is here among us, and anyone may be a secret Satanist. This may be a reflection of anomie and is similar to the phenomenon of the witchcraft craze in earlier times (Ben-Yehuda, 1980).

If the essence of Satanism accusations is the victimization of children by parents and parental substitutes, then this is a rather ancient idea. The perception of the child as the victim in the family situation isn't a modern invention, or a minority viewpoint. It is an essential component of the universal Oedipal mythology. Myths of infanticide are part of the general pattern of the myth of the birth of the hero (Rank, 1914). This pattern includes the Oedipal story, but it may be one variant of the theme of the danger to children from parental aggression.

Returning to antiquity and to foundational myths means returning to the basic religious question of the proper sacrifice to the right god. Are Satanists accused of sacrificing children because we are all opposed to such a horrifying idea, or do the foundational myths teach us that the idea of child sacrifice could and should be celebrated when the imaginary transaction is done with the right god? (Tatlock, 2006). The question of the correct human sacrifice to the right god is not limited to Judaism. The encounter of Europeans with the religions of the New World raised the same issue (MacCormack, 2000).

It is worth looking at ever-present images of human sacrifice and child sacrifice (Isaac, Jesus) that have played a major role in Western culture over the ages. The privileged presence of these images means that echoes and reverberations are experienced by many, even inadvertently.

Going back to antiquity means encountering not only ancient narratives but also the traditions built around them over millennia. If we want to discuss Abraham offering his son Ishmael to be sacrificed, what comes to mind immediately are images of hundreds of thousands of pilgrims in Mecca celebrating the myth, and hundreds of millions around the world holding public ceremonies of ritual slaughter. These acts are performed in addition to texts and folk traditions, commemorating and celebrating foundational myths. Still, most of the ancient narratives may be just as shocking to us as the allegations about Satanic sacrifices.

6

A Child Is Being Sacrificed

The title of this chapter is a paraphrase of the title of Freud's (1919) paper on sadomasochistic fantasies that center on the image of a child being beaten (or "abused," as we would say today). He concluded that these fantasies of a child being beaten, humiliated, and punished by an adult brought about "satisfied excitation" of a masochistic kind. Freud dealt with the question of why and how such a fantasy would be tied to sexual arousal and concluded that the answer is to be found in the experiences and anxieties of early childhood, and in attachments to parents. The image provides the child with proofs of its father's love and survives into adulthood.

To be repeated and circulated, shared fantasies must be gratifying. When we hear a narrative, even a rudimentary one, who do we identify with? We should approach narratives that tell us about children being tortured or sacrificed by looking at the experience of those who hear them for the first time.

Most often this is determined by history and institutions. The narratives about the Binding of Isaac, or Ishmael, or Jesus, heard by billions of religious believers, are inspiring, and so the believers identify with Father Abraham, or YHWH, and with Isaac, Ishmael, or Jesus, according to the tradition they grew up with. Experiencing and interpretation are guided by official doctrines, taught, and relearned through liturgy and powerful rituals such as the Moslem animal sacrifice.

Why do some people take seriously Satanism narratives? The readiness to believe in such cases may be related to personality traits or psychopathology (Furnham and Grover, 2021; Imhoff and Lamberty, 2018), but we should focus on common factors, shared by many. Why would anybody tell stories about children sacrificed to Satan, and why would anybody listen to such stories?

A pall of sadness, madness, and anger hangs over Satanism stories. Plausibility and coherence, for those who tell the stories and those who believe them, depend most prominently on the belief in malevolence as the force animating events around us. Hacking (1995) wanted us to accept this belief.

We are faced with the challenge of explaining the power and the plausibility (to some) of child sacrifice (and other "Satanic") themes. We need to look at the dynamics of stories so often repeated.

The challenge is not the failings of mental health (or "mental health") professionals, but the power of an imagery. What is it about babies being sacrificed that gets some people involved and committed? Images of child sacrifice were part of an infusion of "Christian sensibilities and symbolism" (Goodwin, 2018: 283) into the secular setting of psychological treatment and the mass media.

Judaism, Christianity, and Islam all present variations on a myth of child sacrifice. What hidden needs or fantasies do these stories gratify? There seems to be a universal agreement on portraying parents as menacing and children as victims. Objectively, children are powerless compared to their parents. At the same time, they are highly valued. Mythological narratives tell us that some children are under threat as soon as they are born. The formula is one of threat and a miracle that saves the child from parental hostility. We watch with suspense and horror a father approaching his son with a drawn knife or an evil king ordering the killing of a newborn baby or all newborn babies. This is what happened to Perseus, Moses, Isaac, and Oedipus, among others.

What lies behind the unlikely power of these narratives that makes them so plausible for some?

We are going to discover, if we don't know it already, that both ritual abuse of children and ritualized blood drinking are found not in Satanic cults, but in major religions, such as Judaism and Christianity. So, it's not a hidden Satanist conspiracy, but mainstream religious traditions that sanctify these repulsive practices. In these established traditions, it seems that the idea of human sacrifice and the drinking of human blood are acted out more symbolically than literally. This preoccupation with human sacrifice and blood drinking on the part of Judaism and Christianity is conveniently forgotten and denied when Satanism is discussed. We may speculate that the blatant denial of what we all know, but choose not to think of, makes the Satanism hysteria possible.

On the other hand, we will learn that the idea of child sacrifice has most often appeared in Western history as a tradition of accusations and condemnations. This naturally happens when the sacrifice is made to the wrong gods.

It seems that humanity has often been ready to believe allegations of human sacrifice and ritual infanticide in the form of libel against an out-group. This story turns out to be the first libel, or the universal libel, usable and useful against any group (or individual).

Contemporary Satanism stories contain the elements of incest, pedophilia, cannibalism, and blood drinking, which have all appeared in many stories in various cultures. Sacrificing your own children is also spelled out, to avoid any mistakes. Frankfurter (1994) identified the alleged core atrocity as cannibalism. Punt (2008: 152) stated that

> "Those guys kill kids" has been a reliable slander against one's enemies throughout all known history. It's been applied to Jews living under Christendom … and even nowadays, by a certain fringe, to American Democrats."

Stories differed on whether the children sacrificed were yours or other people's. Sacrificing your own kids is "credible as an accusation" (Douglas, 1996: 38).

There is an attractive fantasy that combines atrocities and appears repeatedly.

> The trio of ritual atrocity (human sacrifice, cannibalism, and sexual perversion) has a long history in discourses of the other and the trio raises its head again not only in accusations against Jews, "heretics," and witches in the medieval and early modern periods, for instance, but also in the more recent "Satanic ritual abuse" scare of the 1980s. (Harland, 2007: 73)

We must discuss ancient fictions because they are alive in the believers' experiences and are embedded in institutional traditions, but we have encountered some new fantasies with little or no institutional support. Looking at Satanism narratives, we should ask why humans create fantasies in which other humans are abused and murdered. We must assume that psychic gratification is involved.

The gratification question is obvious. Why is the image of a child being sacrificed gratifying? In the case of the child being beaten, we know Freud's explanation. Those who enjoy the fantasy reached a masochistic excitation. In the case of child sacrifice fantasies, we must inquire what the source of gratification is.

The modern accounts of child sacrifice are similar to some stories told over millennia, but they are not part of a dominant cultural transmission. Then, the question is about an inherent power or attraction that makes these stories not only plausible but also compelling.

Individual Response Level

What happens when you hear a Satanism story? The mechanisms of regression in the service of the ego, and identification operate. We put ourselves inside the story. This could have happened to us! Could my parents have done this?

The first conscious reaction is one of shock and condemnation. Moral judgment provides its own gratification. By putting a distance between ourselves and the monsters carrying out these acts, we feel safe and even superior.

Plausibility judgments have to do with real experiences and with our generalized fantasies about parents and about people in general. They may also have to do with current conscious and unconscious anxieties. The fantasies are always ready and waiting but get activated in times of stress. It may be that such fantasies reach greater visibility in times of crisis in the form of personal testimonies. It is always there in the form of impersonal myth and legend, but now it becomes personalized.

Preoccupation with Satanism allows both gratification and anxiety reduction through projection and through vicarious satisfaction. This is the same process through which we enjoy crime stories in the mass media. We sometimes hear the comment "Such stories sell newspapers," and they indeed do, but why? Newspapers sell when they print stories of monsters, human and otherwise, space aliens, and perversions. That's what we like to read stories of cruelty, lust, and wonder. We like to watch reports of sleaze, blood, and gore on television, but why? We do like bizarre sex acts and murder stories in the tabloids, but why?

One main factor is arousal, in fantasy and under control. Emotional arousal leads to social transmission and sharing (Berger, 2011). Why do we need fantasies of evil and evil deeds? The fantasy does it just right. It is evil done in the right way, with the right proportions and the right ending.

Twitchell (1985) suggested that the attraction of horror stories is tied to the following elements:

1. Anxieties lead to counterphobic or a vicarious overcoming of fear. Horror stories are like a roller coaster, letting you get frightened without getting hurt.
2. Projection of desire. Horror expresses the most unacceptable impulses in an acceptable way. These are our desires. Otherwise, we wouldn't want to hear them and pass them on.

Gratification is possible not only in terms of sadomasochism or other sexual enjoyment but in terms of expressing aggression as well. The poor victim being sacrificed is also the target of displaced aggression and projection. Evidence from many cultures, from ancient Greece to the European witch craze and to those accused of witchcraft today in Africa or Oceania demonstrates that those chosen to be sacrificed or lynched are the powerless and marginal. Evidence also shows that such scapegoating phenomena are tied to social tensions, economic problems, or crises in religious organizations. A range of stimuli may lead to aggression, which finds the weakest targets.

We can assume two tracks of responding to the images shared by those who want us to believe in the reality of Satanism. Denouncing cruel reality when I believe that Satanism is real is a conscious, normative, reaction we can all share. Most people are sincerely shocked to hear about Satanic torture. When I read about children being sacrificed by the Aztecs, my reaction is one of horror, and I find this experience, part of my academic research, just something I am forced to do. At the same time, I am trying to understand the Aztec belief system.

The other track of responding to horrifying images involves another kind of arousal, which is wholly positive. Some individuals seek and enjoy horrifying images that they consciously (and unconsciously) enjoy, such as the sadomasochists mentioned by Freud. Imagining cruelty offers a way of expressing aggression without hurting anybody. Thus, visualizing nonexistent Satanists engaged in torturing and killing children may be highly gratifying for some people.

In the case of foundational religious myth, such as the Binding of Isaac, I may consciously identify with Abraham, and then again feel morally upright and superior, compared to those who do not share this tradition.

Could ritualized aggression or fantasy aggression provide vicarious tension relief, a catharsis? Konrad Lorenz (1966) argued that the spectators in organized sports events experience a vicarious outlet for their aggression, thus reducing the level of violence in society. This hypothesis has been disproven hundreds of times. The more puzzling cases involve fans rioting in response to their team's victory. Thus, eight people were killed in Detroit on June 15, 1990, after the Detroit Pistons won the NBA title. Research on sports events and violence concluded that spectators follow the conflict they observe, and the effect spills over to domestic violence and homicide. College athletes are also more likely to commit sexual assaults. Some may suggest that vicarious violence achieved through sports aids social integration. In the same way, we can assume that ritualized violence and fantasy violence contributed to social integration in ancient times. This includes real sacrifices and sacrifice fantasies.

Humans are capable of murdering conspecifics, but invest much more in fantasies about killing, done by themselves or by others. Fantasy is better than real murder, in an official war or in informal violence. In most cases, fantasy ends in fantasy. Exposure to violent narratives does not lead to real violence.

If we accept the notion of catharsis, or of fantasy relief through storytelling, we must take the next logical step. Why do some individuals enjoy hearing stories about fornication with the devil or child sacrifice? And we do enjoy them; otherwise, they would just die off and be forgotten. If the stories are so horrifying, why do we retell them?

Satanism stories may provide us with vicarious gratification of our own fantasies, be they heterosexual, homosexual, homicidal, parricidal, or infanticidal.

If we take seriously the idea of projection, then, in the stories we tell, we speak of ourselves and our own impulses only. We can only project internal experiences and internal wishes. Fantasies about other religions and about other people say something about us, and our fantasies of human evil, as Hacking (1995) demonstrated. How much evil are we ready to ascribe to fellow humans?

The projective function of Satanism narratives is to locate and bind evil, to name evil. What they tell us is that evil is among us, but not in us. We want to have the world neatly divided into good and evil spheres, but that is difficult. If the Satanist group isn't easily identifiable, then it's even more dangerous, because the Satanists are us, in every family. How do you know who is a Satanist? Anyone could be!

"True" stories are formed through displacement, projection, and rationalization. Guilt is externalized, and internal balance kept. The demons are first and foremost inside us, but all cultural traditions and all human psyches share the mechanism of projection, which tells us that evil, rather than coming from us and tied to our moral control, is under the command of timeless demons. Our unacceptable impulses are projected on others, on outsiders, real or imaginary. It's good to know that evil is out there, and evil people are out there, not us, not within us. What is being projected in the form of Satan and Satanists? Our own impulses, or our bad father, or bad mother, which have become internalized.

Believing that such things have happened relieves anxiety. Maybe it doesn't, because all these Satanists are around, but now we know about them and can be alert to the danger. What is the conscious moral of the story? Is this a morality play? Do the evil ones get punished? If there are people out there doing these terrible things, I am feeling better, because (consciously) these are not my own impulses. There is here a conscious social comparison effect. When I read some true horror reports, I feel relieved to realize how normal I am (relatively speaking, of course). If I can believe that there is indeed a religion of Satan, committing all these despicable acts, then I can feel superior and safe.

Contemporary Satanism allegations express a rebellion against the whole institution of the family, but this rebellion is ancient, nay eternal. The tension is always there. Sometimes real atrocities are carried out, but mostly it is fantasies that express fears and the perception of hostile impulses.

The psychological approach leads us to broader questions and deeper structures. Why is this motif so prevalent over time and place? The image of the child being sacrificed seems to be always with us. Classical psychoanalysis claims that the unconscious pattern of incest, murder, and cannibalism lives on in all of us, as children and as parents. Children are no angels; they are also capable of hostile fantasies, if not actual cruel deeds.

Psychoanalytic theory would suggest that these fantasies are so common because the impulse is always there, and exactly because acting on it is so rare. If action is common, there is no need for fantasy.

The projections reveal common fears and common plots. The fantasies, much more common than actions, still reflect basic unconscious urges and concerns. A continuum of passions, anxieties, and solutions gives rise to certain common gestalts, which can be found in all human cultures.

For any individual who embraces a Satanism fantasy, we should ask whether, and how, such fantasies empower or gratify. Imagining young children being sacrificed not far from you, and this is what the Satanism conspiracy is about, must be horrifying, and will still attract some people.

Would it be improper to suggest that those involved in sharing stories about cannibalism and sexual perversions derive some gratification out of the process? Such gratification may not be conscious or acknowledged, of course. Embracing the Satanism conspiracy may provide additional gratification and empowerment.

Before this discussion becomes too general and too abstract, let us turn to a statement quoted already in this book. Valerie Sinason, a psychotherapist who has led the British version of the Satanism Craze, in an interview in 2011, chose to describe some of what Satanists do in their spare time:

> Sinason talks of a popular ritual in which a child is stitched inside the belly of a dying animal before being "reborn to Satan." During other celebrations, "people eat faeces, menstrual blood, semen, urine. There's cannibalism." Some groups have doctors performing abortions. "They give the foetus to the mother and she's made to kill the baby." "And the cannibalism—that's foetuses?" I clarify. "Foetuses and bits of bodies." "Raw or cooked?" "The foetuses are raw." "Not even a bit of salt and pepper?" I ask. "Raw. And handed round like communion. On one major festival, the babies are barbecued. I can still remember one survivor

saying how easy it is to pull apart the ribs on a baby. But adults are tougher to eat." (Storr, 2011)

We may suspect that she was enjoying this cannibalistic fantasy, and this enjoyment may be shared by others. Sinason also chose to mention the similarity to the Christian communion. Sinason's cannibalistic fantasies lead us to many narratives and allegations throughout history.

Hacking's fantasies are more general:

> I think it is possible that there have been and will be ongoing satanic rituals by organized sects in which children are viciously abused. I know that in my hometown, which has an undeserved reputation for being the most decent, safe, urbane and dull large city in North America, goats are sacrificed to Satan on the roofs of warehouses only a few streets from my home. I fear that once any idea, no matter how depraved, is in general circulation, then someone will act it out. Even if a decade ago no goat-sacrificing Satanists tortured children, my lack of faith in human nature leads me to think it possible that some do so now. When vile stories are rampant, minds that are sufficiently confused, angry, and cruel will try to turn fiction into fact. It is possible that some local secret society, with loose relationship to other groups in other places, has gone completely off the deep end. Perhaps somebody, somewhere, has used an adolescent to breed a baby for human sacrifice. I sadly do not think it impossible for such things to happen—or even terribly unlikely. Hence in my view a person could in principle have rather accurate memories of such events. (Hacking, 1995: 284)

Seduced by stories about multiple personalities and Satanic crimes, Hacking decided to share with us his malevolent fantasies, warning us about his lack of faith in human nature. "Goats are sacrificed to Satan on the roofs of warehouses only a few streets from my home." Like Doris Lessing, Hacking believes in humanity's inevitable decline into Satanism. I can assure the readers that neither goats nor babies have ever been sacrificed to Satan on any roofs in Toronto.

"When vile stories are rampant, minds that are sufficiently confused, angry, and cruel will try to turn fiction into fact." Billions of people have been exposed to vile stories about fathers willing to sacrifice their children to YHWH. Very few of them were inspired to repeat the act.

What Hacking does not know is that humans do not act out violent fantasies, but they do enjoy imagining them.

In apocalyptic fantasies, which describe how the infidels are to going to meet their just end on Judgment Day, we consciously enjoy the final triumph of justice. Beyond that, the visions of destruction provide a righteous outlet for our violent drives.

Could anybody enjoy the genocidal fantasies in the book of Joshua? I once had a conversation with an observant Jew, who told me that if somebody could prove to him that the Palestinians were descended from the Amalekites, destined for extermination in the Hebrew Bible, he would start exterminating them right away.

The moral condemnation in Satanism stories bolsters the self, just like the identification with Abraham, Isaac, Ishmael, and Jesus, mythological heroes whose sacrifices maintain the cosmic order. Identification with the protagonists in the sacred narratives about Jesus, YHWH, and Isaac is empowering, but not universally emancipatory. There is aggression toward those who do not share the Good News together with superiority feelings.

In narratives about modern Satanism, the message is that everybody except the victim is implicated in this conspiracy, including not only parents and caretakers but also the police and the highest levels of government. A popular British book promoting the Satanism conspiracy tells us that "there is a common allegation contained in the disclosures of both adult and child survivors today that senior politicians are sometimes involved" (Tate, 1991: 86) and that "a number of survivors independently gave the name of a particular MP [member of the British Parliament] as being involved" (Tate, 1991: 340–1).

Satanism becomes tied to the upper classes in a display of justified bitterness.

Our evident fascination with evil does not lead to worship, in most cases. It leads to horror, together with the wish to observe it closely. The preoccupation with Satanism stories is an expression of unconscious admiration for breaking all laws, the fantasy of totally liberated impulses. While consciously we react with horror, at another level we salute the celebration of the idea in the retelling of an eternal tale.

In one of the best-known Satanism texts, published with the imprimatur of the Roman Catholic Church, Michelle Smith described a case of infanticide-by-crucifix (Pazder and Smith, 1980). The power of Christian mythology is very much in evidence here, and to explore it we need to go back in time to ancient traditions and practices.

The Child as Victim: Reality and Fantasy

Children are uniquely insecure, always wary of abandonment. They are indeed weak and vulnerable, being always the potential victims of parental sexual and aggressive drives. There is much abuse going on, of all conceivable and inconceivable kinds. Cruelty exists, both spontaneous and ritualized. Ritualized cruelty is expressed through initiation rites, for example, genital mutilation of males and females, found all over the world (Bettelheim, 1954). Cruelty to children exists also in spontaneous and individual cases of abuse, physical and sexual. There is no shortage of evidence for the bitter reality of child victimization in all its forms. Parental cruelty and rejection have always been part of human experience, and abandonment has always been part of reality (Boswell, 1988; Ransel, 1988).

We are sensitive to any hostility on the part of our parents, and in addition our own hostile impulses may be projected on them. But you wouldn't know it looking at traditional lore. Legend and myth are infantocentric. In legend and myth, the child is the victim, and child sacrifice, child rejection, and abuse abound. Mythologies, whether Mesopotamian, Egyptian, Greek, or Hebrew, are replete with accounts of the family as the site of abuse, incest, rape, and murder.

The abandonment of children is a major theme in myth, legend, and fairy tales. The latter are full of bad mothers and bad mothering, children thrown out and eaten by witches. The figure of the swan maiden of legends turns into a witch, a succubus, or a homicidal mother, like Medea (Leavy, 1994). There is always a threatening forest, where children are in mortal danger, and someone has been ordered to kill them, or they are living with a cruel stepmother, clearly guilty of child abuse.

While searching for useful analogies, we discover that the distant past is not distant and that echoes of ancient stories are still being heard and listened to. As we look at Satanism stories, we encounter not only echoes and shadows of ancient legends but also of surviving rituals. The pervasive historical legacy of beliefs and practices that have formed Western traditions made possible the Satanism epidemic.

Mythology and folklore are made up of a limited number of repeated themes and categories across time and space, histories, and cultures. Where do insane rumors about parents sacrificing their children come from? Straight from the sacred writings of some well-known and respectable religions. The modern delusions of Satanism are inexplicably (or not) related to foundational myths celebrated by the West, such as the Binding of Isaac and the Crucifixion.

The legacy of human sacrifice narratives is universal, but local parts of it are closer to us and impact us today. The Aztecs are also part of human heritage, but Judaic and Christian ideas are more directly implicated, because we are still immersed in them. The issue is both the historical presence of violent sacrifice as a fantasy and its immense psychological attraction.

To a nonreligious eye, ancient child sacrifice narratives are just as absurd as modern fantasies about Satanists in our midst. The artistic quality of the narration makes the unfolding chain of events to the believing reader or listener so dreamlike as to become part of one's own memory.

7

Sacrifice Fantasies

Religious acts are formed by the wish to communicate with/negotiate with/ encounter spirit entities, to ensure a good life and afterlife. Religious praxis is based on the fantasy of communication and exchange. Sacrifice is an attempted negotiation, taking many forms, including any investment of time, effort, and tangible resources guided toward reaching the spirits.

This book is about sacrifice narratives and not any acts of sacrifice, but any act of sacrifice is based on at least three attractive fantasies:

1. Actual offerings may take many forms, from mutilating one's body to prayers, incantations, or avoiding speech for long hours, and a great variety of materials are gifted to the spirits for their nourishment, from bananas to sheep.

    Beyond the substances or life form involved, it is the idea of reciprocity that creates the practice of sacrifice. This fantasy, which holds that humans create an obligation in spirit entities, is the condition for the procedure.
2. The fantasy that an act of destruction will restore order and balance.
3. Maintaining hegemony: The fantasy of the priesthood that this ritual will serve the goals of institutional power.

The reciprocity fantasy is created by natural anthropocentrism, which leads us to regard spirit entities, whether ancestors or deities, as acting and thinking just like ourselves (Beit-Hallahmi, 2015). Among humans, gifts create an obligation and an assumption of reciprocity. The fantasy of an exchange between the living and the dead may also help explain the practice of continuous ancestor worship. This is seen as a reciprocal relationship, within a larger system of exchange. Fantasies of reciprocity also imply that spirit entities, such as ancestors, are dependent on sacrifices by the living for their well-being.

Despite the prevalence of violence and competition among humans, it is everyday reciprocity and cooperation that make human survival possible

(Høgh-Olesen, 2006). Cooperation, reciprocity, and altruism are fundamental aspects of all biological systems, from bacteria to primates. Biological imperatives push organisms to coordinate their activities with those of conspecifics, and even with members of other species. Restraints on individual behavior are necessary for social life and have been naturally selected because of their survival value.

Most humans claim to follow a morality of reciprocity, which expects both sides to keep a deal and follow an agreement. This morality becomes, known as the *do ut des*, is basic to dealing with ancestors and spirits. Humans have always understood the exchange structure, which makes possible the transactions with higher powers, ancestors, gods, and local spirits.

To clarify the actions involved in religious traditions everywhere, we can start with definitions of ritual in general and go on to describe blood sacrifices.

Douglas (1966: 128) called ritual "an attempt to create and maintain culture." Proper order and structure enable the ritual to restore cosmic or tribal stability and ensure their continuing presence. "Ritual is about the cosmic order and its preservation, and the right act will save humanity, the cosmos, and each one of us" (Jay, 1992: 19). Ritual is often apotropaic, designed to protect humans from evil spirits and evil intentions.

We can all think of the rites of passage, easing transitions and offering structure where its absence will raise anxiety. Individual and collective ritual acts achieve renewal, recommitment, and a celebration of triumph and unity.

Sacrifice is a special case of ritual, in which the occasion is not just a human transition, but a structure of worship. A spirit entity is addressed, and an imaginary negotiation opens. Sacrifice is believed to constitute an act of imaginary communication with the spirits, but really affects the humans who are directly involved. Stories of sacrifice are told as testimonials of successful transactions.

How to make a deal with the gods through an effective transaction, that is a question addressed in all traditions. What is the right kind of offering?

In a sample of contemporary adolescents, common examples of active religious sacrifices included attending religious meetings, praying, reading religious texts, serving others, and sharing one's faith. Examples of passive religious sacrifices included giving up time, food, entertainment, language, drugs or alcohol, peer relationships, or a preferred style of dress (Dollahite et al., 2009).

Even in ancient times, sacrifice did not always involve killing, and the latter may appear peripheral to its main public presentation (Frankfurter, 2011). Bread and bananas could be offered to vegetarian gods, of course, but our discussion here does begin with blood rites, that is, killing or at least the spilling of blood, as in circumcision. "Sacrifice is the killing of animals for the purpose of honoring the gods, enacting reciprocity and acquiring food" (Ullucci, 2015: 415). Killing rituals give rise to relief, guilt, and exultation, as an encounter with death is understood to be an affirmation of life.

Black and Green (1992: 30) defined sacrifice as "a religious rite by which an object, animal or person is offered to a divinity in an attempt to establish, maintain or restore a satisfactory relationship of the individual, group of individuals or the community in general to that god," while Fortes (1980: xiii) defines sacrifice as "a special ritual procedure for establishing or mobilizing a relationship of mutuality between the donor (individual or collective) and the recipient."

Public infliction of suffering on the self as a form of sacrifice is found in many traditions. Bloodletting was routinely practiced by the Aztecs (Couch, 1985). Sitting Bull (c. 1831–90), a Lakota Sioux holy man, pierced his body with skewers when performing the sun dance in honor of the goddess White Buffalo Woman (Uttley, 1993). The Sioux Sun Dance was, essentially, self-inflicted torture, performed by men. Among Australian Aborigines, blood sacrifice is traditional: "men open veins in their arms, or pierce the skin of their scrotum or navel, in order to make the rite more effective. They believe that blood animates the embryos of the totem animals or plants with which they identify" (Mol, 1979: 383). Piercing with skewers can be observed today among Shiite Moslems in West Asia, Hindus, Tamils, and Buddhists in South Asia (Cohen, 2012; Jegindø et al., 2013). Blood shedding in the genital mutilation of children is practiced in various cultures as part of puberty or prepuberty initiation rites and is sometimes sanctioned as a religious duty.

Sacrificing one's private life is a dramatic religious act. Religious ideals of renunciation, which involve giving up attachments and family ties, are found in many cultures, and individuals are called upon to make a major offering by consecrating their lives as clergy, monks, or nuns. In some communities around Ghana, young girls are donated by their families to serve as temple slaves for life. Behind this is the belief that somebody in their family sinned, and slavery is the atonement. In recent decades, a movement is struggling to liberate these women (Martinez, 2011).

The consecration of virgins in the Roman Catholic Church is an ancient tradition, reestablished in 1970. As of 2011, there were 400 consecrated virgins in Italy (Turina, 2011). Consecrated virgins make a public promise of perpetual virginity during a special ceremony, conducted by a bishop, which celebrates marriage to the mythical Jesus Christ. They live alone or with their families, have regular jobs, and are part of the community.

In South Asia, we find the phenomenon of middle-aged men who commit themselves to severing all personal attachments. Laungani (2007) discusses the case of a former High Court Judge in India, who has renounced the material world, abandoned his large and loving family, and has become a sanyasi to atone for guilt feelings and in search of enlightenment and nirvana.

In antiquity, martyrdom was a form of sacrifice leading to sainthood, or at least to recognition: "For many, torture and death were the prerequisites for elevation to sainthood, or for the mediation between human and divine existence" (Andriolo, 1981: 274). As we all know, martyrdom has become a contemporary phenomenon, to the surprise and shock of Western powers. Suicide bombers are certain that killing themselves and others as part of a religious-political campaign will ensure their eternal rewards (Beit-Hallahmi, 2003; Neria et al., 2005; Strenski, 2003).

Fantasies about transactions with spirits are uniquely generative, and sacrifice narratives include variations on the interactions between humans, spirits, transactions, and rewards. What is the psychological effect created by fantasies about mythic rituals? Once they become part of a continuous tradition, their impact on individuals is assured. Such a tradition, whether Judaism, Christianity, or Islam, offers its followers the fantasy of an eternal covenant, through Abraham or Jesus, which they should naturally celebrate.

Rituals emerge from a combination of the individual's need for the release of aggressive and libidinal drives and the community's need for binding acts, contributing to group cohesion and adaptation. Any blood sacrifice is a ceremony of violence, in which aggression is not only structured but also choreographed. Impulses are let loose, but kept under control, for the benefit of ego and community. Walter Burkert argued that "civil life endures only by giving a ritual form to the brute force that still lurks in men" (Burkert, 1983: 45) and that "society is built on the impulses of aggression controlled by ritual" (Burkert, 1966: 112). One might say that in the drama of blood sacrifice aggression is handled creatively and realistically. The solution offered by the ego enhances self and community.

Animal sacrifice used to be a dramatic part of many traditions. The relationship with the sacrificial victim is often complex and ambivalent, as the animal may be worshipped as well as sacrificed. An example is the worship of the bull-God, found in Mediterranean cultures as well as in South Asia. Bulls were deified, but sometimes also killed, and worshipped while being consumed. The ritualized killing of a bull survives to this day in a secular form in Latin America, Spain, and Southern France as bullfighting.

What is the proper offering to the spirits? According to the authors of the Hebrew Bible, YHWH was no vegetarian (even though cereals were sometimes offered to him), and meat offerings are best to pacify him.

Vide his reaction to the offerings of Cain and Abel in Genesis 4:

> 2 And she again bare his brother Abel. And Abel was a keeper of sheep, but Cain was a tiller of the ground.
>
> 3 And in process of time it came to pass, that Cain brought of the fruit of the ground an offering unto the Lord.
>
> 4 And Abel, he also brought of the firstlings of his flock and of the fat thereof. And the Lord had respect unto Abel and to his offering:
>
> 5 But unto Cain and to his offering he had not respect. And Cain was very wroth, and his countenance fell.

This narrative is reinforced by the story of Noah, where the right kind of sacrifice results in YHWH's promise never to destroy humanity. Just how precarious human existence is we learn in Genesis 6. While individuals may worry about their own death, humanity is worried about total extinction, resulting from godly anger.

In Genesis 6, we observe YHWH in his wrath, regretting the creation of humans:

> 5 And God saw that the wickedness of man was great in the earth, and that every imagination of the thoughts of his heart was only evil continually.
>
> 6 And it repented the Lord that he had made man on the earth, and it grieved him at his heart.
>
> 7 And the Lord said, I will destroy man whom I have created from the face of the earth; both man, and beast, and the creeping thing, and the fowls of the air; for it repenteth me that I have made them.
>
> 13 And God said unto Noah, The end of all flesh is come before me; for the earth is filled with violence through them; and, behold, I will destroy them with the earth.

Evidence of the way humans believe they could placate angry spirits is found in Gen. 8:20-22. After the punishment of the Flood, meat served to YHWH leads to an eternal promise: Humanity will survive together with the seasons of nature and with agriculture.

> 20 And Noah builded an altar unto the Lord; and took of every clean beast, and of every clean fowl, and offered burnt offerings on the altar.

21 And the Lord smelled a sweet savour; and the Lord said in his heart, I will not again curse the ground any more for man's sake; for the imagination of man's heart is evil from his youth; neither will I again smite any more everything living, as I have done.

22 While the earth remaineth, seedtime and harvest, and cold and heat, and summer and winter, and day and night shall not cease.

This is presented as humanity's great achievement, an eternal covenant for our survival, and all because of choosing the right offering. The "sweet savour" is mentioned at least five more times in the Hebrew Bible.

This carnivore perspective reflects the West Asian pastoral cultures in which fantasies about successful transactions with the gods were created by priests surrounded by herds and concerned about fertility and survival. Bountiful herds ensured against famine and offered a steady supply of good meat cuts to the priesthood. The ram caught in a thicket marked the continuity of pastoral rites.

The tradition of the mythological scapegoat, described in Leviticus 16, lives on in Orthodox Judaism, where the custom of sacrificing a chicken on the eve of the Day of Atonement for every member of the family (hens for females and roosters for males) is still prevalent, and hundreds of thousands of fowl are sacrificed every fall in Jewish communities all over the world. The belief is that human sins are transferred to the animal, which will pay for them with its life. In this case, as in others, the projection of sins on a victim is conscious. While holding the fowl, the sacrificer declares, "This rooster will go to death, and I go to a long, good life."

Any animal sacrifice is horrifying to Western sensibilities (Boaz, 2019), and today it is most common in Islamic and African cultures, as well as in Afro-Caribbean and Afro-American traditions, such as Vodoun. The Gadhimai Hindu festival in Nepal, held once every five years, involves the one-spot largest public killing in the world, with tens of thousands of animals going to their death. In Nepal, animal sacrifice is also found among Buddhists (Owens, 1993).

Islam has its most important holiday, a feast of sacrifice (Id al-adha), which involves public killings of tens of millions of animals by hundreds of millions of believers. The experience of the sights, sounds, and odors of public killing is shocking (Weddle, 2013).

Kiev (1962) interpreted a Voudon sacrifice as a totem feast. On one level, it was a symbolic murder of a divinely possessed animal. It maintained social controls, exercised by the priest, by allowing the followers some emotional relief. It was also a threat, as the priest reminded his followers of his presumed "supernatural" ability to kill them.

Walter Burkert suggested the guilt felt by prehistorical hunters as the motive that led to the development of ritual sacrifice (1983). There is much evidence of guilt over the killing of animals, expressed in taboos and rituals among hunters (Luckert, 1975).

Such rituals, which consist of negotiating with the souls of animals, can be found in cultures that rely on hunted or domesticated animals for survival. They involve apologizing to the hunted species and expressing hope for its preservation and its continuing fertility. Thus, members of the Yurok tribe were described praying to the salmon:

> Tearfully they assured their prey that they meant no harm to his essence, that they were eating only that fleshy part of him that he could well afford to lose, and that they would let his scales return downriver and out into the ocean where they came from, so that from them new salmon could grow—and continue to come into the Yurok's nets. (Erikson, 1964: 104)

Among the Cherokee, interactions with nonhuman living creatures and their ghosts might have serious consequences:

> Hunters who failed to offer prayers after killing a deer might expect to be struck with rheumatism or other diseases by Little Deer, a ghost-spirit who was the head of the deer tribe ... Another common source of illness was from the tsgaya, or disease-causing insects or worms that inhabited the body and caused swelling, boils, or skin irritations. These were not visible creatures but small invisible powers who were regarded as the ghosts of tsgaya who had been killed unthinkingly by humans. (Irwin, 1992: 243)

The Cherokee concern about any living being is reminiscent of the Jain tradition in India.

Some cultures tell stories about the migration of souls from humans to animals, found in strikingly different settings. According to beliefs held by the Wari', an Amazon basin tribe, the spirits of dead go to an underground world, and return in the form of fish or peccaries, pig-like animals that are a major source of meat for the tribe. The ancestor-peccaries then seek out hunters from their own families and offer themselves to be shot, ensuring that their meat will go to feed the people they love (Conklin, 2001). Among Hassidic Jews, members of a tradition that started in Eastern Europe in the eighteenth century, there has been the belief in the souls of just men transmigrating into kosher beasts, which

Jews may eat. These beasts need to be slaughtered only with the sharpest knives, otherwise causing the just men unnecessary suffering. Such notions express the confidence in continuing relationships with the dead, gratitude for their aid, and the guilt about killing animals to feed humans.

Even if Burkert is mistaken about the origins of animal sacrifices, we can see that humans have been concerned about animal souls and felt guilty about killings. Ideas about the fear of revenge by the souls of hunted or slaughtered animals lie at the root of slaughter rituals, which are best known today in Islam and Judaism (Frazer, 1922).

The Reality of Human Sacrifice

> Caesar must bleed for it! And, gentle friends,
> Let's kill him boldly, but not wrathfully;
> Let's carve him as a dish fit for the gods,
> Not hew him as a carcass fit for hounds.
> —William Shakespeare, *Julius Caesar*, ed. Oliver Arnold
> (New York: Longman, 2010), 2.1.167–75.

Real blood sacrifice is truly violent, as a living creature is put to death, and fictional sacrifice narratives are violent as well, as they force us or lead us to imagine a killing or averted killing of an animal, an adult, or a child. Thus, we are led to imagine Jephthah's nameless daughter being slaughtered and then burned by her father, or Abraham holding the knife over his bound son.

First, we should recall that killing, sanctioned by authorities, or defined as criminal, is not sacrifice. Humans are killed every day by kin and by strangers, but the thought of a transaction with deities is never there. In sacrifice, victims must be offered to a deity (Noegel, 2016), and the act is a celebration: "Half gods are worshipped in wine and flowers. Real gods require blood" Hurston (2006: 145). Structuring death in accordance with religious fantasies offers the believers both a successful transaction and a way of imaginary coping with death. A sacred killing takes place without rage, in cold blood, under control, with a prescribed order of action, incantations, and specified roles. It is this predictable order that gives the ritual its power to affect a deal with powerful spirits.

A rare phenomenon of voluntary death among old men and women, when they feel that living should end, is found in the Siberian Chukchi culture. The old person involved is killed by a relative, usually a son. According to Willerslev

(2009), this is a form of a ritual blood sacrifice, conceived by participants as an exchange of soul-stuff with deceased ancestors.

During ritual killing (of an animal or a human), the officiants and the audience are not only transformed and moved but shocked as well, identifying with the killers and the victims, engulfed in fantasy and in the reality of dying. They also believe that the transaction between their community and the spirit world will ensure their survival, prosperity, and cosmic peace.

It is also possible that those who are habitually involved in sacrifice, or in ritual slaughter, develop a state of moral disengagement, which neutralizes any emotional reaction. In a study of individuals engaged in executions in the United States, this state of disengagement was found (Osofsky, Bandura, and Zimbardo, 2005). When we read the descriptions of hearts being torn out of the chests of victims in Inca human sacrifice, we can imagine the priests to be in such a state.

Human sacrifice has been a worldwide practice, but the archaeological evidence for many of the prehistoric cases is in doubt or in dispute. Kansa et al. (2009; cf. Carter, 2012) found evidence for what seems like sixth-millennium BCE feast that included cannibalism in Neolithic Anatolia, but we still are not sure how the human victims were killed. In Central Europe, there is evidence of human sacrifice and cannibalism dating back to 5000 BCE (Bauer et al., 2016; Meyer et al., 2018). At Umm el-Marra, Syria, excavators found thirteen humans killed by a blow to the head, *c.* 1600 BCE and deposited under eleven strata of animal skeletons. The exact circumstances of the violent deaths are unknown (Schwartz, 2013).

In addition to remains that present an ambiguous story, there are numerous locations around the world where the findings are unequivocal. These include the Aztec culture in Central America, ancient Mesopotamia, Egypt, sub-Saharan Africa, China, India, Southeast Asia, and Oceania. New World cultures, such as the Pawnee, the Maya, and the Inca stand out because of the massive evidence, both qualitative and quantitative, for traditions of human sacrifice. In the case of the Aztecs, the numbers are staggering and the rituals bloodcurdling. Human sacrifice, including child sacrifice, was performed on several Polynesian islands, such as Tahiti and Tonga, up to the nineteenth century, as attested in many contemporary reports.

Politics and Human Sacrifice

Public ceremonies of violence, and especially human sacrifice, are an affirmation and an assertion of authority and power: "The best way to demonstrate one's potency is to sacrifice the most valuable object or objects one can. If a state or leader is very potent, then presumably it or he can afford to sacrifice human heads when important projects are undertaken, such as opening fields" (Barnes, 1993: 155). Using data on the evolution of ninety-three Austronesian culture, Watts et al. (2016) concluded that human sacrifice legitimized class stratification and political authority. In the Aztec empire, mass sacrifices of war captives were carried out in response to natural disasters, or to demonstrate power in response to rebellions (Carrasco, 1999). Winkelman (2014) suggested, based on cross-cultural data, that the presence of human sacrifice as a normal part of culture is explained by population pressures and a desire for intergroup intimidation.

A statement by one of the principal actors involved shows his awareness of the social and political consequences of these human sacrifices:

> King Kpengla of Dahomey, in an explanation of human sacrifice offered to a European enquirer in the 1780s, avowed … "You have seen me kill many men at the Customs … This gives a grandeur to my Customs, far beyond the display of fine things which I buy. This makes my enemies fear me and gives me such a name in the bush." (Law, 1985: 75)

The same sentiment is expressed in the statement from a nineteenth-century king of Asante: "If I were to abolish human sacrifices, I should deprive myself of one of the most effectual means of keeping the people in subjection" (Wilks, 1975: 594). It appears therefore that the central point of the Annual Customs in Dahomey, during which human sacrifices took place, was to assert and reinforce royal power.

Gruesome violence could be a way for the perpetrator to signal formidability. The perpetrator is trying to convince any spectator that he can escalate his violent actions without thinking twice, and this display is quite effective (Scrivner et al., 2020).

Examples of gruesome displays were as follows:

> In Africa, the former requirement that the Rukuba king's installation ceremony included him ingesting small pieces of two different human beings, his deceased predecessor and an infant killed for this propitious event and thereby insuring the longevity of his reign. The tie between human sacrifice and the palaces of royal families was expressed in the Abomey where the king's house was built over the entrails of a conquered enemy chief. Sacrifices became the very stuff of the buildings as when human blood from ritual killings was mixed with the earthen materials used to build the palace walls. (Carrasco, 2013: 214)

Ritual violence has been serving the maintenance of political control, and the emergence of early states was often accompanied by an increase in rituals of sacrifice (Swenson, 2014). This is reflected in what is known as retainer sacrifice.

The tombs of the first dynasty of Egyptian pharaohs (3100–2890 BCE) were each surrounded by an entourage of graves representing the royal court (Morris, 2014), and the royal cemetery in Ur, dating to 2500 BCE, contains the skeletons of hundreds of attendants, who were killed and buried near the tombs of presumed members of the royalty and nobility (Baadsgaard, Monge, and Zettler, 2012; Woolley, 1934). Evidence for the practice of retainer sacrifice is found all over the world, but is it really a form of sacrifice or just a cruel show of ruler potency?

Conceptually, having retainers and wives accompany the ruler or local chief in death seems like an extension of the notion of grave goods, first interred with dead humans about 100,000 years ago (Mayer, Vandermeersch, and Bar-Yosef, 2009). Grave goods or retainer sacrifice are first an investment in the economic sense, made for the benefit of the dead, equipped and provisioned for the afterlife.

Accompanying the chief in death means ritual murder, understood and justified within the religious discourse on preparing for the afterlife. "Ritual murder is the killing of a human being for religious purposes, repeated in specific circumstances in a prescribed fashion that marks it off from profane killing" (Schultz, 2010: 518).

There are many forms of sacrifice benefiting the dead, especially relatives and ancestors, including special prayers, lighting candles, or burning fake paper money and other objects. Killing a human to accommodate the dead, by making the transition to death easier, seems appropriate in the local culture, because of the higher status of the dead person.

We are not surprised to learn that in Tonga, when a chief died, his wives were strangled and buried with him. In some cases, female relatives of the wives were also sacrificed (Filihia, 1999). "At the funeral of the Maharaja of Jaipur in 1818, the royal barber was one of the 36 victims burnt upon the pyre, so that he might continue to shave his lord in the next world" (Morris, 2014: 74). The cruelty of such practices and their political cost led in some cases to their rejection and disappearance within the culture.

While Barnes (1993) argues that human sacrifice proves the potency of the ruler, Carter (2012), Pongratz-Leisten (2012), and Weber (2012) emphasized that it is, more importantly, believed to be the right means to reach the gods and restore a relationship with them.

Human Sacrifice as a Necessity

Certain needs and predicaments were believed to justify human sacrifice and even child sacrifice. Narratives in many cultures tell of situations where a calamity befalls a nation, a tribe, or a clan, and only a human sacrifice would avert or stop the disaster. Catastrophes such as plagues, famines, or an impending defeat, caused by a transgression, must be righted by a penance in the form of human sacrifice. Storms and winds that prevent smooth sailing are another occasion for human sacrifice. This is an ad hoc ritual and not part of regular worship.

Other cultures offered similar ideas of necessity. The Kalika Purana, composed in Northeast India in the eleventh century, states that human sacrifice is permitted only when the country is in danger and war is expected (Lawrence, 1976).

And in another continent,

> in some ancient African societies human beings were sacrificed to carry a direct message to the ancestors. In times of national crisis such as war and drought, a human was sacrificed to provide the community with direct line to the other world. (Thomas, 2005: 17)

This sacrificial act follows the "Emergency formula," "heir sacrifice," or "sacrifice of distress" (Monroe, 2013). We will see it applied to children being sacrificed by their fathers when disaster strikes and offering the child is believed to be the only solution.

Every story about human sacrifice, or child sacrifice, in response to a serious crisis, is a triumph of the cosmic order and a recognition of a divinity's power to ward off chaos.

Thinking about Child Sacrifice

The reality, or fantasy, of child sacrifice, like all sacrifices, is created by specific beliefs about transactions between humans and spirits. The images of child sacrifice are horrifying, but the idea is common. Narratives of child sacrifice as an imaginary transaction are so well-known that they appear as motifs in classical folklore collections.

In Thompson (1955), we find the following motifs:

S263.2 (child sacrificed to gain favor of gods)

S263.2.1 (god furnished substitute for child sacrifice).

Agamemnon's sacrifice of Iphigenia is (S263.2).

A child may be sacrificed as a foundation sacrifice (S261).

The basic plot is of filicide, commanded or accepted by deities. There are countless stories in which children are killed in a variety of transactions with gods.

In some Greek stories, children are offered and cannibalized. Tantalus wanted to test if the gods really knew everything, so he killed and cooked his own son Pelops and planned to serve the dish to the gods, but the food looked suspicious. Tantalus was punished for eternity.

A generation later, Pelops' son Thyestes was served the flesh of his own children at a banquet given by his brother Atreus.

Lykaon, the mythical king of Arcadia, was reported to have sacrificed a baby (in some versions one of his own sons or his grandson) to Zeus and became a wolf as a punishment. Another version of the story claims that human flesh was offered to Zeus, testing his omniscience. Zeus overturned the table in anger.

Norse mythology offers several stories of sons being sacrificed by their fathers. The mythological Swedish king Aun gained ten years of life for every son he sacrificed, and so sacrificed nine of his own sons to Odin in exchange for longer life, until the Swedes stopped him from sacrificing his last son, Egil.

At least two versions of a story about Heidrek the Wise involve sacrificing a son. When the land suffers a famine, it is determined by the priests that the most noble young man must be sacrificed to Odin. The chosen young man turned out to be Heidrek's son, Angantyr. In return for his son, Heidrek would be granted half the army, but then he rebels, kills the king (his father-in-law) and the king's son (his brother-in-law), and wins the whole kingdom.

In another version of the story, Heidrek agreed to sacrifice his son in exchange for commanding a fourth of the kingdom. He then seized the entire kingdom and prevents the sacrifice of his son.

Killing children is horrifying, but humans will make allowances when it is ordained by gods and leads to salvation.

> In several ancient texts, be they biblical, Greek, or Roman, human—and especially child—sacrifices are described as the ultimate solution to get out of a desperate situation. Very often, one offers to the gods that which is most precious and valuable—one's children—in order to have the deity intervene (unless it is the deity itself that requires the sacrifice, generally through an oracle). (Berthelot, 2007: 152)

In all narratives of human sacrifice or child sacrifice, the transactions work out, whether the victim dies or not. The most shocking deal saves the city, the king, or the covenant. We observe a template, in which every case of child sacrifice or intended child sacrifice was a successful transaction, or a double miracle when the child survived, and the transaction worked out. Children selected for sacrifice in mythology are princes, but in reality, unprotected children, as well as upper-class youngsters, may end up dying for others.

In Tonga, we hear about a child being sacrificed to save his ailing father. When a chief was seriously ill, a child was sacrificed to secure healing. It was a child fathered by the chief with a low-status woman. In 1797, the supreme leader of Tonga was dying. One of his sons was tricked and killed as a sacrifice. The leader had fifteen wives, and the victim was by one of the low-status spouses. The sacrifice was arranged by another son, by a higher-status consort (Filihia, 1999).

A recent case of child sacrifice reflects a substitution fantasy encountered in so many cultures. It was reported in Nepal in 2015. Four men were arrested after a father whose own child had been sick arranged for a ten-year-old child to be sacrificed following advice from a shaman (CNN, 2015).

In the Inca empire (1438–1533) "human sacrifices seeking atonement were conducted on sacred summits in response to natural calamities (such as volcanic eruptions)" (Ceruti, 2015: 9; cf. Reinhard and Ceruti, 2005).

Five centuries later, in the same region of South America, "the last human sacrifice that has been recorded among the Mapuche took place in the surrounding areas of Puerto Saavedra in 1960, after a huge, devastating earthquake. An abandoned small child was sacrificed in order to 'calm down deities' and to bring an end to the destruction" (Gonza´lez-Galvez, 2012: 134).

Dreams of Purity

New World cultures distinguished themselves in carrying out large-scale human sacrifices, including child sacrifice. Between 3,500 and 5,000 years ago, in what today is the Central United States "several dozen babies—apart from the infanticide victims—among the 480 were ritually sacrificed for rain falling/fertility rites, a rebalancing rite, a hunt god rite, and world renewal rites" (Claassen, 2013: 307). The Aztecs engaged in child sacrifice "on the mountains" (Guilhem, 2004; Hogg, 1966). Aztec children were drowned as an offering to the rain god and were also sacrificed to the fire god (Tannahill, 1975). Children were also sacrificed to insure fertility (James, 2002).

Detailed and horrifying descriptions of child sacrifices in the Inca empire are offered by numerous sources. Reading these descriptions teaches us about the reality of child sacrifice.

The capacocha was a sacrifice in which

> human victims who were described as "Chosen Ones," boys and girls under the age of fourteen, were offered to a deity. The capacocha was also performed at times of special need, such as pestilence, earthquake, famine and war. (MacCormack, 2000: 120–1)

Why were children selected?

> Children were not the subject of sacrifice due to their marginal status as less than adult, but rather the opposite—that due to their very young age which afforded them proximity to the ancestors and the gods, they were one of the most precious offerings available. (Ardren, 2011: 133)

Choosing the proper victims was done with care:

> The preferred victims were unblemished and of unusual beauty. They were seldom newborns; they could even be adolescents ... Upon death, these innocent victims might attain a status of guardian and protector of the region. (Lantigua, 2018: 302–3)

> The chroniclers report that children were selected to serve as messengers to the gods because their "purity" made them the most fitting mediators between humans and deities. (Ceruti, 2015: 7)

A moving story tells of a father offering his daughter to be sacrificed, with political gains to the whole clan:

> Sometime in the mid or later fifteenth century, the curaca Caque Poma from Ocros ... committed himself to offer his only daughter, who was "beautiful beyond exaggeration," as a capacocha sacrifice in return for the Inca's help in constructing an irrigation canal ... the girl thus walked in solemn procession to Cuzco, arriving there along with other such delegations ... After days of celebration, those of the "chosen ones" who were to die in Cuzco were given to eat and to drink one last time, and were then strangled or put to sleep and placed in shaft graves as offerings to the Maker, to Pachamama, Mother Earth, and to other deities of the Incas. (MacCormack, 2000: 125)

> For the curaca of Ocros and his beautiful daughter, who, like other chosen ones, was to die in her homeland, a last act followed, which was the long and solemn return home. By the end of this journey, the girl ... appears to have arrived at a

> sense of closure, for on coming back to Ocros ... she said, "Finish with me now, because the celebrations which they did for me in Cuzco are quite sufficient." So, dressed in the finest clothes, she was lowered into a shaft grave with a supply of ornaments ... and was left there, on a mountain peak that was visible from far and wide ... Her father Caque Poma, as a result of all this, has his "seat and lordship" confirmed by the Inca, and ... Caque Poma's descendants followed in peaceful succession long after the Inca's empire had been destroyed by the Spanish. As for Tanta Carhua, she became "the guardian and protector of the entire province." (MacCormack, 2000: 126)

A similar case is reported by another source:

> Chronicler Hernandez Principe specifically mentions that a local leader from the Peruvian sierra (seeking to increase his political standing), volunteered his ten-year-old daughter for the state sponsored ritual of capacocha and was granted special privileges by a grateful Inca emperor because of his "generosity." (Ceruti, 2015: 9)

The sacrificers sought to sanitize the reality of killing: "Capacocha channeled and contained the violence of human sacrifice within very strictly defined limits ... the death of capacocha victims appears to have been a gentle one, in so far as death by sacrifice can ever be gentle" (MacCormack, 2000: 132).

It is interesting to note the parallels between the beliefs in the purity of the ideal victims, babies and young children, hundreds of years ago in the Inca empire and in fantasies about Satanists in the late twentieth century. The accusation that Satanists prefer the killing of babies because of their purity was made in several publications (e.g., DeMause, 1994; Feldman, 1995). The same accusation was made (by Christians) about Bedouins in fifth-century West Asia, as quoted by Frankfurter (2021: 204): "[These people] especially like to offer children distinguished by beauty and the bloom of youth. These they sacrifice on piles of stones at dawn." The purity fantasy resonates with humans everywhere.

The historical evidence of child sacrifice in several cultures demonstrates the same psychological dynamics illustrated in mythological stories. Fathers will protect their children, if they can, but will accept cruel social pressure in the interest of community and nation. Beyond the family, child sacrifice is celebrated by the community, and the dead children are considered the nation's emissaries. New World cultures, and especially Aztec and Inca, provide us with the best documentation of child sacrifice.

We can also find evidence about the acts of parents whose children were sacrificed:

> The parents of sacrificial victims were expected to surrender their children willingly and were encouraged by the Inca to consider the selection of their offspring for capacocha as a great social honor as well as being an act of pious devotion. (Ceruti, 2015: 7)

Under what circumstances would parents hand over their child to be sacrificed? It is not the same as killing one's own child, but it's absolutely, knowingly, close. In the case of Inca child sacrifice, of which much information is available, children were selected, and parents told they were being honored.

> The Inca sacrifice of Andean children would have been ideologically presented as having an important "mission" in which these "chosen ones" would continue living among the celestial and mountain deities as intercessors on behalf of the Inca emperor and for their own people.
>
> Their parents, their kinsmen, and local communities would have been encouraged by the Inca to believe that the payment of this type of "tribute" (consisting of their own children) was not only a religious obligation but more importantly, it was a great social "honor" as well. (Ceruti, 2015: 7)

According to many sources, parents accepted the official narrative and probably did not have much of a choice (MacCormack, 2000). Parental reaction in this situation may be regarded as a rationalization, which involves the realities of power among the Inca and the Aztecs, together with the parents' own guilt and unbearable suffering.

Despite the religious beliefs and the political pressures, there is evidence of parental suffering:

> But in one instance, commenting that some individuals "gave" their children to be buried alive, he added: "He who gave his child went about weeping." (MacCormack, 2000: 134)

There are also reports of children escaping after being buried alive.

Coping with the loss of children has led parents, millennia ago or today, to seek meaning and rationalize. Accepting the idea of the sacrificed children as the perfect emissaries for family and community that is an integral part of their religion is one form of rationalization. Modern parents may find benefits in disasters and use religious beliefs to have the energy to get up in the morning, telling themselves that their dead children are up in heaven, with the angels (Davis and Nolen-Hoeksema, 2001; Holland, Currier, and Neimeyer, 2006; Lichtenthal et al., 2010; Matthews and Marwit, 2003; Stein et al., 2009).

I have personally watched televised testimonies by Orthodox Jewish fathers who, after losing a young child, calmly stated that this was the result of the child's soul ending its migrations and being ready for the next stage. The child died young because his soul was close to perfection and needed just a short time for a final stage of preparation for "nirvana."

Bereaved parents, whose world seems to be crumbling, find consolation in the idea that a cosmic order has preordained the death of their child, who may be assigned a role in humanity's negotiations with the gods. Such fantasies, which occur to parents who have not experienced bereavement, are clearly connected to child sacrifice narratives, in which the child is essential to reaching miraculous responses from the gods. In most child sacrifice fantasies, the child is lost, but lives on in his role as the one who saved his father, the kingdom, or the whole nation.

8

Human Sacrifice in West Asian Heritage

This chapter offers observations on twenty cases of sacrifice, two involving adults whose sacrifice is unrelated to family ties, and fourteen narratives in which parents are responsible for child sacrifice, in most cases the firstborn son. A father is the sacrificer, and the circumstances are dire. No one can defy the gods, and humans end up snared, defeated, and helpless, but they survive, unlike their children, who often perish. The connection to the myth of the Binding, and to the myth of Jesus, is obvious.

Staubli (2015) states that actual human sacrifice was never a reality in West Asia, so where do sacrifice scripts come from? One plot started with the intention of sacrificing a child and then a substitution miracle took place. Why is a miracle needed, and where does the sacrifice fantasy come from? We do not get an answer, but we do get significant connections to traditions of child sacrifice stories.

Staubli (2015) presented an ancient artistic depiction of imaginary scenes where a child is saved from being sacrificed through the actions of a goddess and the miraculous appearance of an animal to be offered. This tradition possibly contains both murderous designs and triumphant compassion.

> From Mesopotamia and Syria came the story, expressed without words in works of art, of a human who is about to be killed or sacrificed to an evil god, and then miraculously saved when a benevolent goddess produces an animal, most often a sheep or goat seemingly dropped from heaven, to take its place as the victim. Works of art depicting this theme were created already in the nineteenth century BCE ... an ancient Babylonian, Syrian, and Canaanite tradition ... combining a priori the possibility of human sacrifice (as an unsurpassable measure of devotion) with the redemption of it by a divine gift (as an unsurpassable measure of grace).
>
> It shows that the pagans of the ancient Near East were able to confront and to question mighty human feelings, conceived of and shaped as gods: righteous

zeal with its willingness to murder; compassion and love with its willingness to find a less violent solution. (Staubli, 2015: 99–100)

Both human sacrifice and the substitution miracle appear early in Mesopotamian art, and thus might have influenced other traditions.

In West Asia, there were stories telling of the miracles of child sacrifice, and despite the tragic context, the stories are optimistic in the sense of relating successful transactions with the spirits. Whether the child dies or is miraculously saved, the sacrificer, who is usually the father, gets his reward. This survey of sacrifice stories shows that they all share a belief in the right offering, leading to crisis resolution.

Greeks, Phoenicians, Hebrews, and later Christians living in the Eastern Mediterranean shared the same stories and traditions of the sacred killings landscape, and the logic of sacrifice is identical. Here is one reader's comment: "The echoes of Hebrew sacrificial thought are uncanny, to say nothing of the passion narrative" (Wyatt, 2009: 426).

Exchanges were bi-directional. Not only did Greece affect the world, but "it now seems clear that many of the Greek gods and myths existed in Asia Minor and Phoenicia and even further east before they existed in Greece" (Williams, 1968: 10). If cultural borders do exist, they are extremely permeable, and certain fantasies travel easily.

The firstborn formula for solving extreme crisis is found in the landscape, or the cultural climate, around West Asia, where we observe echoes and similarities to beliefs and practices from Mesopotamia to Greece (Sparks, 2007). In this shared sphere, neighboring cultures are in contact, which leads to both conflict and influence. It is first and foremost a miracle fantasy about being saved from extinction. Cultures may share the formula and then naturally express commonality, as well as emphasizing their own respective uniqueness (Blakely, 2018; Edrey, 2018; Niehr, 2008; Noegel, 2007; Stern, 2003).

Roman and Greek Stories about Phoenician Child Sacrifice

Silius Italicus (*c.* 26–101 CE) wrote a long poem titled "Punica," which contained a story about child sacrifice in Carthage. The firstborn sons to be offered were determined by lots. One selection fell on Hannibal Barca, who had to offer his only begotten son. The child was saved when Hannibal sacrificed calves instead.

Diodorus Siculus, a Greek historian of the first century BCE, described Carthage being under siege by Agathocles of Syracuse, which led to mass child sacrifices. Diodorus claimed that certain Phoenicians had bought children and substituted them for their own children, selected for sacrifice. This ruse was noticed by the gods, and only when the originally selected children volunteered to be the victims was the siege lifted.

These stories reflected the prejudices and stereotypes promoted by the Romans at the time and can be regarded as the repetitions of ancient templates (Barcelo, 1994; Prag, 2010).

Sacrificing a King or a Virgin

According to Bremmer (2002, 2015), in cases of necessity, when a city was facing ruin, self-sacrifice was an important part of Greek sacrificial ideology, expressed in many mythological narratives. The gods always initiate the sacrifice through an oracle.

King Kodros of Athens saved his city by sacrificing himself to be killed by an invading army, following a message from the Delphic oracle.

In Thebes, it was Menoeceus, son of Creon, and grandson of Oedipus, scion of a tragic, long-accursed family, who, following a prophecy by the oracle Tiresias, sacrifices himself by jumping off the walls of the city to stop a siege. The curse started with his great-grandfather Laius, who raped a handsome youth and was cursed for that.

Numerous stories relate the heroic fate of virgins willing to die for their city. During the reign of Erechtheus, king of Athens, there was a war with Eleusis. An oracle declared that the survival of Athens depended on the sacrifice of one of his three daughters. One daughter volunteered to die. The remaining sisters are said to kill themselves. They remain nameless and known only as the virgins, immortalized by the Parthenon in Athens. In Euripides's *Erechtheus*, Queen Praxithea encourages her husband the king to sacrifice one of his daughters and says, "I hate a woman who holds her child's life above duty."

Macaria was the daughter of Heracles. After Heracles died, King Eurystheus of Tiryns pursued his children, who fled to Athens, and were sheltered by King Demophon. Eurystheus arrived with an army to the gates of Athens and demanded that Heracles's children be surrendered. Demophon refused and received an oracle's message that promised victory for Athens if a virgin was sacrificed to Persephone. Macaria volunteered and committed suicide.

Hyacinthus was a Lacedaemonian who moved to Athens. To deliver the city from famine and plague, an oracle advised the sacrifice of his four daughters, which was done.

The story of Leos and his daughters is similar. Leos was the son of Orpheus and father of a son and of three daughters. Obeying the Delphian oracle, he had his three daughters sacrificed in order to relieve the city of famine.

A Distinguished Citizen and His Daughters

The city of Thebes was at war with the people of Orkhomenos. An oracle promised victory if the Theban citizen of the most distinguished descent would commit suicide. Antipoinos, who had the most illustrious ancestry, was reluctant to sacrifice himself for the city. His two daughters, Androkleia and Alkis, were ready to kill themselves as substitutes for their father. They were buried in the Artemis sanctuary, and their sacrifice was honored by the city and by Herakles, who led the army to victory.

Andromeda and a Mother's Arrogance

Cepheus and Cassiopeia were the king and queen of ancient Ethiopia. Cassiopeia boasted that she was more beautiful than the Nereids, fifty sea nymphs living in the depths of the Aegean Sea. This pretension led Poseidon to send a sea monster named Cetus, which started decimating the Ethiopians. An oracle tells King Cepheus that he must sacrifice his virgin daughter Andromeda to the monster, so his subjects may be spared. Andromeda is chained to a rock in the sea to atone with her life for her mother's vanity. She is then saved by Perseus, a great hero and the son of Zeus, who kills the monster. Andromeda becomes his wife, and they are blessed with many illustrious descendants, including Heracles.

The Tragedy of Athamas

Athamas was the king of Boeotia and had married Nephele, a cloud-goddess who had been created in the image of Hera by Zeus. From Nephele, Athamas begot a son, Phrixos, and a daughter, Helle. Later, Athamas repudiated Nephele and took another wife, Ino, daughter of Cadmus. Ino hated her stepchildren and plotted to have them killed by their own father. She bribed messengers who told Athamas that the oracle of Delphi wanted him to sacrifice his son to Zeus on Mount Laphystion in order to end famine in their country.

Just as Athamas was about to sacrifice Phrixos, Zeus (or Hermes, or Nephele, depending on the version) sent a golden winged ram, that took Phrixos and Helle on its back. Helle fell into the sea, and the ram brought Phrixos safe to Colchis (Georgia). There, to thank Zeus for saving his life, Phrixos sacrificed the ram, and hung its golden fleece on an oak. This story is the prologue of the epic of the Argonauts, who will come to Colchis years later to bring the famous Golden Fleece back to Greece. (Wajdenbaum, 2010: 132)

Frazer (1990) discusses various stories about Athamas in the context of a custom of sacrificing the firstborn son. In one version of the narrative, Phrixos was a willing victim, whose readiness to save his community from famine was praised in plays and artworks (Tiverios, 2014).

As ordered or requested by gods to kill his son, Athamas was a tragic figure, whose firstborn son was saved, but then lost his other children. Then an oracle had ordered Athamas himself to be sacrificed for his country. He was saved at the last minute, just like his firstborn son Phrixos, but went mad and killed his son Learchus. Next, he tried to kill his remaining son Melicertes. The son was saved and went to the island of Tenedos, where, interestingly, "babes were sacrificed to him" (Frazer, 1990: 163). Because Athamas escaped being sacrificed, it was commanded by the gods that the firstborn son in every generation of his descendants would be sacrificed if he set foot in the town hall. Many tried to avoid their fate by exile, but homesickness led to the death of others.

The basic Athamas template shows how he was fooled to commit a senseless killing of his children. This story contains extremes of family hate and love, ending with the punishment of Athamas and his descendants.

In earlier versions, only the sacrifice of the firstborn son to Zeus was mentioned, and Phrixos volunteered to die in order to save the kingdom (Krappe, 1923). Athamas, as the king, was supposed to be the victim:

> The basis of the Phrixos story is undoubtedly an Old Greek belief of holding the king responsible for the failure of the crops. The result was that the king was sacrificed to mitigate the wrath of the gods whenever a famine threatened. (Krappe, 1923: 145)

Bremmer (2008) suggests that the message coming from Delphi implies that the king was guilty of grave offenses against the gods, which was the real cause of the famine. There is an interesting parallel in the Hebrew Bible (2 Samuel 21), discussed later in this chapter.

In times of famine, human sacrifice becomes necessary, and the king or his son will be sacrificed. The firstborn son will die to avoid catastrophe, or end of the kingdom, which to the rulers equals the end of the world. Then, the only beloved son needs to be offered (see the case of Mesha).

Various plot lines have become connected with Athamas, some of which were turned into stage plays, written by Aeschylus and Sophocles, among others. Athamas, the child killer, and an intended victim himself, was saved miraculously but punished by having firstborn sacrifice run in his family forever. Athamas is the victim of "fate," that is, the will of the gods. His willingness to obey the oracle and sacrifice his son was supposed to be rewarded, but negotiations with the gods turned out to be a failure.

Hellenized Phoenician Legends

There are two ancient paragraphs, quoted by many scholars (e.g., Frazer, 1922), which claimed to reflect ancient Phoenician practices of child sacrifice in an emergency. They are taken from *Praeparatio Evangelica* by Eusebius of Caesarea (265–339) and attributed to Philo Byblius (*c*. 64–141):

> And when plague and destruction came, Kronos offered his only begotten son as a whole burnt offering to his father Ouranos and he circumcised himself, compelling his allies to do the same thing also along with him. (translated by Williams 1968: 110)

> It was the custom with the ancients, when great dangers befell them, that the rulers of the city or of the nation, instead of permitting the destruction of everyone, gave their most beloved child to be slaughtered as a ransom to the avenging gods. And those who were given were sacrificed with secret rites. Kronos, then, whom the Phoenicians called Elos, being king of the land, and later, after his death, being consecrated as the star of Kronos, had an only son by the nymph of that country who was called Anobret. For this reason, they called the son Ieoud, as the only son is still called even today by the Phoenicians. Now when very great dangers from war befell the land, he adorned his son in royal fashion, prepared an altar and sacrificed him. (translated by Williams, 1968: 120)

This is not only a story of firstborn sacrifice, but Kronos is told to have circumcised himself, sacrificing his prepuce, and forced the mutilation on his allies. This is reminiscent of the text of Gen. 17:23-27, where Abraham circumcised himself and then all male members of his household.

The Strange Story of Jonah

The quest for calm seas and smooth sailing is tied to other stories of human sacrifice. Dangers at sea or even on a river were recognized in ancient times when every trip was a risk. The idea that the spirits that control calm seas or rivers demand human lives to let sailors survive is found in many cultures.

Storms, disasters, and shipwrecks have been universally believed to be caused by personal sins or pollution, just like disease.

> In Hellenistic thought the working out of retributive justice was often complicated by belief in the possibility of religious pollution. According to this idea, the innocent, if they associate even unknowingly with a person guilty of a religious crime, are so endangered by him that they may become engulfed in whatever disaster it is by which the guilty is punished. A particularly relevant example of this belief from the Judaic tradition is, of course, the story of Jonah. (Miles and Trompf, 1976: 261)

The Greeks were a seafaring people and were constantly concerned about safe sailing. Human sacrifice to pacify the winds for sailing is mentioned together with the sacrifice of Iphigeneia, and the sacrifice of Polyxena. It is also reported in a story about Menelaus, king of Sparta and brother of Agamemnon. During a visit to Egypt, Menelaus sacrificed two children, to ensure favorable winds on his trip back. This led to universal condemnation (Vandiver, 2012).

> In the fourth-century Characters of Theophrastus, the coward is defined as the sort of person who on shipboard, as soon as a great wave hits the side, asks "whether there is someone uninitiated on board," uninitiated, that is, into the cult of Kabiri, the Samothracian patron saints of sailors. (Ladouceur, 1980: 443)

We find such beliefs in modern times:

> During the sinking of the Titanic, when Olive Schreiner was being lowered into a lifeboat, one of the passengers cried out, "Don't put her in here. She is an Atheist and will sink us." (Ladouceur, 1980: 440)

Even sailors on the Volga believed that sacrificing a young woman to the river was a good idea. One of the best-known Russian folksongs is a ballad about Stenka Razin, the Cossack leader executed in 1671. Razin sacrifices a young woman, a "Persian princess" to Mother Volga after a night of lovemaking. The beautiful melody in so many renditions is not equal to the horror story of apotropaic killing.

In Japan, not only storms at sea required human lives to be calmed, but even construction of bridges over water needed to be secured this way (Noritake, 1918). Rarely mentioned among ancient stories about human sacrifice is the case of Jonah, who is cast at sea to stop a raging storm. How Jonah was saved from drowning is celebrated in countless interpretations, but the fact that he was thrown off to stop a raging sea is neglected like an afterthought.

Jon. 1:4-15

> 4 But the Lord sent out a great wind into the sea, and there was a mighty tempest in the sea, so that the ship was like to be broken.
>
> 5 Then the mariners were afraid, and cried every man unto his god, and cast forth the wares that were in the ship into the sea, to lighten it of them. But Jonah was gone down into the sides of the ship; and he lay and was fast asleep.
>
> 6 So the shipmaster came to him, and said unto him, What meanest thou, O sleeper? arise, call upon thy God, if so be that God will think upon us, that we perish not.
>
> 7 And they said every one to his fellow, Come, and let us cast lots, that we may know for whose cause this evil is upon us. So they cast lots, and the lot fell upon Jonah.
>
> 8 Then said they unto him, Tell us, we pray thee, for whose cause this evil is upon us; What is thine occupation? and whence comest thou? what is thy country? and of what people art thou?
>
> 9 And he said unto them, I am an Hebrew; and I fear the Lord, the God of heaven, which hath made the sea and the dry land.
>
> 10 Then were the men exceedingly afraid, and said unto him. Why hast thou done this? For the men knew that he fled from the presence of the Lord, because he had told them.
>
> 11 Then said they unto him, What shall we do unto thee, that the sea may be calm unto us? for the sea wrought, and was tempestuous.
>
> 12 And he said unto them, Take me up, and cast me forth into the sea; so shall the sea be calm unto you: for I know that for my sake this great tempest is upon you.
>
> 13 Nevertheless the men rowed hard to bring it to the land; but they could not: for the sea wrought, and was tempestuous against them.
>
> 14 Wherefore they cried unto the Lord, and said, We beseech thee, O Lord, we beseech thee, let us not perish for this man's life, and lay not upon us innocent blood: for thou, O Lord, hast done as it pleased thee.
>
> 15 So they took up Jonah, and cast him forth into the sea: and the sea ceased from her raging.

The authority and power of several gods are recognized by the authors of this Biblical fantasy. The story arrays several gods who have their followers on the ship. Religious identities were in place and in play. Jonah must make a deal with his god, who had caused the storm, and so he is (willingly) sacrificed. The transaction is successful and the storm ends, but YHWH intervenes again, and Jonah survives. There is a perfect match between the victim and the god. The right victim was cast out to sea, and the right god stopped the storm in a double miracle for Jonah.

Loving Daughter, Warrior Father, and Smooth Sailing

Iphigeneia's story is well known, in several inconsistent versions. Most agree that there was no miracle, and Agamemnon sacrificed his daughter.

> Agamemnon, following the advice of Odysseus, sends for Iphigenia, promising her marriage with Achilles. The sacrificed child does not get the chance to utter any protest: When Iphigenia becomes aware of her father's treachery, the priests at Aulis gag her mouth, stop her from uttering a word. (Tucker, 1999: 33)

In Aeschylus' *Agamemnon*, the goddess Artemis demands the sacrifice because of the bloodshed before the fleet was planning to leave for Troy. According to another version Artemis demanded a sacrifice "in propitiation for a stag which Agamemnon has killed in Artemis' sacred grove" (Burkert, 1985, p.151). In another version, the goddess Artemis is angered by the Greeks' plan to destroy Troy, holding the fleet at Aulis and demanding a virgin in sacrifice before the right wind will let the ships sail. In the miracle versions of the narrative, used by Euripides, a deer or a bear took the daughter's place and she survived.

> In some versions she is killed by her father, in other versions an animal is substituted for her, and she is taken away by the goddess to serve her as a virgin and priestess. Curiously the substitution pattern seems to be older than the death pattern ... Both patterns can be found in Euripides' tragedies. (Römer, 1998: 34)

Iphigenia's killing led to a long chain of revenge murders. Iphigenia's mother, Clytemnestra, slaughters Agamemnon. Her children, Orestes and Electra, vow to avenge their mother's murder of their father, which takes place when he comes home from the Trojan War. The family is cursed, as murders follow murders across generations.

If stories were told about Iphigenia's miraculous survival and her new life as priestess or goddess, they were still horrifying. She was busy now carrying out the sacrifice of shipwrecked sailors and prisoners of war in mythical Tauris.

The Jephthah Sacrifice

The basic plot of the leader who makes a vow, unthinking, and ends up killing a loved one is well known, and listed among universal folklore motifs. It appears in Thompson (1955) as S241 ("first thing you meet").

A Greek story tells of Maeander, the son of Cercaphus and Anaxibia, who, while at war with the Pessinuntines, made a vow to the mother of the Gods. If he emerged victorious, he would sacrifice the first person that came to congratulate him. The first that met him following his victory were his son Archelaus, his mother, and his sister. He sacrificed all of them, but then committed suicide by jumping into a river that now bears his name. This story comes to us from third to fourth century CE (Pseudo-Plutarch, 2008).

In a melancholy narrative, Jephthah, an Israelite hero, sacrifices his daughter to fulfill a vow he had made to God in exchange for military victory over the Ammonites. The story is bleak, and the daughter's name remains unknown. Still, the sequence of events is clear and straightforward.

Judg. 11:29-40

> 30 And Jephthah vowed a vow unto the Lord, and said, If thou shalt without fail deliver the children of Ammon into mine hands,
>
> 31 Then it shall be, that whatsoever cometh forth of the doors of my house to meet me, when I return in peace from the children of Ammon, shall surely be the Lord's, and I will offer it up for a burnt offering.
>
> 32 So Jephthah passed over unto the children of Ammon to fight against them; and the Lord delivered them into his hands.
>
> 33 And he smote them from Aroer, even till thou come to Minnith, even twenty cities, and unto the plain of the vineyards, with a very great slaughter. Thus the children of Ammon were subdued before the children of Israel.
>
> 34 And Jephthah came to Mizpeh unto his house, and, behold, his daughter came out to meet him with timbrels and with dances: and she was his only child; beside her he had neither son nor daughter.
>
> 35 And it came to pass, when he saw her, that he rent his clothes, and said, Alas, my daughter! thou hast brought me very low, and thou art one of them that trouble me: for I have opened my mouth unto the Lord, and I cannot go back.

36 And she said unto him, My father, if thou hast opened thy mouth unto the Lord, do to me according to that which hath proceeded out of thy mouth; forasmuch as the Lord hath taken vengeance for thee of thine enemies, even of the children of Ammon.

37 And she said unto her father, Let this thing be done for me: let me alone two months, that I may go up and down upon the mountains, and bewail my virginity, I and my fellows.

38 And he said, Go. And he sent her away for two months: and she went with her companions and bewailed her virginity upon the mountains.

39 And it came to pass at the end of two months, that she returned unto her father, who did with her according to his vow which he had vowed: and she knew no man. And it was a custom in Israel,

40 That the daughters of Israel went yearly to lament the daughter of Jephthah the Gileadite four days in a year.

The tragic Jephthah story is presented by the authors as part of tradition, not an aberration. The father's idea of sacrifice is not a personal innovation or invention:
"What's missing in this story is any indication that child sacrifice, painful to father and offspring alike, was inappropriate from God's standpoint. Quite the opposite: Jephthah's actions are intelligible only on the assumption that his daughter (he had no son) could legitimately be sacrificed as a burnt offering to Yhwh" (Levenson, 1993: 14). The narrative takes its course, with no authorial comments, and the religious legitimacy of the act is never in doubt (Logan, 2009).

The story is a shocking parallel to the Binding of Isaac, and it seems clear that the author of Judg. 11:30-40 knows Genesis 22 well and follows its structure (Römer, 1998). The unnamed daughter is an only child, like Isaac, but no ram appears to save her. If Abraham made a deal and won a blessing and a covenant, Jephthah won a war because of his vow, and there was a true *do ut des*, as in the Mesha story below (Tatlock, 2006). Abraham won countless descendants, while Jephthah will have none.

Römer (1998) claims that not only was the author of the Jephthah story familiar with Genesis 22, but he was also at home in Greek culture and knew the story of Iphigenia, sacrificed by her father Agamemnon. This nameless author wished to present Jephthah's daughter as the Hebrew Iphigenia and the vow narrative in Judges 11 represents a very late addition under Hellenistic influence. Gnuse (2020) points to the obvious similarity between the two maidens being sacrificed, Iphigeneia and the unnamed daughter of Jephthah. Another virgin willingly sacrificed in Greek narratives is Polyxena, the princess sacrificed next to the tomb of Achilles at the end of the Trojan War (Bremmer, 2002).

In his treatise *Panarion*, written around 377 CE, Epiphanius of Salamis discusses cults associated with Jephthah's daughter that evidently existed in his day:

> In Sebasteia, which was once called Samaria, they have declared Jephthah's daughter a goddess, and still hold a festival in her honor every year … For in Shechem, that is, the present-day Neapolis, the inhabitants offer sacrifices in the name of Core [Persephone], supposedly because of Jephthah's daughter, who was once offered to God as a sacrifice. (Epiphanius of Salamis, 2013: 79)

This testimony runs counter to the impression of Biblical scholars, who could find no evidence in Jewish sources for the mourning tradition mentioned in the book of Judges (Shoemaker, 2008).

The earliest Christian reference to Jephthah appears in the book of Hebrews, where he is listed alongside other military leaders and righteous men (such as David); no mention is made of his daughter (11:32).

Idomeneus and Exile

A close parallel to the Jephthah story is that of Idomeneus, who, while coming back from the Trojan War hit a huge storm. He then made a vow to Poseidon to sacrifice the first living being he encountered when getting home, if only Poseidon would save the ship. The first living being he met was his son. When Idomeneus carried out his vow, the gods got angry and his kingdom, Crete, was hit by a plague. He then was exiled and died away from Crete. Another version of the story tells of Idomeneus losing his throne to Leucus, his foster son, who had seduced and then killed Idomeneus's wife Meda. Apparently, some Greeks were partial to Oedipal plots.

Idomeneo, a 1781 opera seria by Mozart, is based on the story of Idomeneus's return to Crete. In this version, Poseidon (Neptune in the opera) spares Idomeneo's son Idamante, on the condition that Idomeneo relinquish his throne to the new generation

The Mesha Narrative

The king of Israel, the king of Judah, and the king of Edom went to war against Mesha, king of Moab. The prophet Elisha promised them a total victory. They were indeed triumphant, destroyed Moab, and laid siege to Mesha's capital. Then came a dramatic turn of events:

2 Kgs. 3:26-27

> 26 And when the king of Moab saw that the battle was too sore for him, he took with him seven hundred men that drew swords, to break through even unto the king of Edom: but they could not.
>
> 27 Then he took his eldest son that should have reigned in his stead and offered him for a burnt offering upon the wall. And there was great indignation against Israel: and they departed from him and returned to their own land.

This is one of the most stunning passages in the Hebrew Bible. Here the authors tell us that the Israelites, supported by their god YHWH and promised a victory by the great prophet Elisha, were defeated by the Moabites, supported by Chemosh. This only happened after Mesha sacrificed his firstborn son to Chemosh.

There is no other case in the Bible where YHWH is defeated in an encounter with another god. The authors seem to assume that their readers are familiar with the practice of such a burnt offering. In this case, Mesha's child is the firstborn, just like Isaac and Jephthah's daughter.

David and Saul's Sins

Several Hebrew Bible narratives express the belief that when disaster strikes, such as a famine, or a plague, which must be is the result of human sin committed by the king, only a human sacrifice will satisfy YHWH and will save the people.

2 Sam. 21:1-14 tells a sad story about a drought and a resulting famine in the days of the mythical King David. It turns out that while the reigning king was David, the sin that caused the drought was committed by King Saul. To right Saul's wrongs, two of his three surviving children and five of his grandchildren are killed. Saul's concubine keeps watch over the exposed bodies of her children, waiting day and night for the coming of the rain. The executions do not end the drought, and the rain returns only when the bones of Saul and his son Jonathan are buried in the family plot, together with the bones of Saul's other children (Darshan, 2013).

Is the killing of Saul's children a sacrifice? It might be called a ritual murder, because it is done with the purpose of settling a divinely judged royal wrong. Whether it was the killings, or the act of burying the bones of Saul and Jonathan, these acts were being addressed to the gods, and seemingly recognized and rewarded. This is unlike killings in war and is part of the king's authority (or cruelty).

Lessons to Be Learned

Because every disaster or threat is tied to gods and ancestor spirits, humans need to negotiate and offer a deal. Giving up treasured possessions may ensure our survival. The narratives are straightforward: miracles can be produced through human sacrifice. The special case of firstborn sacrifice works under rare, dire circumstances, but the sides play their roles. The gods, whether YHWH or others, provide victories, and the cosmic order is kept.

Attempts to control nature and human threats through human sacrifice are, according to religious narratives, always successful. The narratives offer an obvious causality. Either a vow that is kept after the desired outcome (Jephthah, Idomeneus), or a public sacrifice (Agamemnon, Mesha, Kronos, Athamas) operate to affect major changes in natural and human events, as gods are moved to interfere.

Stories may appear like a distant rumor but are consistent. King Mesha, faced with imminent defeat, was able to defeat Jehovah. Kronos, in dire straits, was victorious. The stories of Athamas and Abraham (discussed later) prove that the readiness to sacrifice a firstborn son counts just as much as the actual sacrifice. Athamas saved his people and his son, and Abraham won eternal glory. The narrative is shocking but offers a way out of annihilation and into redemption. The protagonists move from fatalism and helplessness to triumph and safety.

When faced with emergencies and existential threats, these narratives of successful transactions may be useful in keeping up hope among the desperate. Disaster stories turning into miracles encourage salvation fantasies. The overall message of the stories as religious lessons is the emphasis on obedience, reward, order, and justice.

This all happens among males, whether humans or deities. We find the fraternity of men versus women in all stories in which where they are mentioned. The exception is in the case of Jephthah, where the daughter, while nameless, is the equivalent of a son because her death will leave him without seed.

If we examine the Hebrew Bible narratives, the Binding of Isaac, Jephthah's daughter, Mesha's son, and Jonah, each one is unique. As the Bible is clearly an anthology, we can ask about the religious significance of a narrative. Why and how was it created and chosen to be canonized? Not all cases are exemplary tales, and two cases, those of Mesha and Jonah, express henotheism. Both describe Israelites in an encounter with the world, and both recognize other gods.

In Judges 11, we find another acceptance of henotheism. In negotiations between Jephthah, as the Israelite leader, and the Ammonites, he states, "Wilt not thou possess that which Chemosh thy god giveth thee to possess? So whomsoever the Lord our God shall drive out from before us, them will we possess." Thus, the Moabites live by, and with, their god Chemosh, while Israelites coexist with YHWH edicts and gifts.

The ubiquity of the miracle-by-sacrifice plot is clear. Child sacrifice is a common, if not a universal, idea. We will find it in Oceania, Africa, and the Americas, and we are going to be touched by reading about the Inca belief in beautiful children, who would serve as the best emissaries to the realm of the gods after they are sacrificed.

The Accusation: Father's Double Culpability

Child sacrifice narratives relate

a. an existential emergency,
b. need for an extreme act of sacrifice, in which a child is offered to the gods.

Most of the dramatic plots focus on (a) and (b) and demonstrate a king's cruelty in deciding to sacrifice his child (or children).

Another issue is implied, and it is even more serious.

Humans explain any misfortune or serious threat, whether it is a plague, famine, or imminent defeat, as resulting from human transgression. A king's sin may cause the whole kingdom to be punished. Many ancient stories mention a king's responsibility for the fate of his kingdom, and how he was expected to be sacrificed in case of plague or famine. They also refer to the king's willingness to relegate being sacrificed to his children.

Here is an inherent father–son conflict, which may be driving the plot of some child sacrifice narratives. Above, I presented the horrifying story of David and Saul (2 Sam. 21:1-14). Saul sinned, and his descendants pay with their lives. David, Saul's adversary, son-in-law, and heir, meted out the sentence.

In addition to the substitution miracle, where an animal is sent by the gods to be sacrificed, in the case of Athamas, and Abraham, when a ram appears, offering children to the gods instead of self is another miracle. In the case of

Kronos, his heir is sacrificed, together with his prepuce, Abraham was ready to sacrifice his son, and did also circumcise himself.

All variations of the child sacrifice narratives imply a father's sin against the gods, which starts the chain of events leading to the killing or averted killing. Then, in response to a catastrophic emergency, the displacement of the lethal punishment from father to child takes place, which makes it all the more horrifying. There are rare cases (discussed earlier) in which the king is indeed the victim and saves the nation. So, children must die because of their fathers' sins. There is one case mentioned above in which a daughter, Andromeda, is offered to be killed to atone for her mother's arrogance.

The Historicity Question

Human sacrifice and child sacrifice, as ways of dealing with the gods, are a major theme in both the Hebrew Bible and the New Testament.

But do such stories, especially the notion of firstborn sacrifice, reflect history or fantasy? It has been argued that the many references to child sacrifice in the Hebrew Bible, and the narratives under discussion here, reflect a reality of child sacrifice as part of an early YHWH tradition.

Are there or have there been any religions or cultures that have practiced child sacrifice as rituals? There is plenty of evidence for that, some presented above. What the record shows is the occurrence of human sacrifice and child sacrifice in numerous cultures. There is no evidence of fathers sacrificing their children, but only of fathers offering their children to be killed.

While unequivocal evidence for human sacrifice is found in many parts of the world, it is rare in West Asia and the Mediterranean. Most archaeological finds in the form of unusual burials lead to uncertain conclusions (Schwartz, 2013). The best-known case of human sacrifice in West Asia is that of the royal cemetery in Ur, dating to 2500 BCE, where a group of servants and soldiers were found buried together with some musical instruments and gold jewelry, next to a VIP tomb (Baadsgaard, Monge, and Zettler, 2012; Woolley, 1934).

The seeming preoccupation with child sacrifice in the Hebrew Bible has led some scholars to argue that the texts alone, including the numerous condemnations and the positive commandments regarding the firstborn sons, are sufficient to assume that child sacrifice was once a historical reality.

We can understand how the phrasing of some condemnations in the Hebrew Bible may be regarded as evidence for the reality of child sacrifice. Condemnation and proscription are evidence of existing practices, otherwise why condemn and forbid? Attempts at suppression show that a phenomenon may be real. What is more interesting are some condemnations that imply that child sacrifice commands were being attributed to YHWH.

Jer. 19:5

> They have built also the high places of Baal, to burn their sons with fire for burnt offerings unto Baal, which I commanded not, nor spake it, neither came it into my mind.

Jer. 32:35

> And they built the high places of Baal, which are in the valley of the son of Hinnom, to cause their sons and their daughters to pass through the fire unto Molech; which I commanded them not, neither came it into my mind, that they should do this abomination, to cause Judah to sin.

Jer. 7:31

> And they have built the high places of Tophet, which is in the valley of the son of Hinnom, to burn their sons and their daughters in the fire; which I commanded them not, neither came it into my heart.

Jeremiah 7.31, 19.5, and 32.35 state that Yahweh did not command the sacrifice of children, a protestation which implies these very claims were made (Gilmour, 2019: 66).

Ezek. 20:25-26 tells us that YHWH achieved personal satisfaction from recognition as the Lord by those who committed child sacrifice:

> 25 Wherefore I gave them also statutes that were not good, and judgments whereby they should not live;
>
> 26 And I polluted them in their own gifts, in that they caused to pass through the fire all that openeth the womb, that I might make them desolate, to the end that they might know that I am the Lord.

Mic. 6:7 presents child sacrifice as an atonement offering, which raises the question of official sanction again.

> Will the LORD be pleased with thousands of rams, or with ten thousands of rivers of oil? shall I give my firstborn for my transgression, the fruit of my body for the sin of my soul?

As noted above, together with such condemnations, Biblical authors show complete equanimity when narrating some cases of human sacrifice, such as Abraham, Jephthah, or Jonah, where the intended recipient is YHWH. The claim that Israelites were engaged in child sacrifice to demons (Ps. 106:37), that is, foreign gods, and that they were punished with exile, is repeated in two of the Dead Sea scrolls (Reynolds, 2006). Hahn and Bergsma (2004) correctly point out that there is no archeological evidence of child sacrifice among the Israelites, so where does the Biblical preoccupation come from?

Over the past seventy years, more and more scholars have argued that child sacrifice was part of the reality of Judaic worship in ancient West Asia (Ackermann, 1992; Day, 1989; Dewrell, 2017; Finsterbusch, Lange, and Diethard Römheld, 2007; Green, 1975; Heider, 1989; Lange, 2007; Levenson, 1993; Noort, 2002; Ruane, 2013; Smith, 1975; Stavrakopoulou, 2004; Tatlock, 2006). Interestingly, these claims by Hebrew Bible scholars recall the assertions by psychoanalysts, who were almost identical (e.g., Lustig, 1976; Schlesinger, 1976).

Here is a relatively early claim about the historicity of human sacrifice among Israelites:

> Any religion that required sacrifice would practice human sacrifice if the theory behind the system were driven to its logical conclusion. For the more valuable the sacrifice the more "power" it would have for the one who offered it. (Sales, 1957: 112)

Niditch (1995: 50), when discussing the Biblical ban (*Herem*) as sacrifice, suggested that it implies "a God who appreciates human sacrifice," and that those engaged in it during a war "would presumably have something in common with those who believed in the efficacy of child sacrifice."

Van Seters (2003) argued that child sacrifice used to be central in Israelite religion, but then a transformation occurred, which was reflected in certain stories around the mythical Exodus. The story of the tenth plague and the story of the paschal lamb were invented by anonymous authors to end the custom of firstborn sacrifice. Thus, the myth of the paschal lamb liberated the Israelite firstborn.

Winkelman (2014: 48) stated that both Judaic and Christian myths grew out of a prevalent "sacrificial-cannibalistic complex":

> For example, in the Old Testament, Abraham was instructed by God to sacrifice his son Isaac (but then stopped by an angel upon passing a test of obedience). Christianity also has symbolic remnants of this ritual sacrificial-cannibalistic

complex (Levenson 1993). This is exemplified in its Saviour, Jesus Christ, who was sacrificed in atonement for the sins of humanity.

Relying on Biblical texts alone, other scholars suggest that child sacrifice was typical of early Judaic culture, and that the Passover sacrifice was a substitute for the firstborn sacrifice. They claim that this theme is found often in Judaic texts and rituals, though in muted form. The springtime festivals that marked the beginning of the year have been suppressed, except for Passover, and now the Judaic year starts in the fall. Making the death of Jesus occur on Passover contributed to the success of Christian mythology about Jesus as the Messiah.

Some scholars today believe that the evidence points to child sacrifice being part of the YHWH rites until the seventh century. Tatlock (2006: 237) regards the year of Jerusalem's fall to the Babylonians, 586 BCE, as the "watershed moment in the history of innocent heir immolation in Yahwism."

The problem with using religious texts as historical sources is that the stories in these texts are fictional. When the narratives we read describe the actions of gods, angels, and other spirits, they cannot be taken seriously. This is true for the Hebrew Bible, the New Testament, or the Mahabharata. Secular stories may be just as fictional, and need to be checked, as they are every day. The allegations by Bennett Braun about the underground Satanic network, quoted earlier, are both secular and purely fictional.

Some Biblical scholars have suggested that archaeological finds from Carthage confirm claims about ancient child sacrifice in West Asia (Day 1989; Heider 1985). However, the findings have not been beyond dispute. The debate over the Carthage Tophet has been raging, but any suggestion that child sacrifice was a reality in the West Mediterranean Phoenician colonies seems unsupported by evidence (Azize, 2014; Garnand, 2013; Schwartz et al., 2017; Smith et al., 2011; Xella, 2017).

It is possible, of course, that the Binding narrative or the Jephthah narrative grew out of other fictional stories, and it is also possible that both a reality of sacrifice and imaginary stories have contributed to their creation. The problem is the lack of relevant evidence.

Stories about human sacrifice go back millennia. What Staubli (2015) describes is a scenario of human sacrifice averted at the last minute, created by humans more than 4,500 years ago, and around the same time we know of human sacrifice in Ur.

Some have argued that behind an ancient story there may be is a memory of even more ancient practices. The story about Cronus eating his children, according to this claim, reflected a very ancient reality of cannibalism (Douglas, 1996). Relying on human memory, especially of ancient times, is always risky.

If we encounter the stories about Isaac or Jesus, they appeared after millennia of possible occurrences of human sacrifice, and traditions of sacrifice narratives, but this does not guarantee their connection to reality. Ancient texts may refer to sacrificing a prince or a martyr. It might have never happened, but, if we can read it now, the plot must have been significant.

The story about the crown prince who is sacrificed by his father King Mesha of Moab, told in 2 Kings 3 is astounding by any measure, and why it was included in the Hebrew Bible is puzzling. It might have never happened, but it is still gripping.

The Greek Case

If we suggest that Hebrew texts show an obsession with human sacrifice, the same could be said of Greek texts. There are many Greek narratives of human sacrifice, some even related to Hebrew stories, but scholars agree that there is no historical reality behind them. The consensus is quite clear.

Hughes (1991) argued that the countless references to human sacrifice in Greek writings are no evidence for actual practices, in the absence of archaeological evidence. In the search for evidence, ancient texts may relate ancient fictions, and archaeological finds may be decisive, but they are absent (Henrichs, 2019).

Rives (1995: 75) stated that "human sacrifice was in the Graeco-Roman tradition always characteristic of 'the other,'" and Parker (2016) stated that human sacrifice occurred only in myth and scandalous stories.

Watts (2011: 11) argued that

> a similar claim can be made about the prominence of sacrificial themes in Greek tragedies. They portray human sacrifice as extraordinary and perverse when practiced by Greeks (e.g., in Euripides' *Iphigenia in Aulis*) and routine only when practiced by barbarians, where it attests to their depravity (as in Euripides' *Iphigenia in Tauris*).

Weiler (2007: 37) stated,

> The practice of human sacrifices is often imputed to the respective enemies, but also to political agitators. However, it can be noticed that the contemporaries shrank back from these acts more and more, considered as cruel and uncivilized.

We might mention that not only is the Hebrew Bible preoccupied with human sacrifice, but so is Norse mythology. When it comes to evidence of actual sacrifices, the picture regarding Norse mythology is different, and enough archaeological finds allow us to determine that in this case mythology is tied to some reality (McLeod, 2018; Walsh et al., 2020).

Many Biblical references to child sacrifice are originally presented as accusations. How should they be judged?

Douglas (1996) suggested that Biblical accusations about child sacrifice are no more credible than the Blood Libel. Garnand (2013) argued that stories about child sacrifice targeted Phoenicians, who for the Greeks were on the edge of the civilized world. Thus, the Phoenicians were another slandered group, like the Canaanites.

Very often, allegations have nothing to do with the actions of those targeted, and everything to do with those making them. Bremmer (2013) demonstrates this in the case of early Christians, accused of cannibalism and incest, just like many other groups. Witchcraft accusations, targeting the weaker in society, included allegations of sexual perversion, infanticide, and cannibalism, repeated recently and targeting nonexistent Satanists (Harland, 2007). We have seen already how contemporary allegations of Satanism, presented with the help of first-person testimonies, were purely fictional.

It would be easy to collect examples of fantastic accusations targeting the oppressors as well as the oppressed. In nineteenth century Africa, European Whites were accused of kidnapping African children to use their meat in cannibalistic feasts (Douglas, 1996).

How does the historicity debate affect my work in this book?

Let's assume that there were indeed cases of child sacrifice in ancient West Asia. If this is true, the acts were based on beliefs about imaginary transactions, held by the participants. If we assume that no such cases of child sacrifice occurred, the imaginary narratives still reflect the same beliefs about imaginary transactions with spirit entities.

I have read with great interest the relevant archaeological literature, but this book is about fantasy. Whether there were really child sacrifice cases or not, the significance is in the fantasies, the narratives that survive and attract believers.

The fantasies about a major transaction and a covenant express the idea that a violent, unprecedented, transaction that includes an unnatural death (or many such deaths) is needed to maintain or save the cosmic order. Such fantasies are found in many cultures and have been spelled out by Hebrews, Christians,

Aztecs, or Inca. We are on safe ground when we ignore all claims to historicity and stick with the fantasies.

Some narratives have become foundational, and first and foremost among them is the Binding of Isaac, which remains enigmatic, frustrating, and powerful. Possibly because of tradition, it still pulls us into its orbit.

9

The Binding

The Binding of Isaac has been told and retold, in most cases by those who saw themselves as the spiritual or physical descendants of Abraham and were committed to his religious heroism. Fatherhood, violence, power, and miracles are the building blocks of this fantasy. The Binding narrative has been embraced and celebrated as a model for billions of believers.

The Binding of Isaac (or Ishmael) has been presented in major religious traditions (Judaism, Christianity, and Islam) as the model of faith and devotion. It is told from the father's point of view, with the child just as obedient as the father, and Abraham remains the hero of the story. Obedience is the beginning of group loyalty, and horrifying stories become a way of building up identity, as the myths are celebrated and remembered, and each member of the religious community is tested, proving (or not) that they find the explanation for the horror convincing. Living out the fantasy in their imagination becomes an experience of election and pride. Our ancestor was chosen, and we follow his example, say the believers. The Abrahamic example is common to Judaism, Islam, and Christianity, while each tradition and its followers will naturally emphasize their uniqueness and superiority.

The audiences for the mythical narratives are made up mostly of believers and have been socialized to accept the framework of obedience and divine compassion, but even to some of them the story may be baffling. The narrative of the Binding comes to us with the entire religious establishment of Judaism, Christianity, and Islam united behind it in their wish to teach us just one lesson from this mythical interaction with YHWH. Jews, Christians, and Moslems agree and celebrate this startling mythic narrative, which is designed to engage the self and create commitment.

The Binding of Isaac

Gen. 22:1-19

1 And it came to pass after these things, that God did tempt Abraham, and said unto him, Abraham: and he said, Behold, here I am.

2 And he said, take now thy son, thine only son Isaac, whom thou lovest, and get thee into the land of Moriah; and offer him there for a burnt offering upon one of the mountains which I will tell thee of …

6 And Abraham took the wood of the burnt offering, and laid it upon Isaac his son; and he took the fire in his hand, and a knife; and they went both of them together.

7 And Isaac spake unto Abraham his father, and said, My father: and he said, Here am I, my son. And he said, Behold the fire and the wood: but where is the lamb for a burnt offering?

8 And Abraham said, My son, God will provide himself a lamb for a burnt offering: so they went both of them together.

9 And they came to the place which God had told him of; and Abraham built an altar there, and laid the wood in order, and bound Isaac his son, and laid him on the altar upon the wood.

10 And Abraham stretched forth his hand, and took the knife to slay his son.

11 And the angel of the Lord called unto him out of heaven, and said, Abraham, Abraham: and he said, Here am I.

12 And he said, Lay not thine hand upon the lad, neither do thou any thing unto him: for now I know that thou fearest God, seeing thou hast not withheld thy son, thine only son from me.

13 And Abraham lifted up his eyes, and looked, and behold behind him a ram caught in a thicket by his horns: and Abraham went and took the ram, and offered him up for a burnt offering in the stead of his son.

Sharp-eyed readers of the Hebrew Bible have noticed that the appellation Elohim, which appears in the first part of the chapter, changes to YHWH (Adonai) in v. 11. This leads to asking whether the latter part, with Isaac being saved, is an added insertion. In the early version, there was no ram and no miracle, and the only son was indeed sacrificed (Tatlock, 2006). Gen. 22:15-18 is also considered a latter insertion (Lemański, 2021).

Staubli (2015) interprets the Binding narrative as a variation of the substitution miracle plot, involving two deities:

> The story of Genesis 22 is likely founded on the same constellation: (1) a deity (ĕlōhîm) asking for (2) a human sacrifice, and (3) another deity, represented by its messenger (mal'ak yhwh) providing (4) an animal substitute. (Staubli, 2015: 100)

This is an intriguing possibility, connecting the Binding to earlier Mesopotamian art. Regardless of the redaction process, what we have now is the official version, which was destined to move and inspire, and became the received version of this foundational myth.

The narrative is so unique, striking, and weighty that it demands a reaction. The story of Isaac is designed to surprise, to shock, and to bind. Who will fail to be moved by a young boy who is being led by his father to a place where sacrifice is about to be performed, and does not suspect that he is the intended victim, when he says, "Behold the fire and the wood; but where is the lamb for a burnt offering?" (Gen. 22:7). The authors would have us believe that the child had witnessed animal sacrifice and knew the procedure. This knowledge creates a moment of intimacy between son and father, but the father cannot tell the truth, because he is a victim, just like his son.

Verses 7-8 are the human and dramatic climax of this literary masterpiece. At this stage of the story, these verses are not necessary. The son suspects that things are amiss, and the father tells him that his fate is in the hands of YHWH and his angels. This father–son exchange makes the narrative real and authentic, but also subversive. Who is the sadist that invented this script? This is great literature, and a puzzling myth.

Gen. 22:1-19 is arguably the greatest short story in the Hebrew language, but its aims are not artistic or aesthetic, of course. The narrative was created to impress on us the superiority of faith over death.

One natural reaction to this narrative is to add it to the long list of mythological stories in which a child (often a newborn baby) is subject to murderous intentions by fathers, uncles, or grandfathers. Here the connection is more intimate, as the child communicates with his father and knows that a killing is about to take place. The narrative is shocking, as the covenant between father and child is breached, with the father hiding what he already knows. This is unlike stories about Romulus, Perseus, Moses, Krishna, or Jesus, where the intended killing is impersonal. The narrative introduces us to a plot that is outside the common pattern of attempts by father figures to kill the young upstart. The child is saved miraculously, escaping death at the last second.

At first blush, Abraham's motivation may be classified as Oedipal and infanticidal, and later in this book, this question will be discussed at some length.

Religious apologists have tried to sanitize the Binding story for millennia (Kalimi, 2010; Levenson, 1998), and one of their most common claims is that the story describes a great historical transformation, from human sacrifice to the killing of animals. On what evidence? The apologists would have us believe that there is one author or one mind behind the text. If this is true, there is no need for the Binding story to appear and steer the Israelites away from the horrors of child sacrifice, because the practice is condemned often enough in various parts of the Hebrew Bible, and YHWH's position is supposedly clear, and set against it.

If the message of the story is the end of human sacrifice (or child sacrifice) and the substitution of animal sacrifice, why is it never expressed, directly or indirectly? There is simply no hint of that. The narrative does not contain any message about the end of human sacrifice, even though Biblical authors are never shy about issuing explicit commands or prohibitions. If the message is the end of human sacrifice, it implies that until that point it had been a regular part of YHWH worship.

Genesis 22 has no comment, criticism, or condemnation of human sacrifice, just like the other narratives of actual human/child sacrifice in other books of the Hebrew Bible. There is no comment on abolishing human sacrifice in Judges11, where Jephthah sacrifices his daughter, or when Jonah is thrown into the raging sea, or when David kills Saul's children in 2 Samuel 21. Ska (2013) points out that none of the condemnations of child sacrifice ever mention the Binding, which seems natural if it was indeed meant to denounce the practice.

We can contrast the Biblical narratives with a story in Indian mythology that proclaims an end to human sacrifice (Manring, 2018; Shulman, 1993). Here is one version of the narrative:

> Haris´candra … had one hundred wives but no son … Haris´candra then placates the god Varuna, who does grant him a son, Rohita … Varuna immediately asks that the boy be sacrificed to him, as Haris´candra had promised, but Haris´candra equivocates … he stalls repeatedly, insisting that a child would not make a fit sacrifice until he is ten days old; then, until his teeth appear; then, until his baby teeth fall out; then until his new teeth come in; and finally, until he is old enough to bear arms. By this time the child himself realises what is happening, and refuses to participate, running off to the woods. Varuna is not pleased and knows he will have to resort to trickery to get his due … Rohita meets a starving brahmin family headed by Ajagarta Sauyavasi. The family has three sons, and Rohita persuades them to sell him Sunahs´epa (Dog Penis), the

middle son, to serve as stand-in for himself in the sacrifice, to save his own life and redeem that of his father Haris´candra. The family agrees, for a fee. Varuna also agrees to accept the substitution … Preparations for the sacrifice begin. Ajagarta is also present, suspecting … that there may be yet more money to be made. For a price, he offers to bind his own son, and for a further price, to slaughter him for the ritual. Meanwhile Rohita begins praying to one god after another. Indra gives him a gold chariot and instructs him to pray to the twin gods the As´vins, who in turn send him to pray to Usas, goddess of the dawn. Finally, Varuna is satisfied … neither child is actually slaughtered or sacrificed. (Manring, 2018: 190)

The story starts with a god's cruelty and ends with compassion.

One common element in the Hindu story and in the Abraham drama is the miracle that led to the birth of the long-awaited son. This miracle, granted by a kind deity, is about to be reversed, because of a divine caprice (Ska, 2013). The deity insists on getting back what he had gifted. This element is found in the Binding of Isaac, in the story of Haris Candra (Manring, 2018), and in the myth of Jesus. Of course, the turn in the plot may only seem like a divine whim. In the case of Abraham, it is a divine test, and in the case of Jesus the divine intention is to offer a sacrifice that will change humanity's destiny. The tension is resolved when the three sons are saved from death.

Dealing with any living tradition, we should ask about the role of any myth in the religious system of worship. When is the myth told? How is it celebrated? What form does memorization take? The answers are clear in the case of the Binding because it is a narrative that found a central place in Judaic liturgy. Gen. 22:1-19, is part of the morning prayers recited by every observant Jewish man every morning. Rabbinical authorities recommend reading it even when it is not part of the prayer texts. In addition, the story of the Binding of Isaac is read on one of the holiest days of the Jewish calendar, the second day of New Year. The ram's horn is sounded during the High Holidays, and this is interpreted as a reminder of the ram sacrificed by Abraham. Following Reik's (1951) hypothesis, we may suggest that the preoccupation with this narrative reflects doubts and difficulties.

Among Muslims, each of the five repetitions of daily prayer ends with a reference to Abraham. In the Catholic mass, the officiant prays, "Look with favor on these offerings and accept them as once you accepted the gifts of your servant Abel, the sacrifice of Abraham, our father in faith, and the bread and wine offered by your priest Melchizedek." The reference to Abraham is puzzling, as the actual sacrifice of the beloved son was not accepted. Nevertheless, Abraham's willingness to offer his son was recognized and rewarded.

You may imagine that adults would spare their children such narratives, but in religious families, children hear the story without any signs of trauma. There are also special picture books that transmit the religious message of the Binding to Jewish and Christian children in the United States and seem to do well in terms of sales. The books are attractive and the colors vivid. They emphasize obedience and love and soften the horrific details without hiding them. Christian picture books not only describe the Binding but also mention Jesus and his sacrifice (Sasser, 2017).

The Binding is now part of digital, global, culture in the form of a video game known as *The Binding of Isaac*. In this game, released in 2011, it is the mother who wants to kill her son. It has won enormous popularity, with millions of copies sold, together with some objections from defenders of tradition.

The obedience teaching may be interpreted by believers in ways that run counter to the religious establishment. Sigel (2009) describes some difficulties in teaching the Binding formally to twelve-year-old students. The intended message was one of promoting faith and devotion, and Isaac's readiness to be sacrificed was naturally presented as an inspiration. In one class in Israel, a student compared the devotion of a Palestinian suicide bomber to Isaac's, which did not please the teacher.

The Binding narratives may be read as subversive, undermining confidence in parents and authority for some believers. For some, a subversive reading leads to the desire to rebel against all authority. There are those who read the Binding narratives and raise a moral outcry against the fathers, who may not offer human sacrifice, but are responsible for the deaths of their sons in war.

Fromm (1973: 179) stated, "The fact that, in the case of child sacrifice, the father kills the child directly while, in the case of war, both sides have an arrangement to kill each other's children, makes little difference." Here Fromm is clearly wrong about sacrifice.

The reality is that young males everywhere are being sacrificed in war to defend the survival and success of their clan, tribe, nation, or revolutionary ideas inspired by older men (Peterson, 2015). Dying in battle is not a sacrifice to the gods, but the Binding narrative has inspired great protest poetry.

Wilfred Owen, who was killed in France on November 4, 1918, aged twenty-five, wrote the following poem in July 1918.

The Parable of the Old Man and the Young

So Abram rose, and clave the wood, and went,
And took the fire with him, and a knife.
And as they sojourned both of them together,

> Isaac the first-born spake and said, My Father,
> Behold the preparations, fire and iron,
> But where the lamb for this burnt-offering?
> Then Abram bound the youth with belts and straps,
> And builded parapets and trenches there,
> And stretchèd forth the knife to slay his son.
> When lo! an Angel called him out of heaven,
> Saying, Lay not thy hand upon the lad,
> Neither do anything to him. Behold,
> A ram caught in a thicket by its horns;
> Offer the Ram of Pride instead of him.
> But the old man would not so, but slew his son
> And half the seed of Europe, one by one

Owen's text, and subtext, are of intergenerational, "Oedipal," conflict. The old men don't really care about the young, who are destined to be slaughtered. Unlike Abraham, they are not concerned about losing half their seed.

A tense father–child dynamic, inspired by the Binding, is revealed by Oates (2010). An impatient father, in a walk through a forest with his son, holds a big stick and starts pronouncing, in a deserted stage, dramatic texts related to fathers and children. First, Edmund in *King Lear*, refusing to accept his lower status as illegitimate (act 1, scene 2). Then, McDuff about his family being killed (*Macbeth*, act IV, scene 3). The son is already frightened, and the father chooses to loudly pronounce some of the well-known verses of Genesis 22. Starting with "and it came to pass that God did tempt Abraham," he stops after "and Abraham stretched forth his hand and took the knife to slay his son" (Oates, 2010: 306), criticizing his son for taking things literally.

Next, the father describes his son as being spoiled and disobedient, "for his father is not of God's Hebrew chosen" (Oates, 2010: 308). The father jokingly offers to sell his son for $100.99 to an ugly, homeless man. Even though the four-year-old knows it's a joke, he hides from his father and gets lost, possibly forever.

We see that the father's sadism and carelessness lead to the loss of his son. In the case of Abraham, it was the angel that prevented the loss, but in this world no angel will intervene.

Most readers of the Hebrew Bible, and even some scholars, ignore Genesis 21 when they think of the Binding narrative in Genesis 22. We should be grateful to the scholars that remind us how significant Genesis 21 is in telling the story of the firstborn son, Ishmael, sent to his death by his father Abraham and saved by an angel (Lemański, 2021).

Hagar and Ishmael Driven Out

Gen. 21:8-21

8 And the child grew, and was weaned: and Abraham made a great feast the same day that Isaac was weaned.

9 And Sarah saw the son of Hagar the Egyptian, which she had born unto Abraham, mocking.

10 Wherefore she said unto Abraham, Cast out this bondwoman and her son: for the son of this bondwoman shall not be heir with my son, even with Isaac.

11 And the thing was very grievous in Abraham's sight because of his son.

12 And God said unto Abraham, Let it not be grievous in thy sight because of the lad, and because of thy bondwoman; in all that Sarah hath said unto thee, hearken unto her voice; for in Isaac shall thy seed be called.

13 And also of the son of the bondwoman will I make a nation, because he is thy seed.

14 And Abraham rose up early in the morning, and took bread, and a bottle of water, and gave it unto Hagar, putting it on her shoulder, and the child, and sent her away: and she departed, and wandered in the wilderness of Beersheba.

15 And the water was spent in the bottle, and she cast the child under one of the shrubs.

16 And she went, and sat her down over against him a good way off, as it were a bow shot: for she said, Let me not see the death of the child. And she sat over against him, and lift up her voice, and wept.

17 And God heard the voice of the lad; and the angel of God called to Hagar out of heaven, and said unto her, What aileth thee, Hagar? fear not; for God hath heard the voice of the lad where he is.

18 Arise, lift up the lad, and hold him in thine hand; for I will make him a great nation.

19 And God opened her eyes, and she saw a well of water; and she went, and filled the bottle with water, and gave the lad drink.

20 And God was with the lad; and he grew, and dwelt in the wilderness, and became an archer.

21 And he dwelt in the wilderness of Paran: and his mother took him a wife out of the land of Egypt.

The heartrending story of the mother and child sent out to the desert is an exact parallel of the Binding. It is not the first. In Genesis 16, during her pregnancy,

Hagar is first driven out to the desert by Sarah's hostility, meets an angel, and receives the same promise "I will multiply thy seed" that Abraham would receive in Gen. 22:17. The authors of Genesis 22 seem to know well Genesis 16 and 21, if they are not the same persons, and Genesis 21 might have been authored later than Genesis 22 and modeled after it (Lemański, 2021).

Tens of thousands of words have been written about the Binding. Most of the authors involved in writing about it ask religious questions and engage in moral criticism. Most writers ask about the motives of YHWH or Abraham.

Kaufmann (1961: 73–4) states,

> We have no right whatever to admire Abraham, as the great paragon of faith … unless we are prepared [Kierkegaard says], to look up with an equal reverence to a man who in our time is prepared to murder because God commands him to—or rather because he believes that God commands this sacrifice … What Kierkegaard sanctions is in effect fanaticism. (cf. Kierkegaard, 1843)

Gibson (2009: 133) similarly states,

> The absoluteness and purity of Abraham's faith and decision carries a violence and a madness that cannot be justified. Such an attitude is consonant with the behavior of contemporary terrorists, individuals who also act in the name of a faith or a wholly/holy other that cannot be mediated.

When we encounter such stories as the Binding of Isaac or the sacrifice of Jephthah's daughter, two questions need to be asked: Why were these horrifying stories invented, and why were they preserved and included in the final version of the Hebrew Bible? I do not believe in a guiding divine hand determined to teach us anything, so I must ask about the conscious (and unconscious) intentions of those who were creating these shocking narratives. The same questions could be asked about narratives created by the Greeks, or any other culture.

The questions that need to be raised are about the humans that created the story and their motives, as well as about the believers who are keeping this story alive. If you believe in YHWH and in the story about the Binding of Isaac, you may still be baffled by this sadistic narrative, which one believer has called "exquisite mental torture" (Kellner, 2014: 154). If you don't believe in any stories about the spirit world, the question is still there: Why was this story created?

The Binding narrative seems to seal the covenant with Abraham and his descendants, following a series of tests and sacrifices. What has also been sealed is the idea of sacrificing the firstborn son. As we have seen, firstborn sacrifice is supposed to remove an existential threat. What is the threat in this case? For Abraham, it is losing his seed. For his tribe, it is losing the covenant.

What we have here is a deal involving a sacrificed child in return for blessings and an eternal covenant. Genesis 15 tells the story the Covenant of the Pieces (known also as a Greek or Hittite custom) where animals are cut into halves. There are other expressions of the covenant in Genesis, and Genesis 17 presents circumcision as Abraham's sacrifice.

An ancient Hittite text combines cutting animals in half with a human victim, most likely a prisoner of war:

> If the troops have been beaten by the enemy they perform a ritual "behind" the river, as follows: they "cut through" a man, a goat, a puppy, and a little pig; they place half on this side and half on that side, and in front they make a gate of … wood … and in front of the gate they light fires on this side and that, and the troop walk right through, and when they come to the river they sprinkle water over them. (Gurney, 1962:. 151)

Against the background of blood sacrifices that must accompany covenants and ensure good fortune, the story of an averted firstborn sacrifice was created. It was a test of Abraham's loyalty, passed with ease and rewarded by an eternal promise. The universal myth of the hero includes serious tests, ordeals, and challenges. Abraham passed other tests, but this one can only be described as inhuman. Jacob was also subjected to tests, which he passed, but his trials cannot be compared to the shocking story of the Binding. The authors tell us that an inhuman test had been needed for the final election, being a real proof of superiority.

But we can imagine how the test narrative became central, as it justified the covenant and the superior position of Abraham, the mythical wanderer turned into the father of a nation. The Binding is a story of a double miracle, with the intended victim saved from dying, with the full reward for total obedience still given to his father.

The Binding Narrative: Dating and Motives

Reading ancient stories, preserved forever for their religious centrality, which we seek to interpret and decipher, we ask what led to their creation. The goal is to make the stories comprehensible in terms of the motivation of their unknown authors.

The texts we are now reading reflect both struggle and triumph. When it comes to ancient stories, found in the Hebrew Bible or in the New Testament, we don't know their ultimate origins, or how a decision was made to include them, or who were the authors who wrote them. Research on the history of texts, as they were stitched together, revised, and redacted until they gained the form we know today, helps us determine the era in which they were first created. A small group of scribes was involved, and the readers were also the writers. The texts were not exposed to a wide audience.

The Binding of Isaac, this fantasy about an extreme sacrifice, leading to an eternal promise, reflects the desires and beliefs of its authors in a particular moment.

Before discussing possible motives, the first task is dating the writing of a text. Ben-Zvi (2019) stated that most books in the Hebrew Bible were formed in the late Persian/early Hellenistic discursive setting. Wellhausen already suggested that the final form of Genesis was reached in the fifth century BCE. Later generations of scholars have suggested that further changes were made in the Hellenistic period (Barstad, 2001; Grabbe, 2001; Römer, 2015).

Adamczewski (2021) argued that Genesis was written toward the end of the Persian period *c.* 350–340 BCE. Scholars have connected some stories about Abraham to the historical figure of Sanballat, governor of the province of Samaria in the middle of the fifth century BCE (Adamczewski, 2021; Edelman, 2013).

Finkelstein and Römer (2014) suggested that Genesis 22, the Binding, is a product of the Persian period, with additions from the Hasmonean period (including the name Moriah). Lombaard (2008) dated the Binding narrative to between 400 and 250 BCE, and Lombaard (2019) argued that the idea of being tested by the gods, which plays a major role in the Binding narrative, did not appear before the Hellenistic period (332–63 BCE). Lipschits, Römer, and Gonzalez (2017) suggested that the appearance of an angel from heaven in Genesis 22, as in Genesis 21, but unlike Genesis 16, indicates a late date of composition.

Römer (2012: 9) noted that the

> Hebrew term used in Genesis 22, Verse 1 to denote God is "ha-elohim," and not "Elohim" (literally "the God"), and the same holds true for verses 3 and 9. This lexeme appears frequently in texts from the late Persian and early Hellenistic period, and especially in the book of Qoheleth.

As another argument in favor of a very late date for Genesis 22, Ska (2013) points out that the Binding is mentioned only in very late, apocryphal Jewish writings such as 1 Macc. 2:52 or in the New Testament. Apparently, this narrative was not known to writers active earlier.

After establishing an approximate date, we can discuss possible motives.

What we do know is that there were several communities of Yahwists during the Persian period (538–332 BCE). In addition to the Jerusalem temple, built by the returnees from Mesopotamia, and the Samaria temple, there was also a least one temple in Egypt, destroyed in 410 BCE by its Egyptian neighbors (Granerød, 2019), There are indications of other shrines in Samaria, Idumea, or Babylonia (Leith, 2020).

Looking back at the situation around 500 BCE, we can think of groups of self-proclaimed Yahwists all over the map of the Persian empire. We have reason to believe that the Southern Egypt group was quite friendly toward the groups of Yahwists in Jerusalem and Samaria, as shown in their writings (Granerød, 2019; Leith, 2020).

The canonical writings of the Jerusalem Yahwists eventually became, hundreds of years later, the beginning of what we know today as rabbinical Judaism. The future of this YHWHism at the time was uncertain. No one could predict that it would eventually win out over other traditions and schools.

The Judean group of scribes responsible for the Hebrew Bible as we know it saw itself as part of a small people, objectively weak and buffeted by strong empires around it:

> The reality for the returners from Babylon was a world in which promises had been broken. They characterized their exile as divine punishment for their failure to meet Yhwh's standards, and they also believed that Yhwh had broken Yhwh's promises … sovereignty was being exercised by Persia, while homes and agricultural land had been claimed by others in their absence. (Warner, 2017: 489)

Nevertheless, the returnee leaders were persistent in their sense of superiority and election, as the keepers of the true Torah. Superiority, purity, and election are the terms that reflected the spirit that animated their vision.

Stories are invented to express imagined goals, such as power, obedience, order, psychological release of aggression, revenge, or justice. The story of the Binding was created and embraced in a time of weakness, with a great yearning for security and power. A believer's self-esteem was offered support through belonging to an elect group.

It has been suggested that the Binding narrative expressed the existential anxiety of the small returnee community in Yehud about their mere survival.

The myth of an eternal covenant, which concludes the narrative, is designed to inspire confidence about the future. It repeats the promise of progeny made in reference to both Isaac and Ishmael. Abraham passed the test, and thus was Israel elected. The story assured Judeans they had a promise, not just a dream, of triumph and redemption. The Creation of the Judaic identity was a response to trauma, exile, and helplessness.

What we know about the authors' motives is quite clear in one way. A tiny group of scribes was motivated to assert the authority of the small community of returnees from Mesopotamia over the large majority of Judahites who stayed in the land and survived as peasants.

The group of returnee scribes claimed to be in possession of the true tradition attributed to ancient lawgivers and tied to momentous events. They expressed the ideals of superiority and purity, whereas the peasantry did not display what was now determined to be Judaic identity markers. Not only did they intermarry with other nations, but they disregarded the keeping of the Sabbath. Boundaries had to be established to preserve the kingdom of priests.

The strategy of establishing the returnees from exile over the stable peasantry led to the creation of stories about Abraham, a migrant from Mesopotamia who was the actual father of the nation. Those returning from Mesopotamia in the Persian period needed the story about his coming from the same place (Ska, 2009).

Details about Abraham's family of origin and his travels were added to various old stories. His own trek was turned into the national history.

> Abraham, an indigenous local and patriarch turned into a newcomer, a wanderer arriving from Ur of the Chaldeans, who trustfully followed God and His promises. (Lemański, 2021: 222)

The mythological nation of Abraham's descendants reflected the reality of the migrants from Mesopotamia. The people of the land, who resented the attempted takeover by a small group of newcomers, was being told that the father of the nation was an outsider crossing rivers and deserts, and that the whole nation was a community of outsiders engaged in conquest and a struggle for purity.

The narrative of wanderings, exodus, and holy conquest was invented to justify the returnees' claims to the ownership of revelation. The description of Ezra reading the Book of the Law before the assembled Jerusalem congregation parallels and finalizes the sequence of revelations to the mythical Moses and Josiah.

The group of priests and scribes represented by the mythical Ezra claims the right to rule. It is unclear how successful they were in establishing control, but they crystallized the shape of the Hebrew Bible. Other small groups carried on the vision of knowing the whole truth about purity and the right to power. Eventually, through the creation of the Mishnah and the Talmud, this became rabbinical Judaism, still alive today.

The Hebrew Bible is a collection of traditions and superiority assertions, including story cycles coming from various and competing sources. While the Abraham story cycle was developed in the Southern Kingdom of Judea, a Jacob story cycle was created in the Northern Kingdom, which described Jacob-Israel as the father of the nation. The scribes now combined the two cycles. Jacob became Abraham's grandson, but his wanderings followed the same mythological geography. Jacob had the stories about Bethel and the angel, together with his name change. How do you counter that? With the narrative of the Binding. The Abraham cycle defeated the Jacob cycle, and he became the great Father (Blum, 2012; Pury, 2006). The postexilic scribes tied emerging Jewishness to the great Father of the nation, who withstood the test and won the covenant.

Belonging to a committed tribe is both rewarding and costly, a burden and a prize. The burden for every individual believer is asking oneself whether you could be like Abraham the hero-martyr. The martyr not only shames common believers but also inspires them to demonstrate unwavering loyalty and self-renunciation in submission. Some may find such pressures oppressive. The individual is pressured to conform and demonstrate loyalty. Within the believing community he will enjoy protection, belonging, safety, and the joy of being among the elect. The price of belonging is unshaken devotion and obedience. The leaders struggled to steer the group toward this goal, excluding those seen as failing. Being chosen to share a cosmic mission promotes group cohesion and solidarity.

From Athamas to Abraham

As we discuss the sources and the context of the Binding of Isaac, the tragedy of Athamas demands our attention. The basic Athamas narrative bears some unmistakable similarities to the Binding of Isaac. It is noteworthy that it is not better known, given its parallels to the Abraham narratives.

Is the Athams story the source of the Binding story? Is it a template copied? We don't know, but there are overlapping pieces that are unmistakable.

> This tale, too, has Biblical echoes in Sarah's envy of Ishmael (Genesis 21:10) and Abraham's barely averted sacrifice of Isaac, in which the ram is a stand-in, not a get-away vehicle. (Griffith, 2001: 228)

The Athamas narrative starts with two jealous women, clearly paralleling Hagar and Sarah. Then the kingdom faces catastrophe, which can be avoided through sacrificing the firstborn son. Athamas is ready to kill his children and save his community. At the right moment, Zeus, just like YHWH, introduces a miracle. The message is that filicide is caused by warring women and their jealousy.

In the Binding of Isaac narrative, Abraham is devout and strong, while Sarah is evil, like Ino, Athamas's second wife. Both manipulate an unlucky man who becomes a victim, and children are killed or saved miraculously by the ram. The victimized father, in his madness, becomes guilty of both filicide and the readiness to sacrifice his son (like Abraham).

In the case of Athamas, we find two warring, jealous, women, who destroy the lives of their children and bring about death and eternal suffering to the blended family. The intended victims to be sacrificed are saved, but the gods are angry and demand punishment.

In the case of Abraham, we find two warring women who cannot abide each other, and (as a result?) the two children of the two mothers are in danger, but both are saved miraculously. Ishmael, who is the first son born to the first wife (or concubine), is sent into the desert to die (Genesis 21).

Then, the women's jealousy is forgotten and the challenge from YHWH is unrelated to any family conflict. The father's readiness to slaughter his son leads to reconciliation, affirmation, and covenant. The two sons are promised a great future for their seed, but only Isaac is the chosen one. The story of Athamas was not only reimagined but also reborn and re-created.

The cultural landscape around the Mediterranean offered other stories of child sacrifice, of course. The prevalence of similar stories does not explain the creation of the Binding narrative, because it is marked by the Judaic elements of the test and the election. We can speculate about the pressures that led to the new narrative, and the historical setting of the Persian period.

If there has been a borrowing, or influence, the authors of the Binding narrative transformed the Athamas plot into a test that seals the series of Abraham's covenants. Such narratives are part of the official Judaic profession of superiority, letting us know that one formulation of sacrifice works better than others. If protection and prosperity are not always guaranteed, election is, and it belongs to a minority.

Who was it that decided to convert the narrative of firstborn sacrifice, portrayed as an emergency sacrifice in the cases of Athamas, Kronos, or Mesha, into a divine test of obedience? We obviously cannot know.

The justification for the firstborn sacrifice is usually a dire situation with threat of extinction. What is the threat? "In the case of Abraham, there is no emergency, no impending disaster" (Sarna, 2001: 153) The Abraham story is different because the sacrifice is an order from YHWH, to serve the goal of establishing absolute obedience as the norm. If we follow the book of Genesis, the command from YHWH to Abraham to sacrifice his son seems arbitrary, unlike the case of Athamas, whose act will stop a catastrophe. The Abraham narrative is not about catastrophe, but about the ultimate test, which involves the fate of Isaac, and by implication, that of the whole tribe.

Looking at the Kronos Phoenician template, presented above, the firstborn sacrifice comes about to avoid a catastrophe, but the sacrifice is accompanied by the father circumcising himself, which is also attributed to Abraham in Genesis 17. What happens to Kronos, who sacrificed his firstborn son and his prepuce, is what happens in all child sacrifice stories, as we have seen above. The transactions worked, and the fathers were rewarded by the gods.

The Athamas case seems uniquely similar to that of Abraham, for more than one reason. In the two cases of Athamas and Abraham, it was explicitly the readiness to sacrifice the child that was recognized and rewarded. The two sons, Isaac and Phrixus (or Phrixus and Helle in some versions) were saved at the last second in the same way. The substitution miracle, celebrated already in Mesopotamia millennia earlier, is made possible by a ram, provided by divine mercy.

The Athamas narratives, which end with an eternal curse on his descendants, are tragic and show humans to be helpless in the face of fate, while Abraham's is shocking, but delivers more than a kingdom saved from famine, in the form of an eternal covenant with the descendants being the elect. The message of the Bible is that the trials will never end. Isaac's averted sacrifice ensures a conditional covenant that must be obeyed.

In both cases, the resolution is a display of obedience, which leads to a miracle. Athamas demonstrates obedience, as he follows oracles and gods' commands, thus keeping the cosmic order. He is acting to stop a catastrophe by sacrificing his beloved children. Here, his loyalty is first to the people of his kingdom, who are affected by the famine.

Abraham and Athamas were both ready to sacrifice their sons, following instructions from gods and oracles. We regard Athamas as manipulated and victimized, but possibly because of the power of tradition as formed by the Hebrew Bible and the New Testament, Abraham is praised for making a choice.

He is a potential victim turned hero because of his presumed choice and his leading the chosen, but if we look at the narrative, the authors tell us about a man who is helpless in the face of omniscient, omnipotent, YHWH, so he is still a victim. In the Athamas case, gods are sadistic and brutal, and humans helpless. With Abraham, YHWH designed this cruel test, deliberately tricking him. Eventually, Zeus had pity on Athamas, the poor father tricked into killing his son, just like YHWH, who saved Abraham from the same act.

The Judaic story tries to move from "fate" to a test of total obedience. This new message supersedes all other stories of child sacrifice.

If the Binding narrative is meant to lead to a happy ending for father and son, why is its tenor seemingly so cruel? While nothing is said about changes in sacrifice practices, what Abraham receives is a new covenant in a highly successful transaction (Schlossman, 1966). Athamas does not receive a new covenant, but the famine that afflicted his land ends, following his proven willingness to sacrifice his children. Like the Biblical ones, these Greek stories of child sacrifice do not contain any censure or disapproval.

The Firstborn Reversal

While in the Athamas narrative sacrificing the firstborn son is the punishment his family will carry forever, the Hebrew Bible turns this curse around. As the Hebrew Bible authors lead us through the mythical wanderings from one ordeal to the next, the narrative includes a firstborn sacrifice averted by a miracle, universal male circumcision, and the killing of all Egyptian firstborn.

This last miracle, and passing over the Israelite firstborn, must remind us of the attention paid to the Israelite firstborn, who are expected to be sacrificed, or consecrated. While the command regarding the firstborn may seem ambiguous to some readers, it must remind the believers of the Binding narrative.

The Hebrew Bible text makes 118 references to the firstborn. The phylacteries that all Jewish males are supposed to tie to their body every weekday contain four selections of the Law. Two of them are the sections dealing with the firstborn sacrifice (or sanctification) Exod. 13:1-10 and Exod. 13: 11-15.

Exod. 13:1-2

And the LORD spake unto Moses, saying, Sanctify unto me all the firstborn, whatsoever openeth the womb among the children of Israel, both of man and of beast: it is mine.

Other commands prescribe that the tribe of Levi is to take the place of the firstborn.

Num. 3:12-13

12 And I, behold, I have taken the Levites from among the children of Israel instead of all the firstborn that openeth the matrix among the children of Israel: therefore the Levites shall be mine;

13 Because all the firstborn are mine; for on the day that I smote all the firstborn in the land of Egypt I hallowed unto me all the firstborn in Israel, both man and beast: mine shall they be: I am the LORD.

Numbers 8

16 For they are wholly given unto me from among the children of Israel; instead of such as open every womb, even instead of the firstborn of all the children of Israel, have I taken them unto me.

17 For all the firstborn of the children of Israel are mine, both man and beast: on the day that I smote every firstborn in the land of Egypt I sanctified them for myself.

18 And I have taken the Levites for all the firstborn of the children of Israel.

What these verses mean is a mystery. The authors of the Hebrew Bible would have us believe that the replacement of the firstborn by the Levites took place in the desert, but we know that any claims about the Exodus and desert crossings are mythical. The book of Numbers is believed by scholars today to have been written in the late Persian period. My own hypothesis is that somebody representing presumed descendants of the Levites wanted to gain status for his group. This was done by dedicating many verses to the laws about the firstborn and their uniqueness, and then inventing the story about their replacement by the Levites, which ended all firstborn obligations.

The Binding and the Appearance of Jewishness

In the period before 586 BCE, Israelites lived in a polytheistic culture. Archaeological finds confirm that the Israelites worshiped Canaanite gods like

El (Elyon), Asherah, and Ba'al, just like their neighbors. We know little about the religion of Judean and Israelite kings before the invention of Jewishness in the fifth century BCE. It has been suggested that the northern, Israelite, kingdom was dominated by the worship of Canaanite gods such as Baal and Asherah, together with Yahweh. In the fifth century BCE Yahweh became, according to some believers, the sole ruler of the cosmos, known as Elohim (Edelman, 1995). Yahweh, who came out of the Canaanite pantheon, won over all competitors in Judaism, and Jews consider him now the one God, surrounded by angels and saints.

The Judean tradition of Yahwism, worshipped in several temples, probably had many beginnings before the invention of monotheism. A silver scroll found in Jerusalem and inscribed around 600 BCE carried the priestly blessing (Num. 6:24-26): "The Lord bless thee and keep thee: The Lord make his face shine upon thee and be gracious unto thee: The Lord lift up his countenance upon thee and give thee peace." This indicates one early beginning of Judean Yahwism.

The returnee scribes started the monotheistic revolution, or at least a major reform, in the Persian province of Yehud (Stern, 2021). They defined Jewishness as loyalty to YHWH monotheism, but most Israelites clearly did not share the idea.

Scholars seem to agree on the reality of major developments during the Persian-Hellenistic era:

> Despite the apparent lack of consensus, there is a general agreement that the second half of the Persian period saw the birth of the Torah and of Judaism as a Torah-related religion. (Römer, 2007: 420)

A more recent view states as follows:

> The scholarly consensus places the emergence of "Judaism" and the writing down and editing of the Torah after the Babylonian exile (ca. 587–539) in the Persian-Hellenistic era. (Feldt, 2021: 134)

The invention of Judaism was initiated by a group of scribes/priests who were committed to Yahwism as a vision of superiority and purity. This exclusionary vision led to the creation of the myth of the Exodus and the conquest, together with the myth of exterminating the Canaanites. This narrative served the goal of separatism and conveyed the idea of the superior outsiders who are unrelated to the surrounding populations. The myth of Israelites as foreign invaders aimed at creating a distance from neighbors who shared kinship and tradition with the followers of early Judaism. In some cases, they even shared Yahwist traditions.

The essence of Judaism as we know it, with the emphasis on purity and separatism, is found in the book of Ezra 9:11-12:

> The land, unto which ye go to possess it, is an unclean land with the filthiness of the people of the lands, with their abominations, which have filled it from one end to another with their uncleanness.
>
> Now therefore give not your daughters unto their sons, neither take their daughters unto your sons, nor seek their peace or their wealth forever: that ye may be strong, and eat the good of the land, and leave it for an inheritance to your children forever.

Moreover, "separate yourselves from the peoples around you and from your foreign wives" (Ezra 10:9).

The Judaic message is one of separatism, superiority, purity, and election. It aims to create a maximal distance between Jews and non-Jews and between "pure" and "impure" Jews. This ideology of separation and exclusion claimed that most of those living in Palestine in the fifth century BCE were "Canaanites," descendants of those accursed and condemned by the ancient Mosaic tradition.

That members of these groups deserved to die was made clear again and again:

> But of the cities of these peoples which Yahweh your God gives you as an inheritance, you shall let nothing that breathes remain alive, but you shall utterly destroy them—the Hittite, Amorite, Canaanite, Perizzite, Hivite, and Jebusite—just as Yahweh your God has commanded you, lest they teach you to do according to all their abominations which they have done for their gods, and you sin against Yahweh your God. (Deut. 20:16-18)

The idea of the autochthonous Canaanites as a negative reference group was invented as part of the myth that sought to present Judaism as a foreign transplant, introduced by wanderers coming from Mesopotamia by way of Egypt rather than the local product that it really was.

The denunciations of "Canaanites," who do not deserve to live, describe the reality of the late fifth century BCE, when the creators of early Judaism aimed at separating themselves from the majority around them, who were devoted to the continuing worship of a polytheistic pantheon or to a differing version of Yahwism. When the Hebrew Bible denounced heathen religious practices, they were not just ancient practices but the majority tradition at the time of writing. Separatist Judaism took shape in the following centuries, after the rise of the Hasmoneans, through the canonization of the purity rules that were to become well-known identity markers, such as the Sabbath, food taboos, and male genital mutilation, sanctioned by the scriptures.

We may be shocked by some Biblical stories and assertions but must keep in mind that they represent religious ideals rather than historical events. There was no genocide committed by Joshua and his army (because there was no conquest and no Joshua), no one was ever executed for gathering sticks on the Sabbath (Num. 15:32-36), and few foreign women, if any, were divorced following the cruel rulings of Judaic leaders (Ezra 9–10). These ideals might have been cruel enough, but we have no reason to believe that they were ever obeyed. The great separatist effort, which created Judaism, insisted on strictness and purity because separatism was so unnatural when traditions were so similar and when tribes and families were intermarried.

Contemporary sociology of religion has found that strictness makes churches attractive (Tamney and Johnson, 1998). We cannot generalize that to the Yahwism of 2,500 years ago, but competition was even then the order of the day. The reward to the membership was in knowing that they belonged to the elect, the few, the happy few, who possess the truth. The position of the happy few was not easily shared.

"Love thy neighbor" is one of the best-known imperatives in the world, and is widely regarded as a call for unconditional, universal love for humanity. However, if we go back to the original source, we discover something totally different. The "Love thy neighbor" commandment quite explicitly covered only members of the tribe. The original verse states, "Thou shalt not avenge, nor bear any grudge against the children of thy people, but thou shalt love thy neighbour as thyself: I am the Lord" (Lev. 19:18). Many other Biblical injunctions commanded Jews to treat in-group members differently than non-Jews.

But we can also find in the Hebrew Bible some remarkable moral lessons derived from the Exodus myth:

> Also thou shalt not oppress a stranger: for ye know the heart of a stranger, seeing ye were strangers in the land of Egypt. (Exod. 23:9)
>
> But the stranger that dwelleth with you shall be unto you as one born among you, and thou shalt love him as thyself; for ye were strangers in the land of Egypt: I am the LORD your God. (Lev. 19:34)

These benevolent and thoughtful messages, unique in the times they were written, call for compassion for those outside the tribe and blunt the edge of exclusion. Remarkable as they are in expressing universalist ideals, they are far fewer than those emphasizing exclusive in-group loyalty.

The struggle between YHWH monotheism and the established Yahwistic practices would continue over hundreds of years and would be reflected in elite writings of the one hand and archaeological finds on the other. What we can observe over the centuries is the persistent gap between the elite writings and mass beliefs and practices evident in thousands of finds, demonstrating the prevalence of polytheistic and decentralized rituals.

Archeological finds demonstrate that a variety of rites were being practiced, including the supposedly Canaanite tradition of having a collection of cult objects and fertility statuettes at home, to be worshipped in the family circle.

de Hulster (2012) points to the fifty-one figurine fragments found in 1978–85 in the Persian stratum in Jerusalem, which most likely were being used by the majority population during the Persian period. Balcells Gallarreta (2017) reviews the archaeological data from Tell en-Nasbeh, a Persian period settlement twelve kilometers north of Jerusalem. "Ritual objects in the collection from Tell en-Nasbeh include human and animal figurines, incense altars, stands, chalices, zoomorphic vessels, rattles, and amulets" (Balcells Gallarreta, 2017: 3). These objects reflect the range of polytheistic ritual acts that represent popular Yahwism before and after the reforms introduced by the returnees. Clay figurines are found all over the territory of ancient Judea and seem to have been a permanent feature of domestic rituals (Kletter, 1996, 2004). YHWH worship continued to be decentralized, not only in the form of domestic rites but even in the form of public altars to YHWH, found in the Hellenistic period (Balcells Gallarreta, 2017).

The chasm between the scribal elite, which later became the rabbinical elite, and the masses is evident in findings that reflect the reality over centuries. In the art displayed in ancient synagogues, built hundreds of years after the invention of monotheism, we observe images that come from pagan cultures, including pagan deities (Magness, 2005). Inside these synagogues, we can also find the pictorial portrayal of women in ways that run counter to stated Talmudic norms (Hachlili, 2013; Wortzman, 2008). At the same time, portrayals of the Binding of Isaac in synagogue art indicate first the centrality of the myth and then its appearance as evidence of loyalty and of authentic Judaic practices.

For centuries following the intense activities of the fifth century BCE, Yahweh worship was shared by several groups, of which the largest and the best known were Samaritans and Jews. These two groups were in bitter enmity between the second century BCE and the ninth century CE. Other religions of Yahweh have disappeared, and now Judaism is identified with the ancient heritage of Yahwism, which preceded it.

Rabbinical Judaism, the historical tradition that has dominated Jewish life for more than a millennium, represents the triumph of the separatist vision, that of creating a "kingdom of priests" over other temples, other Yahwist movements, Greek and Roman cultures, and rising Christianity, being formed at the same time. It first appeared in the days of the Roman Empire, the home of many cultures, religions, and communities where Jews lived in dispersed communities all over the Mediterranean world.

Abraham is the proper hero of the monotheistic revolution, which presents Judaic identity based on endogamy and circumcision (Ska, 2009). Beyond that, the message of the Binding for every believer is one of strength and consolation. No matter what is happening around you, you are a member of the chosen tribe, as proven by the history of countless miracles and sacrifices, above all the Binding of Isaac and Passover.

Significantly, the ideal of absolute loyalty is expressed in the Hebrew Bible by denying any family allegiance:
Deut. 33:9

Who said unto his father and to his mother, I have not seen him; neither did he acknowledge his brethren, nor knew his own children: for they have observed thy word, and kept thy covenant.

Exod. 32:27

He told them, "This is what the LORD, the God of Israel, says: 'Each of you men is to fasten his sword to his side, go back and forth through the camp from gate to gate, and slay his brother, his friend, and his neighbor.'"

Both verses refer to the Levites, portrayed as the enforcers of obedience, and rewarded accordingly.

The New Testament follows the same idea:
Mt. 10:37

Anyone who loves his father or mother more than Me is not worthy of Me; anyone who loves his son or daughter more than Me is not worthy of Me.

These verses are shocking. The denial of natural love to kin in favor of loyalty to the covenant echoes the Binding narrative.

Nonetheless, as the Jewish tradition reads it, the message in the Binding narrative is not only of total obedience but also of compassion, The claim of YHWH's compassion to Abraham and Isaac really implies that the son rightfully belonged to YHWH and should have died, but he made a concession to Abraham and Isaac, which was not a precedent. Jews can claim that YHWH showed a quality of mercy when he pardoned Isaac at the last minute, and Jewish prayers recall this attribute, while Christians may connect Isaac and Jesus, and emphasize that human sacrifice and human blood were essential to reaching salvation and ushering in the Messiah.

Firstborn Sacrifice and Death

Sacrificing the firstborn was the toughest (in)conceivable trial indeed. It was invented as the ultimate test of absolute loyalty to one god. The Athamas story was recast by the Judaic authors within the framework of loyalty to YHWH and his Law. Sacrificing to YHWH was evidence of identity, no matter who or what the victim was. Was the threat of death necessary to reach the covenant?

Firstborn sacrifice narratives offer us miracles, and the most significant is overcoming death. It happens in the Binding of Isaac, as he is never touched by the knife. The Binding of Jesus does much more than that with the resurrection of the dead son, who joins his father in heaven.

10

The Binding of Jesus

The genealogy of the Jesus myth is undoubtedly complex and goes back to earlier narratives and cults of Mediterranean and West Asian deities. But the written traditions of the New Testament explicitly direct us to one source. In the Christian metanarrative, Isaac's sacrifice was an incomplete prefiguration of the complete one, that of Jesus. The Jesus sacrifice (and resurrection) myth aimed to offer the resolution that was not achieved in the Binding of Isaac (Stroumsa, 2004, 2009, 2015). This resolution, a cosmic breakthrough, is the gateway to the eschaton and confirms the identity of the one Messiah.

The authors of the New Testament build on the Hebrew Bible texts as they make the case for the superiority of their myth. Abraham's family drama, and Genesis 22, are at the center. Isaac became Jesus, as the incomplete sacrifice is now done. The offering of Isaac pointed to the Crucifixion of Jesus, and in both cases the sacrifice was a necessary filicide. The many similarities and the crucial differences between the two cases became the topic of many Christian writings.

Melito of Sardis, a Christian bishop who died *c.* 180 CE, described "the difference between Isaac and Christ:

> and he carried the wood on his shoulders
> as he was led up to be slain like Isaac by his Father.
> But Christ suffered, whereas Isaac did not suffer;
> for he was a model of the Christ who was going to suffer.
> But by being merely the model of Christ
> he caused astonishment and fear among men." (Strumsa, 2004: 276)

The Jesus sacrifice myth had in it the correct victim to be offered and the right sacrificer. The correct victim was a son produced by YHWH, and the sacrificer was the father himself, just like Abraham.

In this once-for-all sacrifice, the son was being connected to the Binding as a vital part of presenting him as the correct offering. New Testament authors presented Jesus as a descendant of Abraham and David, on the one hand, claiming a line of descent proper for the Judaic Messiah, and on the other hand, Jesus was the firstborn, only begotten and beloved son of YHWH.

Jn 3:16 may be the most widely quoted verse from the New Testament and has been called "Gospel in a nutshell":

> For God so loved the world, that he gave his only begotten Son, that whosoever believeth in him should not perish, but have everlasting life.

This contains a reference to the Binding, which can be found also in "He that spared not his own Son, but delivered him up for us all, how shall he not with him also freely give us all things?" (Rom. 8:32). Mk 1:11 "And there came a voice from heaven, saying, Thou art my beloved Son, in whom I am well pleased" seems like an allusion to Gen. 22:2 "thy son, thine only son Isaac, whom thou lovest."

Gal. 4:21-31 offers a justification for the way events unfolded in Genesis 21, when Ishmael lost his birthright, and states that all Christians have won, as they are the children of the winning freewoman, Sarah.

> 21 Tell me, ye that desire to be under the law, do ye not hear the law?
>
> 22 For it is written, that Abraham had two sons, the one by a bondmaid, the other by a freewoman.
>
> 23 But he who was of the bondwoman was born after the flesh; but he of the freewoman was by promise.
>
> 24 Which things are an allegory: for these are the two covenants; the one from the mount Sinai, which gendereth to bondage, which is Agar.
>
> 25 For this Agar is mount Sinai in Arabia, and answereth to Jerusalem which now is, and is in bondage with her children.
>
> 26 But Jerusalem which is above is free, which is the mother of us all.
>
> 27 For it is written, Rejoice, thou barren that bearest not; break forth and cry, thou that travailest not: for the desolate hath many more children than she which hath an husband.
>
> 28 Now we, brethren, as Isaac was, are the children of promise.
>
> 29 But as then he that was born after the flesh persecuted him that was born after the Spirit, even so it is now.
>
> 30 Nevertheless what saith the scripture? Cast out the bondwoman and her son: for the son of the bondwoman shall not be heir with the son of the freewoman.
>
> 31 So then, brethren, we are not children of the bondwoman, but of the free.

The exposition in Galatians 4 is unique in its triumphalist spirit and its lack of compassion for the downtrodden. Genesis 21 shows much more sympathy for Hagar and her son. Verse 27 above, quoted from Isiah 54, shows compassion, which is ignored by the New Testament author. Verse 30 here is a quotation of what Sarah says in Gen. 21:10. The argument anticipates any contesting claims from those sympathetic to Ishmael, who was indeed the mythological firstborn, and a "child of promise." Such claims, from Muslims, arose only a millennium after the writing of the New Testament.

The argument in Rom. 9:6-9 recalls the promise to Isaac and assures Christians that they are the seed of Isaac and Abraham, regardless of their parentage in this world.

> 6 Not as though the word of God hath taken none effect. For they are not all Israel, which are of Israel:
>
> 7 Neither, because they are the seed of Abraham, are they all children: but, In Isaac shall thy seed be called.
>
> 8 That is, They which are the children of the flesh, these are not the children of God: but the children of the promise are counted for the seed.

We might suggest that this emphasis on being chosen is identical to the Judaic claim of superiority.

Certain elements in the Abraham-Isaac story are chosen by the New Testament authors because of a transaction that makes sense to those who wish to be the shapers of the new tradition.

In Hebrews 11, we read

> 16 By faith also Sarah herself has received the strength to give seed.
>
> 17 By faith Abraham, when he was tried, offered up Isaac: and he that had received the promises offered up his only begotten son,
>
> 18 Of whom it was said, That in Isaac shall thy seed be called:
>
> 19 Accounting that God was able to raise him up, even from the dead; from whence also he received him in a figure.

Heb. 11:17-19 points to the similarity, or identity, between Abraham offering Isaac and YHWH offering Jesus. Swetnam stated that the author of Hebrews "is thinking of the death and resurrection of Jesus in terms of the sacrifice of Isaac by Abraham as portrayed in Gn 22 (the Aqedah) and as developed in the Jewish tradition" (Swetnam, 1981: 2).

If we are ready to suggest a preoccupation with human sacrifice and child sacrifice in the Hebrew Bible, it certainly was embraced by Christianity, with one big difference. In the Hebrew Bible, narratives of human sacrifice or child sacrifice are found in many places, with many contexts, often ambiguous. The authors of the New Testament focus on one great act of human sacrifice. They also developed the idea of universal atonement by human sacrifice.

A review of modern Christian theology offers the following account: "The New Testament, drawing on Old Testament imagery and expectations, presents Christ's death upon the cross as a sacrifice. This approach presents Christ's sacrificial offering as an effective and perfect sacrifice, which was able to accomplish that which the sacrifices of the Old Testament were only able to intimate, rather than achieve" (McGrath, 2001: 411).

One observer stated that

> Jews, Christians, and Muslims ... have [all] chosen to place the narrative of a father preparing to kill his the heart of their self-understanding. (Feiler, 2002: 108)

Ulreich (2009: 421) points to the difference, and similarity, between Judaism and Christianity:

> The two faith traditions tend to read the story in profoundly different ways. Judaism generally rejects the idea of child sacrifice, whereas Christianity displaces the sacrifice onto the Father God, who "so loved the world that he gave his only Son" (John 3:16). But the patriarchal image of an all-consuming father who demands the sacrifice of his son overshadows both traditions.

The believers are those that keep the Binding and the Crucifixion alive through commemoration. Harding (1987) offers verbatim quotations from sermons in a Baptist church in the southern United States, low on scholarship but filled with genuine faith:

> And the Bible says that Isaac the son said, "Father"—he didn't know what was going on—he said, "Here's the altar, here's the wood, here's the knife, here's the fire, but where's the sacrifice? Where's the lamb?" And Abraham said, "My son, God himself shall provide a sacrifice. A lamb." Now we go down several thousand years into the future, and John the Baptist, when he saw Jesus Christ for the first time, he told the disciples that were with him, he said, "Behold, take a look, here is the lamb of God that will take away the sins of the world." Isaac was not slain. There was a ram caught in the thicket which was a type of substitution. So Jesus Christ died in my place as a substitution for me ... Now God so loved

me that God himself died for me because Jesus Christ is a Very God. (Harding, 1987: 175–6)

The idea of the Passover sacrifice has been embraced by Christianity:

> Clean out the old leaven, that you may be a new lump, just as you are in fact unleavened. For Christ our Passover also has been sacrificed. (Cor. 5:7)

The mythological Crucifixion and Resurrection are said to have taken place during Passover, and its traditions are part of Christianity's foundations. Jesus became "both Isaac and the lamb" (Sherwood, 2004: 828). He was sacrificed not just as the only begotten son, but also as the Paschal lamb.

The Bloody Sacrifice

The authors of the New Testament place the mythical Jesus in the role of the Judaic High Priest on the Day of Atonement, when he entered the Holy of Holies:

> When Christ came as a high priest ... he entered once for all into the Holy Place, not with the blood of goats and calves, but with his own blood, thus obtaining eternal redemption. (Heb. 9:11-12)

The mythical Blood of Christ is even tied to the narrative of the first mythical killing, which had followed the first sacrifice: "The sprinkled blood that speaks a better word than the blood of Abel" (Heb. 12:24). Does the author here mean that Abel was sacrificed?

Earlier in the book, we discussed sacrificial acts that follow the "Emergency formula, heir sacrifice," or "sacrifice of distress" (Monroe, 2013) with children being sacrificed by their fathers when an emergency occurs and killing the child will save the day. What is the emergency in the case of Jesus? It is not a plague, famine, or defeat. If the emergency in the case of Abraham was an ultimate test of obedience, here it is the atonement for all sins.

Redemption will come only through the blood of the Savior who is also the victim, dying in unimaginable torment:

> The purpose of the ultimate sacrifice of God's own child as ultimate and thus final atonement is still predicated upon the satisfaction of a God demanding a blood sacrifice, a human sacrifice, a child sacrifice; and to be frank, the ensuing religion now becomes predicated on the bloody death of the crucified Jesus as ultimate sacrifice. (Punt, 2009: 436–7)

While the Judaic narrative of the Binding allowed us to imagine only animal blood, the Binding of Jesus narrative invites us to visualize torture, pain, blood, and death. Christianity explicitly wants us to see the blood and the suffering, because only blood will atone.

Believers will quote Lev. 17:11:

> For the life of the flesh is in the blood: and I have given it to you upon the altar to make an atonement for your souls: for it is the blood that maketh an atonement for the soul.

We know that treaties in ancient West Asia were finalized with sacrifices and, so, another covenant is sealed in blood. The ancient formula of triumph over adversity through firstborn sacrifice becomes a triumph over sin in Christianity, but this atonement still demands human blood and human sacrifice.

Because of the way the Jesus myth as presented was built on the Isaac myth, the role Christianity assigned to some Hebrew Bible texts could not but affect Jews:

> The importance of Abraham's sacrifice of Isaac among Jews of late antiquity might well reflect its centrality among Christians, for whom Isaac (as well as the ram) was a typos, or *sacramenum futuri*, of Jesus Christ. (Stroumsa, 2015: 113)

This importance of the original Binding led to unexpected adoptions of Christian mythology:

> Philo of Alexandria comes back several times to the significance of the name Isaac. At some point, he even adds, using the esoteric language of the mystics and announcing the revelation of a great secret, that Isaac was not, contrary to appearance, the son of Abraham, but rather of God! The maternity of Sarah is not in doubt, but Philo believes he knows that God, before giving birth to Isaac, miraculously returned Sarah to virginity. Thus, we have from a contemporary of Paul's the idea that Isaac was the son of God and of a virgin. (Stroumsa, 2008: 151)

This is remarkable, but we should keep in mind that narratives about the divine paternity and exceptional birth of great heroes were common (Beit-Hallahmi, 2010b).

The Binding of Jesus grows out of the Binding of Isaac and other sources, with some striking changes. What had seemed like another story of a dying and reviving god became a sacrifice myth leading to universal atonement. Those responsible for the new mythology were a small group of scribes, some of whom knew the Hebrew Bible well and were committed to relying on it.

What believers held to be the true and important key to redemption was the incomplete sacrifice of Isaac, righted by the perfect sacrifice of Jesus. Abraham is being tested and wins the tribal covenant, while Jesus is being resurrected and saves all of humanity. The Christian myth is of sacrifice, death, and cosmic rebirth, telling us that we now live in a new earth thanks to one act of firstborn sacrifice.

In the Christian narrative, God died but is reborn, like Attis and Osiris, and so sacrifice is not a final death, but a demonstration of obedience similar to the case of Abraham.

But a deviation from the perfect obedience of the perfect Son is reported in Mt. 27:46 (and Mk 15:34), where Jesus, before his death cries out:

> And about the ninth hour Jesus cried with a loud voice, saying, Eli, Eli, lama sabachthani? that is to say, My God, my God, why hast thou forsaken me?

This cry is not only disruptive but also subversive and has troubled Christians for 2,000 years. It is also a literary high point, expressing what appears like a moment of human truth. It reminds the reader of the literary high point of the Binding narrative:

> Genesis 22:
>
> 7 And Isaac spake unto Abraham his father, and said, My father: and he said, Here am I, my son. And he said, Behold the fire and the wood: but where is the lamb for a burnt offering?
>
> 8 And Abraham said, My son, God will provide himself a lamb for a burnt offering: so they went both of them together.

Isaac disrupts the journey and the planned event and leaves us shaken. In the Binding narrative, the son's question makes the story more authentic and convincing. Isaac turns to his father with a sincere child's question, and the father hides the truth, as fathers do, to protect their children from the facts of life (and death) (Beit-Hallahmi, 2011).

Judg. 11 offers a parallel scene of intimacy and truth:

> 35 And it came to pass, when he saw her, that he rent his clothes, and said, Alas, my daughter! thou hast brought me very low, and thou art one of them that trouble me: for I have opened my mouth unto the Lord, and I cannot go back.
>
> 36 And she said unto him, My father, if thou hast opened thy mouth unto the Lord, do to me according to that which hath proceeded out of thy mouth;

forasmuch as the Lord hath taken vengeance for thee of thine enemies, even of the children of Ammon.

37 And she said unto her father, Let this thing be done for me: let me alone two months, that I may go up and down upon the mountains, and bewail my virginity, I and my fellows.

Verses 35-37 are a literary and emotional high point. Jephthah is shocked to realize that his daughter is the designated victim. He rent his clothes, a sign of mourning, and then seemed to blame his poor daughter for his own deed but admitted his own fault. The unnamed daughter offers herself for sacrifice because a vow must be respected. This exchange, a moment of intimacy between father and daughter, leads to an agreement, and she is given time to mourn. Bewailing her virginity is an obvious disruption of the victim's complete willingness to die but adds to the psychological authenticity of the narrative.

The father breaks down and grieves, and it is the daughter who takes a fatherly role, supporting him as well as the whole cosmic order.

Jesus strays from his assigned role; his cry is more than disruptive. Unlike Jephthah's daughter's show of responsibility, in the Crucifixion, we discover that a willing victim rebels and rejects the role of the obedient son.

The real mystery here is about the authors and the redactors of the New Testament, who introduced to the telling of the Jesus myth a subversive line of text, which undermines the metanarrative of uninterrupted miracles and final redemption.

If we examine the narratives that were undoubtedly part of the genealogy of this particular myth, and are described above, we realize again that while all human sacrifice stories are shocking, there are sometimes disruptive messages that are contained in the narratives and serve the function of mitigating the listeners' shock.

The ambivalence and disruptive messages reflect the burden that lay on the authors' minds. And so, the readers will encounter jarring details that will interfere with their confidence in the judgment of the gods if not undermine it completely.

When we encounter the Isaac or the Jesus narratives, they arrive with the heavy armor of tradition, which protects them from being dissected. A few, or even many, believers may become baffled, but the power of traditions and institutions is there to shore up the faith. Difficult texts are assigned to religious professionals, and the believers accept the general contours of the great miracle stories without worrying about the details.

Those who created the Jesus myth considered the Binding narrative to be incomplete. In the new telling, an actual killing takes place, but after the torture and death, the victim rises to Heaven, and any conflicts are resolved. A shockingly violent fantasy turns into an eternal triumph and the promise of a cosmic rebirth. We identify with the victim because his victimization is temporary, just like his death.

In Heaven, Father and Son were united, while the mother remains an outsider. The Assumption of the Virgin Mother to Heaven, joining Father and Son, was declared only on November 1, 1950. The Catholic Church emphasizes that Assumption does not equal Ascension. The Son was capable of Ascension, an active step, while the Mother was only taken up to Heaven.

The Binding of Ishmael

Judaism expresses ambivalence as it gives us the myth of the binding of Isaac and saves the chosen son at the last moment (Genesis 22), Islam introduces the possibility that another chosen son, Ishmael, was the intended victim, and is spared as well (Quran, 37: 99-113), while Christianity goes all the way with the myth of the Crucifixion and with the son's sacrifice, which saves the believers.

Pilgrims to Mecca reenact two mythological narratives, which are as follows:

> The binding of Ishmael and the banishment of Hagar. The sequence of acts, moreover, brings about a series of identifications with exemplary persons. The key identifications elicited are with Abraham and the ordeal he faced in having to sacrifice his son, and with his wife Hagar and the ordeal she faced in wandering with her son in the desert with no water to quench his thirst …

> Islamic traditions stress the voluntary nature of these ordeals: Ishmael knew in advance, pilgrims told me, that God had ordered Abraham to sacrifice him and obey His will. Hagar, too, accepted the edict of God … Isma'il said to Ibrahim: "Tie my legs and put my face away [from you] so that the affection [you feel for me] won't stop you [from fulfilling God's will]." (Werbner, 2015: 31–2)

The dramatic phrasing, attributed to a son speaking to his father, is quite horrifying. It is an attempt to convince us of the victim's willingness, an ideal often found in other ancient traditions.

Most Muslims will never visit Mecca, but the world's Muslim population celebrates the Binding of Ishmael annually in Id al-Adha, the Moslem Sacrifice Feast. Here is a report from Istanbul, recorded in 2008: "Kurban Bayram (literally, "Sacrifice Holiday") is a Muslim religious holiday that commemorates the intended sacrifice of Ishmael by Abraham and a similar event in which the father of Mohammed was offered up as a sacrifice by his father; as with Ishmael, he was also rescued from that fate by Allah at the final moment" (Weddle, 2013: 142).

This connection to Muhammad's family is not known to most non-Muslims. In addition to Abraham's readiness to sacrifice his son Ishmael, there was a "near-sacrifice of Muhammad's father, 'Abdullah, in Islamic tradition" (Firestone, 1998: 102). 'Abd al-Muttalib, Muhammad's grandfather, was ready to sacrifice Abdullah, Muhammad's father, who was saved at the last moment by YHWH. The mythological events in Abraham's family are miraculously repeated in Muhammad's family. This adds merit to the mythical Muhammad, who in this way had two ancestors who were nearly sacrificed, Ishmael and Abdullah, Muhammad's father.

The Isaac-Ishmael-Jesus story offers the believers clear moral exemplars. Starting as a potentially disruptive story and a moral failure, Father Abraham, Jesus, and Ishmael all offer themselves. Even today, those that justify Abraham and YHWH feel morally superior. Believers identify with Abraham, Jesus, and Ishmael, hoping for self-transformation so they will be worthy of these heroes' example.

The narrative of child sacrifice by father may be seen as a radical challenge to death. In the fantasy, we can imagine both father and son preparing for the ordeal of meeting death, even if it is only to deliver the son into its waiting hands. "I can face it real close, even stare at its face." Death is defeated in the Isaac-Ishmael-Jesus story, as in all religious fantasies.

The believers are called upon to commemorate the unique sacrifice of Jesus by taking part in it in a shocking fantasy. Every member of the community is the sacrificer, who is expected to imagine the eating of human flesh and the drinking of human blood.

11

In Remembrance of a Mythical Sacrifice

If we want to examine unusual and violent fantasies and the way they develop, the ritual of the Eucharist, which celebrates human sacrifice by partaking of it, is a prime example. It is a case of theophagy, a celebration that involves god-eating and is found in ancient traditions (Frazer, 1922; Griffiths, 1980).

The Eucharist (otherwise labeled as, "Holy Communion," "the Mass," or "the Lord's Supper") may be considered by some to be a relic or even a fossil, and by others, the height of their experiences. Why would the memory of a sacrifice be celebrated with theophagy? The explicit, conscious, message of the Crucifixion and Eucharist draws us into a concrete scene of human sacrifice. Following the fantasy of human sacrifice in the Crucifixion, which invites us to imagine torture, blood, and horrible death, the Eucharist offers an imagined act of cannibalism. It means touching and living the bloody myth.

One New Testament paragraph seems to emphasize its symbolic, but shocking, nature:

Mt. 26:26-28

> 26 And as they were eating, Jesus took bread, and blessed it, and brake it, and gave it to the disciples, and said, Take, eat; this is my body.
>
> 27 And he took the cup, and gave thanks, and gave it to them, saying, Drink ye all of it;
>
> 28 For this is my blood of the new testament, which is shed for many for the remission of sins.

The authors of the New Testament went on to create the Eucharist as we know it:

John 6:51-58

> 51 I am the living bread which came down from heaven: if any man eat of this bread, he shall live for ever: and the bread that I will give is my flesh, which I will give for the life of the world.

> 52 The Jews therefore strove among themselves, saying, How can this man give us his flesh to eat?
>
> 53 Then Jesus said unto them, Verily, verily, I say unto you, Except ye eat the flesh of the Son of man, and drink his blood, ye have no life in you.
>
> 54 Whoso eateth my flesh, and drinketh my blood, hath eternal life; and I will raise him up at the last day.
>
> 55 For my flesh is meat indeed, and my blood is drink indeed.
>
> 56 He that eateth my flesh, and drinketh my blood, dwelleth in me, and I in him.
>
> 57 As the living Father hath sent me, and I live by the Father: so he that eateth me, even he shall live by me.
>
> 58 This is that bread which came down from heaven: not as your fathers did eat manna, and are dead: he that eateth of this bread shall live for ever.

The drinking of the blood and the eating of the flesh has become necessary for salvation (Jn 6:53-58) and reminds us of the sacrificial cults in which the sacrifice must be eaten to obtain union with deity.

The early history of this ritual has been described as follows:

> In strong opposition to post-Yavneh Rabbinic Judaism, early Christianity unabashedly presented itself as a sacrificial religion, although one of a new kind, in which the central ritual was called anamnēsis, a re-actualization, or even re-activation—rather than our weaker term "memory"—of Jesus's sacrifice. It was a religion without temples, in which the same sacrifice was offered perpetually, on a daily basis. (Stroumsa, 2008: 148)

Unlike in Judaism and Islam, in Christianity, animal sacrifice has disappeared, but myth and practice preserve the idea of human sacrifice and theophagy. With the Crucifixion myth comes the idea of ritual cannibalism in the form of a never-ending miracle, where some Christians believe they eat human flesh and drink human blood.

Hundreds of millions of Christians celebrate the Eucharist, which is the most important sacrament in some traditions, "the fount and apex of the whole Christian life" (Paul VI, 1964: para. 11). Why is human sacrifice, which saved humanity, celebrated through imaginary cannibalism? Christian rhetoric has struggled with the problem of this ritual since its early days, and later formulations emphasize the concreteness of the act.

The Fourth Lateran Council issued the dogma of transubstantiation in 1215. In the words of Pope Paul VI:

> The marvelous change of the whole of the bread's substance into Christ's body and the whole of the wine's substance into his blood. (Paul VI, 1965)

The Council of Trent in the 1560s declared:

> By the consecration of the bread and of the wine, a conversion is made of the whole substance of the bread into the substance of the body of Christ our Lord, and of the whole substance of the wine into the substance of His blood; which conversion is, by the holy Catholic Church, suitably and properly called Transubstantiation. The Sacrifice that is offered on the altar is the same sacrifice that was offered in Calvary; it is the same Priest, the same Victim. (Council of Trent, 1848)

The Eucharist in Catholicism is presented as an act of undisguised cannibalism:

> That the consequence of Transubstantiation, as a conversion of the total substance, is the transition of the entire substance of the bread and wine into the Body and Blood of Christ, is the express doctrine of the Church … CANON II If any one saith, that, in the sacred and holy sacrament of the Eucharist, the substance of the bread and wine remains conjointly with the body and blood of our Lord Jesus Christ, and denieth that wonderful and singular conversion of the whole substance of the bread into the Body, and of the whole substance of the wine into the Blood—the species Only of the bread and wine remaining—which conversion indeed the Catholic Church most aptly calls Transubstantiation; let him be anathema. (Council of Trent, 1848)

> CANON VIII—If any one saith, that Christ, given in the Eucharist, is eaten spiritually only, and not also sacramentally and really; let him be anathema. (Council of Trent, 1848).

Here are relevant paragraphs from the catechism.

> The sacrifice of Christ and the sacrifice of the Eucharist are one single sacrifice. The victim is one and the same. The same now offers through the ministry of priests who then offered Himself on the cross only the manner of offering is different.

> The sacrifice of Christ and the sacrifice of the Eucharist are one single sacrifice. The victim is one and the same. The same now offers through the ministry of priests who then offered Himself on the cross only the manner of offering is different.

> The Mass is the unbloody renewal of the Sacrifice of our Lord upon the cross. In it the priest, as the representative of Christ, offers to God the bread and wine,

which he changes into the Body and Blood of our Lord at the Consecration, and then completes the sacrifice by consuming the Host and drinking the chalice at the Communion.

The believers insist that they are engaged in the eating of human flesh and the drinking of human blood. Even if it is all symbolic and sublimated, just an incantation, it is still about the ingestion of flesh and blood. Outsiders see only wafers and wine, but the fantasy is powerful. For the believers, the Eucharist is a reenactment of the Crucifixion and the Resurrection (Sokolowski, 1994). This is a conscious message, and it is rarely deconstructed.

Most of the Protestant churches reject the doctrine of Transubstantiation but retain some understanding of the Eucharist as an occasion where Christ's presence becomes real and tangible along with the bread and wine—but not in the form of actual flesh and blood.

Meanwhile, most Evangelical and Pentecostal Christians consider the Eucharist simply as a memorial meal or an opportunity to experience spiritual communion with Christ. Still, the imagined cannibalism is very much there.

Here is a popular hymn:

Let us eat Jesus every day,
Eating His flesh in such a way
That in the trials great or small
He as a Man will be our all.
    Eat, eat more of Jesus!
Eat, eat more of Jesus!
Why should we undernourished be
When we have His humanity?
2
Let us drink Jesus till we see
That we are human, Jesusly!
Till rivers flood the barren ground
And quench the thirst of all around.
    Drink, drink more of Jesus!
Drink, drink more of Jesus!
Why should we ever thirsty be
When we have His humanity?
3
We must eat Jesus till God can
Have the fulfillment of His plan—
One man expressed for all to see,

> One church in each locality.
> > We'll masticate Jesus!
> We'll masticate Jesus!
> Then to the tent of meeting bring
> Jesus, our real meal offering.

And another one:

> We thirst to drink Thy precious blood,
> We languish in Thy wounds to rest,
> And hunger for immortal food
> And long on all Thy love to feast. (Jones, 1956: 193)

In a 2010 survey of the US population, about half of those polled (52 percent) said, incorrectly, that Catholicism teaches that the bread and wine used for Communion are symbols of the body and blood of Jesus. Just four in ten people answered correctly that, according to the Catholic beliefs, the bread and wine actually become the body and blood. Even many Catholics are unaware of their church's teaching on this topic; while 55 percent of Catholics got the question right, more than four in ten Catholics (41 percent) say the church teaches that the bread and wine are symbols of Christ's body and blood, and 3 percent say they do not know what the church's teaching is. This is an indication of growing secularization, where Catholic identity label is kept, but observance and knowledge decline (Pew, 2010).

Among believers, the Eucharist may serve as an inspiration under the most tragic circumstances. In 1972, sixteen young Uruguayans found themselves in the high Andes after their plane crashed. They survived by feeding on the dead bodies of fellow passengers, who were their classmates and rugby teammates (Canessa and Vierci, 2016; Read, 1974).

To cope with the horrifying ordeal, here is what they said to themselves and among themselves:

> If Jesus, in the Last Supper, offered his body and blood to all the disciples, he was giving us to understand that we must do the same ... what we did was really Christian. We went back to the very source of Christianity ... and ... We swallowed little bits of flesh with the feeling that God demanded it of us. We felt like Christians. (Kilgour, 2014: 150)

Could we point to this tragedy as evidence for the power of religion and its role in coping? These survivors relied on religious ideas to face enormous guilt and horror. This was a group of young males, energetic, optimistic, athletic, and physically fit (before the disaster). We can speculate that even without religious beliefs, this group would have survived and faced their predicament.

Interpreting Theophagy

Some interpreters have suggested that the Eucharist is a sublimation of child sacrifice rituals:

> Child sacrifice was once common, eventually supplanted by the sacrifice of an animal, even further neutralized in the totemic Eucharist, i.e., the eating of Christ's body and blood. (Peterson, 2015: 42)

Grotstein (1997: 207) included the Eucharist among the derivatives of child sacrifice:

> Human sacrifice in general and infant sacrifice in particular have been characteristic of virtually all religions since the beginning of time and up to the present time. Today we may witness its more tepid derivatives in the form of the Eucharist, fastings, circumcision, and so on.

Winkelman (2014: 48) argues that Christian ritual is the sequel to a

> sacrificial-cannibalistic complex… kept alive in … the metaphoric and symbolic act of the officiant and communicant consuming the body and blood of Jesus in the form of bread and wine.

Cannibalistic fantasies are primarily aggressive:

> Do these acts of anthropophagy, literal or metaphorical, merely place an even greater emphasis on the hatred that seethes through the celebrants' veins? Or do they evidence some conceptual overlap between feasting over one's slain enemies and ritual sacrifice? (Noegel, 2016: 289)

Twentieth-century Satanists were accused of cannibalism, and Sinason's fantasy of the Satanist eating of a fetus should raise the same questions. This fantasy is both shocking and illuminating.

The Eucharist, as the main Sacrament of the Roman Catholic Church, has clearly affected European culture. Cannibalism was tied to the Eucharist in the European mind as long as it was central to the culture (Coudert, 2012; Price, 2004). Of course, associations are also a personal matter. Douglas (1996), when discussing the story of Little Red Riding Hood, remarks on how the girl eats soup made from her grandma's blood and eats her flesh. Eating flesh and drinking blood reminds Douglas of sex and menses. The Eucharist would be higher on my personal list of associations (cf. Douglas, 1972).

Kott (1973) interpreted *The Bacchae* by Euripides, in which Pentheus, king of Thebes, encounters the god Dionysus and ends up being killed and dismembered by his own mother, as paralleling the myth of Jesus and the Eucharist. O'Flaherty (1995) ties the Eucharist to Hindu mythology and to Greek stories about Dionysus, who is being torn to pieces and eaten.

The shocking idea of the Eucharist has been routinized and normalized. In a modern novel about anorexia (Grant, 1995), the heroine tells us about her conversion to Roman Catholicism while in high school. She states that the reason was that Catholics had to acknowledge eating someone's flesh, as the Communion bread became actual flesh, according to their beliefs. The seemingly universal aversion to the eating of human flesh and the drinking of blood has been blunted. Is it because the Western world has left myths behind, as O'Flaherty (1995) suggested?

Encountering Human Sacrifice among the Colonized

The discourse about blood sacrifice and the Eucharist has been thrust to the foreground when Christian nations were engaged in colonizing the world and its non-Christian natives. Tatlock (2019) criticized the hypocrisy of Christians, when accounts of human sacrifice among colonized natives were used to justify imperialism in the New World, India, and Africa. To be fair to Christians, they never practiced human sacrifice. They just told a story about it, and then created the Eucharist, which involves the believers in a fantasy about cannibalism.

The encounter between Christian Europeans and the indigenous cannibals, whether in the New World or in Oceania, led to disturbing thoughts about the nature of the Eucharist. Transubstantiation and the Eucharist hung over all discussions of cannibalism in the encounter with native "savages."

Some Europeans interpreted the connection as the work of Satan, who seduced the natives with sweet human flesh:

> In the specific case of the Eucharist, the Devil carried out his copy of transubstantiation to an extreme by making it a bloody sacrifice, as if he wished to outdo the most sacred mystery. Thus the New World became host to the plagiarizing hand of Satan; the unspeakable rites of the Americans were actually perverse copies perpetrated by the Simia dei [God's ape]. (Jáuregui, 2009: 72)

For some Catholics the Other became a mirror, and in indigenous rituals they saw the Eucharist. This was so disturbing that some religionists spent much effort into distancing Christianity from the traditions of savage natives. Other Europeans were ready to justify human sacrifice as part of Christianity. The best-known among them was Las Casas, who stated: "We owe to God the best we can give, which was human life: hence the sacrifice of Abraham" (Las Casas, 1909: 242; quoted in MacCormack, 2000: 117).

Las Casas went on to offer a general justification of human sacrifice and child sacrifice:

> The nations who offered human beings to their gods … formed a better understanding, and a more noble and worthy regard of the excellence and divinity of their gods (than those who did not) … And the most advanced of all were those who for the welfare of their people … offered their own children. (Las Casas, 1909: 244; quoted in MacCormack, 2000: 117)

Similar encounters between the Christian communion and Native American practices took place in North America:

> Quebec, 1730. A priest holds fragments of the Host above a silver and gilt ciborium and places them on the tongues of kneeling worshippers.
>
> Huronia, 1636. A group of Wendat (Huron) men torture an Iroquois captive, drink his blood, eat his heart, then cook the rest of the remains in a kettle to share with the community
>
> … eating one's enemies transformed the bodies of eater and eaten, just as Protestants and Catholics used the Lord's Supper to transform themselves and their communities.

Cevasco (2016: 556, 579) finds these two scenes above to be equivalent and argues that the two sides in the intercultural encounter, natives and settlers, denied the similarity. While the similarity is there, I am struck by the difference between real cannibalism and the Communion. Drinking wine while imagining blood is far removed from eating the heart out of a man's body. The Eucharist obviously represents a symbolization of cannibalism, and the real thing is still much more shocking.

Writing about Herman Melville, D. H. Lawrence criticized squeamish Europeans for substituting a fantasy for the real thing practiced by natives:

> If the savages [of Typee] liked to partake of their sacrament without raising the transubstantiation quibble, and if they liked to say, directly: "This is thy body, which I take from thee and eat. This is thy blood, which I sip in annihilation of

thee," why surely their sacred ceremony was as awe-inspiring as the one Jesus substituted. But Herman chose to be horrified. (Lawrence, 1922: 38)

The colonial encounter and the soul-searching that followed it are not over (Birondo, 2020; Graulich, 2000; MacCormack, 2000; Shullenberger, 2010; Test, 2011). One man, Bartolome de Las Casas, is still the focus of discussion, as he sounds sometimes like somebody from the twenty-first century who landed in the sixteenth. What we observe in him is not just empathy or the belief in equality, but the recognition of the psychic unity of mankind, expressed in the logic of sacrifice, that makes possible encounters and comparison. In this spirit, the commonality of religious beliefs is still being discovered: "The fundamental meaning and end of Aztec sacrifice was expiation of sins or transgressions in order to deserve a worthy afterlife. (Graulich, 2000: 354–5).

Freud's Primal Crime and the Eucharist

In *Totem and Taboo* (1913) Freud offered a description of how conscience, society, and religion were first created in prehistorical times. He connected totemic religion, characterized by the centrality of the totemic animal, symbolizing the clan, and the incest taboo, which applied to all members of the same clan as well as paternal authority.

He suggested that this connection stemmed from human prehistory, when humans lived in large groups, the primal hordes, dominated by one older male, who could monopolize all females (this was first proposed by Charles Darwin). This tyrannical father had been murdered and then devoured by the resentful young males, his sons, who then possessed all females, including mothers and sisters. The murdered father has been then symbolized in the totem animal, which holds the authority within the horde.

The primal crime, and the resulting guilt, were the starting point for civilization, morality, the incest taboo, and religion. The guilt-stricken brothers agreed to a social contract: Stop the war of all against all and prohibit copulations within the clan, thus controlling, if not conquering, the disruptive and destructive impulses of sex and aggression.

The primal crime left a legacy found everywhere in culture. From the prehistorical to the more abstract and symbolic, the functions of commemoration, appeasement, and renunciation of instinct remained integral to the cultural treatment of the Oedipus complex, expressed through religion. Religious myths and rituals obsessively reenacted the killing, and the totemic meal, in which the primal crime was celebrated and atoned for, became the Judaic Passover and the Christian Eucharist.

Freud discussed the totem feast, in which the totem is slain and eaten, as repeating the original primal crime. Filicide is the opposite of, and the atonement for, the primal crime of patricide.

Freud described the Eucharist as a totemic meal and stated: "Thus we can trace through the ages the identity of the totem meal with animal sacrifice, with the anthropic human sacrifice and with the Christian Eucharist" (1913: 154). As one observer stated: "Hence Freud sees Christian communion as one means of perpetuating guilt, which the faithful then expiate by bowing to religious authority, both intellectually and emotionally" (Grünbaum, 2010: 26).

Freud interprets the idea of the "atoning blood of Christ" as follows:

> If the Son of God was obliged to sacrifice his life to redeem mankind from original sin, then by the law of talion, the requital of like by like, that sin must have been a killing, a murder. Nothing else could call for the sacrifice of a life for its expiation. And the original sin was an offence against God the Father, the primal crime of mankind must have been a parricide, the killing of the primal father of the primitive human horde, whose mnemic image was later transfigured into a deity. (Freud, 1915: 292–3)

The projected fantasy of sacrifice is needed to expiate impulses and dreams about actual killings. This explains the centrality of sacrifice fantasies in mythology and folklore, and the Eucharist, because a ritual such as the Eucharist would be envisioned by Freud as a repetition of this primal crime, "a fresh elimination of the father, a repetition of the guilty deed" (1913: 155).

Schuster (1970), following Freud, suggests that the Christian myth is a clear departure from earlier traditions, because the sacrifice is voluntary, and the victim is the son rather than the father. This leads to a resolution of ambivalence about the father and the control of incest and murder. Such speculations may seem bold and unfounded, but keep in mind the reality of the Eucharist and the surrounding fantasies.

While Freud's assertions regarding the events of human prehistory have been rejected by many scholars, his psychological observations regarding the dynamics of male competition and intergenerational violence have gained some acceptance.

Some of the best-known anthropologists of the twentieth century, while doubtful about Freud's thesis regarding the "primal crime," embraced his phylogenetic insights. These included A. L. Kroeber, Ernest Becker (1961) Meyer Fortes, and

Derek Freeman. While rejecting the reconstruction of prehistory presented in *Totem and Taboo*, Fortes (1966) embraced wholeheartedly Freud's psychological insights regarding the connections between totem, taboo, and paternal authority.

Freeman (1967) did not accept the idea of the "primal crime" as a reality, but as a psychological pattern, reflecting the force of aggressive and sexual drives within the nuclear family.

Kroeber (1920) stated clearly that there was no support from anthropological data for Freud's suggestions. At the same time, he considered *Totem and Taboo* "an important and valuable contribution." Kroeber (1939) stated that there was still no support for Freud's central thesis. Nevertheless, Kroeber was ready to accept Freud's idea of the primal crime as a hypothesis and to consider seriously some of the concepts introduced in the book.

Mead (1963) speculated that Freud was, after all, right about the "primal crime," except that this deed was committed much earlier in the evolutionary history of humanity. It was a prehuman horde, when sexual maturity was reached at age seven or eight, and life was much shorter. This deed was committed repeatedly, as each generation got rid of the earlier one over hundreds of thousands of years, until these prehumans became real humans.

Fox (1967, 1994), an evolutionary anthropologist, supported Freud's reconstruction of early hominid history. He argued that contemporary observations of primate social life and knowledge in evolutionary anthropology lend support to Freud's idea of the "primal horde." Among baboons one can find a social pattern of a troop with several dominant males, and young males being excluded from sexual competition. He concluded that the primal crime described in *Totem and Taboo* did occur, over and over, in horde after horde, and constituted a stage in human evolution.

de Waal (2019) reported cases of bloody rebellion against the alpha male dominating primate hordes, and Wrangham (2019) discussed the ability of males to conspire together and decide on a time and a place to dispatch a tyrannical despot who is making their lives miserable. To him, rising up together against the tyrant was the beginning of altruism and democracy.

We find an emerging hypothesis, shared at least by Mead, Fox, de Waal, and Wrangham, about repeated rebellions against the old ruler, occurring among generations of older and younger males competing for mates. Male competition is also the source of energy for creation and development.

Even if the primal patricide never took place, every generation repeats the rebellion, or just fantasizes about rebellion, and celebrates the ancient rebellion in traditional and nontraditional ways. The primal crime sequence of events is repeated and reversed in fantasy, with parents killing children or trying to kill them. The father versus child formula, familiar throughout history, is a reversal of the real process. The child is always presented as the victim, but Freud's Oedipal interpretation tells us that the son initiates hostilities, even if this is denied and reversed (more on this later).

Christian mythology includes not only a father god who sacrifices his only son, but also a virgin mother. Thus, an Oedipal victory is achieved, with the hero being born without the help of sexual intercourse and exclusively possessing his mother. After birth, he survives the threats from an evil king and ends his earthly life by becoming a god. Grünbaum (2010) regarded the Virgin Birth doctrine as direct evidence in favor of Freud's Oedipal formulas. The dogma of the perpetual virginity of the Mother of God, which claims that giving birth to Jesus did not affect her anatomy, is even more of an Oedipal triumph.

The Eucharist and Similar Rituals

Determining the actual emergence of the Eucharist in antiquity is impossible, but similar practices have been observed in ancient times as well as more recently.

The fourth century church father Epiphanius of Salamis accused a certain Christian sect, the Borborites, of ingesting semen and menstrual blood during the Eucharist ritual, and regarding them as the "body" and "blood" of Christ. Augustine accused the Manichaeans of holding the same ceremony. It is impossible to judge the accuracy of these ancient claims, but fantasies about the energies of semen are ubiquitous, while the evil powers of menstrual blood are a global theme. Accusations of swallowing menstrual blood (not semen) have been directed at nonexistent contemporary Satanists (Storr, 2011).

In some preliterate cultures, such as the Ainu of Japan, the bear is considered a god, and rituals of bear sacrifice, in which the celebrants share its meat, play a major role in their traditions (Kitagawa, 1961).

According to Vajrayana Buddhist teachings, pupils can consume their master's semen as a means of transferring wisdom. Zivkovic (2014: 121) described how followers of the Tibetan lama Bokar Rinpoche (1940–2004) ingested red and white pills containing his blood and semen following his death and stated that in this way they can "merge with his mind."

The historical processes that led to the selection of particular practices are unknown. We know that humans fantasize about incorporating the forms of animals they eat as well as their power. In the case of cannibalism, there are fantasies about acquiring positive human qualities such as courage (Conklin, 1995, 2001; Vilaça, 2000). In the case of the Eucharist, the command "Take, eat; this is my body" introduces the cannibalistic fantasy about ingesting the god's flesh, gaining some of his powers and uniting with him. At the same time, as indicated above, this is also a violent fantasy, celebrated publicly.

It has been claimed that the Eucharist had Judaic roots in the paschal lamb meal, but it's unclear how such sacrifices had cannibalistic aspects, even the most remote. Ritual drinking of blood, even in the most sublimated form, is impossible to reconcile with Judaic origins (Cahill, 2002). The origins of this ritual seem to lie in the Greek and Roman cultures, especially in minority and mystery religions (Grant, 1981; Harrill, 2008; McGowan, 2010; Riehl, 2019):

> It was an extremely common belief in the ancient world that by drinking the blood, or, later on, by immersion in or sprinkling with the blood, it was possible to absorb the qualities of the god whose blood was so used. (Guignebert, 1953: 446)

The similarities between Christian mythology and the Mithras religion were noticed when stories about Jesus were quite young.

> Mithras—known to Roman devotees variously as "redeemer"; "savior"; "light of the world" and "Son of God"—was said to have been sent to earth from heaven and born of a divine father and mortal virgin mother on December 25 … He was characterized as a celibate miracle worker who, prior to his death, celebrated a final meal with twelve disciples … Worshippers of Mithras believed their redeemer died, was buried in a tomb, returned to life three days later, and ascended to heaven … As a means of communion with the departed deity and in remembrance of Mithras' last supper with his disciples, devotees would partake of a sacramental meal of bread and wine … Mithras' followers marked their savior's birth with the sharing of gifts each December 25th, and his resurrection and ascension each Spring Equinox (Easter). As early as the second century CE—well before the Christianized Empire's efforts to eradicate the Mithras cult—such remarkable agreement between Christianity and the still-active mystery cults caused considerable consternation for several Church Fathers. (Rempel, 2010: 34–5)

Moreover,

> The adherents of Mithras believed that by eating the bull's flesh and drinking its blood they would be born again, just as life itself has been created anew from the

blood of the bull. Participation in this rite would give not only physical strength but lead to the immortality of the soul and to eternal light. (Reynolds, 1993: 78)

Frazer described the rites celebrating the death and resurrection of the Phrygian vegetation god, Attis, which are very similar to the Mithras blood baptism (Frazer, 1990; Herbert, 2002). In the early days of Christianity, the Eucharist gave rise to rumors and accusations of child sacrifice and cannibalism (Cohn, 1975; McGowan, 1994; Schultz, 1991).

Did the Eucharist appear because of a prehistorical killing or because of persistent tensions and conflicts, pressing to be resolved? Keeping in mind, as we should, that this ritual involves extremely violent fantasies, we may examine more immediate causes for its appearance. It offers the participants a way of releasing aggression and supports individuals struggling with internal impulses and external frustrations.

Freud's (1913) theory may be farfetched and impossible to prove, but more parsimonious explanations are not being offered anywhere. The Eucharist remains a challenge and an enigma, just like the rituals of genital mutilation.

12

Genital Mutilation and Child Sacrifice Fantasies

While Christian tradition presents an explicit cannibalistic rite, in Judaism another blood rite, known as the "Blood Covenant," attracts our attention. Does it take a wild imagination to connect the Eucharist to genital mutilation? It has been done (Grotstein, 1997), and while in the Eucharist violent acts are only imagined, in the case of genital mutilation, blood is actually spilled, and the body is marked for life. The origins of genital mutilation are a prehistoric puzzle (Raveenthiran, 2018). It has become an identity marker for different groups, but reconstructing its beginnings is impossible (Jones, 1969). While genital mutilation of the young males and females is practiced in numerous cultures, we have a no idea about the way in which circumcision, one specific form of mutilation, has become part of the Judaic tradition or the Islamic one.

How do you explain, "The desire by adults to attack the genitals of their infants and young children with sharp knives?" (DeMeo, 1997: 1). Those who share the traditions regard such acts as involving purification or initiation. Cross-cultural research found a correlation between male genital mutilations and the presence of a moralizing high god. DeMeo (1997: 7) states that

> male genital mutilations are found present in a cultural complex where children, females, and weaker social or ethnic groups are subordinated to elder, dominant males in rigid social hierarchies of one form or another.

Rituals of mutilation consist of violent and bloody attacks on a baby or child, and the genital mutilation of children has been regarded more and more often as a form of child abuse. Female genital mutilation has been targeted for elimination by the United Nations, and the genital mutilation of males is coming under increasing criticism (Denniston et al., 2006; Terhune, 1997).

Initiation, sometimes conceived of as a process of death and rebirth, involves sacrifices and ordeals, physical and symbolic. Genital mutilation is obviously about sexuality, believed to prepare the young for marriage and adulthood with their sexual identity clarified and strengthened. We must recall that male genital mutilation is performed by father figures, and for females by mother figures (Bettelheim, 1954).

Initiation rituals from all over the world include scarification and genital mutilation (Matthiessen, 1962). Male genital mutilation is practiced in various cultures as part of puberty or prepuberty initiation rites. These mutilation practices include subincision and genital bisection among Australian aborigines and supercision in Polynesia.

Castration and Devotion

Male genital mutilation has been considered a substitute for castration. Instead of sacrificing the testicles, or the penis, or both, cutting off the prepuce or carrying out an operation that does not impair sexual functioning is still a sacrifice. The image of circumcision, not surprisingly, has often brought to mind castration (Seeman, 2007). Circumcision as a form of sacrifice represents a defense against castration through a token sacrifice. This was Freud's observation (1939), which has occurred to modern medical observers (Mordeniz and Verit, 2009).

Cases of castration or self-castration inspired by religion are well-known. Some are the product of individual psychopathology, while others result from institutional processes (Kushner, 1967). Some early Christians wished to literally follow Mt 19:12:

> For there are some eunuchs, which were so born from their mother's womb: and there are some eunuchs, which were made eunuchs of men: and there be eunuchs, which have made themselves eunuchs for the kingdom of heaven's sake. He that is able to receive it, let him receive it.

If we follow the patristic discourse about celibacy and castration, and find it alien, it turns out that the same ideas were being discussed, and acted out, in the late twentieth century (Murray, 2019).

The leader of Heaven's Gate, Marshall Applewhite, who became known because of the mass suicide of thirty-nine of his followers in 1997, had the exact same concerns about sexuality as some early Christians. Eight of the eighteen male bodies found after the mass suicide were physically castrated (including Applewhite), and a few more were "chemically" neutered (Chryssides, 2016; Raine, 2005).

In 2015, a notorious Indian guru, Ram Rahim Singh, who has been convicted of two rapes and a murder and sentenced to life imprisonment, was accused of inducing the castration of 400 followers, which was supposed to guarantee a "personal connection with God." The castrations began around the year 2000 (*Economic Times*, 2015).

The Jewish Circumcision Ritual

When male circumcision became a Judaic identity marker in the fifth century BCE, as reported by Herodotus (Alonso Serrano, 2021) it was meant to express superiority, purity, and exclusion. One of the stories invented to convey this was about the mythological hero David, who collected 200 Philistine foreskins as a dowry for the king's daughter (1 Sam. 18).

An essential part of the Jewish genital mutilation ritual is the sucking of blood from the baby's penis by the mohel, the religious functionary performing the ceremony. The sucking of blood from the wound seems unique to Jewish tradition, where without it the circumcision is incomplete and invalid. The blood is not swallowed but spit out by the mohel. This custom is rarely discussed, and most Jews today are not even aware of it, as they would not be aware of other Jewish traditions.

Somebody present at the ceremony cannot be blamed for viewing it as an assault on a week-old baby, but then the sucking, a homosexual act (Maler, 1966), may be a mitigation, offering love and support. There is a unique choreography of assault and love.

Michel de Montaigne (1533–92) witnessed a circumcision ceremony in Rome on January 30, 1581, and wrote a detailed description (Cohen, 2005). One thing he commented on was the circumciser's bloody mouth. It is clear from his description that even though the circumciser spits out the blood, some of it was swallowed when he drank the obligatory glass of wine, shared with others.

Another matter de Montaigne commented on was the belief, reportedly held by Jews, that because the circumciser has done the sucking, his mouth will be protected from corruption after death. "The Covenant Blood" is indeed considered to have curative and apotropaic powers, mentioned in Judaic sources through the ages (Hoffman, 1996).

Nunberg (1947) argued that the unconscious meaning of circumcision is tied to conflicts around sexual identity and the genitals. Sacrificing a part of the penis demonstrates love to both father and God.

Wyatt (2009), using evidence about male genital mutilation from Ugarit, found that it might have been related to marriage as a protection for the bridegroom. He also suggested that circumcision

> is a substitute for the killing or castration of the child who might otherwise supplant his father. Near Eastern mythic tradition abounds in accounts of both these alternative scenarios, or of reversals (that is, when it is the father who suffers). (Wyatt, 2009: 426)

The enigmatic story in Exod. 4:24-26 presents circumcision as a substitute for human sacrifice. YHWH demands a human life, but Zipporah, the wife of Moses, cuts off her son's foreskin and YHWH "let him alone."
Exod. 4:24-26

> 24 And it came to pass by the way in the inn, that the LORD met him, and sought to kill him.
>
> 25 Then Zipporah took a sharp stone, and cut off the foreskin of her son, and cast it at his feet, and said, Surely a bloody husband art thou to me.
>
> 26 So he let him go: then she said, A bloody husband thou art, because of the circumcision.

Wyatt argued that this is "the paradigm for how to redeem a firstborn son" (2009: 425).

The Biblical account does not explicitly state whose life was in danger. However, we can reasonably conclude that it was not Moses' life, for he had just received a divine commission to lead the Israelites out of Egypt (Exod. 3:10). It seems unlikely that on his way to fulfil that assignment, Moses' life would have been threatened by God. It therefore would be the life of one of his sons. The law given earlier to Abraham regarding circumcision stated: "An uncircumcised male who will not get the flesh of his foreskin circumcised, even that soul must be cut off from his people. He has broken my covenant" (Gen. 17:14). Moses had apparently neglected to circumcise his son, and thus the boy's life was threatened by YHWH.

The Binding of Isaac is interpreted by Reik (1961) as reflecting prehistorical puberty initiation traditions. This initiation included circumcision and a dramatic enactment of death and rebirth. The myth depicts Isaac, a cult hero, as being attacked by a demon god who demands human sacrifice, as part of puberty rites, in which young boys had to symbolically experience death and rebirth. This is reminiscent of Exod. 4:24-26, discussed above.

Circumcision and Anti-Semitism

Genital mutilation is not just an attack on physical integrity. It is also an interference, real and symbolic, with sexuality. In Europe through the ages, Jews, that is Jewish males, were (quite correctly) perceived as genitally mutilated, and this made them less than full men.

Freud (1939) argued that the custom of circumcision arouses in non-Jewish neighbors echoes of dreaded castration and is therefore one of the most important origins of anti-Semitism. That such acts may be tied to cultural prejudice by outsiders has been suggested more than once. Freud stated,

> The castration complex is the deepest unconscious root of anti-Semitism; for even in the nursery little boys hear that a Jew has something cut off his penis ... and this gives them a right to despise Jews. (Freud, 1909: 36)

The circumcised Jew is often represented as a mutilated person, and this leads to the idea that a mutilated people desire revenge and want to circumcise (castrate) the non-Jew (Fenichel, 1946). We do not need to accept the idea of a universal castration complex to realize that any genital mutilation is naturally frightening. It is likely to be tied to other unfamiliar practices in the out-group and to generate other fearful fantasies.

It was not just a matter of genital mutilation that might have been psychologically significant. It was a question of masculine identity and behavior. There was a socially conceived "effeminacy of the male Jewish body" (Bunzl, 1997: 74). Under conditions of objective and subjective powerlessness, weakness, and insecurity, human dignity and manly dignity are easily wounded (Mosse, 1985). Were Jewish men real men?

The emasculation metaphor has been used and is still being used in connection with many oppressed groups, including women (Greer, 1970). It reflects a male ideal that seems quite universal. While the feminine is judged to be weak and deficient, manliness images are everywhere tied to political and psychological empowerment. Masculinity remains a universal human ideal, not just because of its connotation of physical prowess and bravery, but also because it means reliability, steadfastness, and responsibility. Men are not only violent destroyers but they also help to build and maintain the world around them. Beyond the male physique, there are universally valued masculine behaviors and attributes, such as assertiveness, energy, power, and success.

The Substitution Hypothesis: Mutilation and Child Sacrifice

That the mutilation may be a substitute for a complete child sacrifice has been suggested more than once.

Loeb (1923) argued for a universal connection of cannibalism, circumcision, and human sacrifice, which appeared in that order. Schlossman (1966: 351) argues that the covenant with Abraham and his chosen people was contingent on the "acceptance of the foreskin as a token sacrifice in lieu of the son." The totemic ram becomes the substitute for full sacrifice; and circumcision becomes a token sacrifice. Schlesinger (1976) suggested that circumcision, as practiced by Jews on the eighth day, is a condensation of puberty initiation and firstborn sacrifice, and thus is also a reminder of infanticide.

> Circumcision may well be a remnant of a tradition of human sacrifice, with the foreskin serving as a substitute for a whole human victim. (Ehrenreich, 1997: 63)

Instead of speculating about the ancient origins of genital mutilations and its possibly being a substitute for child sacrifice, we can look at the ritual itself, as it is carried out today. What reactions does it bring up? One natural reaction is fear, and Jewish folklore expresses that with hundreds of jokes. Nonobservant Jews who have been circumcised express resentment, which reflects their ambivalence about Jewish identity (Baum, 2013).

In modern prayers, authored for the circumcision ceremony since the Middle Ages, we can find evidence of what comes to mind if you are involved in the act. The prayers turn out to be violent fantasies.

The hypothesis that circumcision is considered, by believers and officiants, as a substitute for the actual sacrifice of the baby on a divine altar is supported directly by traditional texts that are part of the ritual. The reaction to the ritual is not only fear, but fantasies of greater violence.

One direct affirmation of fantasies that treat circumcision as a substitute for child sacrifice is found in the circumciser's prayer before performing the cutting:

> Master of the universe, may it be your will that this be considered by you—and thus accepted as according to your will—as if I had sacrificed him before your throne of glory. (Hoffman, 1996: 72)

This circumciser's prayer is part of Ashkenazi Jewish tradition. The Sephardi tradition offers another text as follows:

After the circumcision, the father of the child recites the following prayer which is found in Sephardic prayer books: "May it be thy will, oh God, that the blood of this covenant be esteemed as if I had built an altar and offered burnt offerings and slaughtered sacrifices. (Weiss, 1966: 79)

The term "burnt offerings" must remind every observant Jewish father of Genesis 22, where Abraham is commanded to offer just that. Do these prayers express a wish to complete the Binding? What these texts indicate is that the ritual that involves holding a sharp knife over a baby's body and using it on his genitals, and then sucking the blood, may bring to mind ideas about more extensive violence.

The father is just an observer, but he is very close to the action. Observing a violent act may provide vicarious relief of aggressive impulses, according to some theories, but the evidence from the real world, as discussed above, shows that it is likely to stimulate additional violent acts or violent fantasies.

Within the religious context, both the circumciser's prayer and the father's prayer are evidence of total devotion.

We can imagine that during adolescent-initiation rituals, where the images of death and rebirth are explicit, older men who are guiding the procedures have similar fantasies. In the Jewish case, a tiny baby is bloodied in order to be sanctified and initiated, but the assault on his body must be both shocking and provocative for the observers.

It is interesting to note here that while discussions of the Judaic genital mutilation tradition have tied it to child sacrifice (Levenson, 1993), such a connection does not appear very often in the extensive literature on genital mutilation in other cultures.

Genital mutilation among the Aborigines in Australia has been discussed in numerous publications, and Roheim suggested that "subincision of the penis represents the cathartic attempt of old men to castrate the young" (Anderson, 2014: 142; Roheim, 1945). No psychic ties of genital mutilation and child sacrifice have been mentioned by anthropologists in this context despite evidence of cannibalism in the same tribes. We don't know if these ties ever occurred to the Aborigines themselves, but they certainly did not occur to any observers.

Similarly, the literature on genital mutilation in Africa or in Papua New Guinea rarely mentions the idea that this violent act is a substitute for the more violent killing of the child. This might have been different if we had texts written by the indigenes.

The texts written by Jews and offered as prayers provide the kind of data that clearly point to a psychological connection between genital mutilation and child sacrifice. We now come a full circle connecting ancient child sacrifice fantasies and surviving rituals that target children.

Another surviving substitution ritual practiced by Jews involves the redemption of the firstborn. A firstborn son must be redeemed from the priesthood through a ceremonial payment and a firstborn male donkey is redeemed in a mass ceremony.

The survival of *pidyon haben*, the redemption of the firstborn through a token payment to a priest is significant:

> Indeed, Jewish self-perception has developed into viewing the Jewish tradition as a culture that had distanced itself early on from human sacrifice, and later on, gave up on the sacrifice of animals, as well. One would have expected Jews to erase all traces of the offering of children to God and give up on a ritual that came to exempt first-borns from being offered, even if only symbolically, to the service of God. Yet, the ritual has survived, and so has the role of priests in performing it and accepting the ransom. (Ariel, 2007: 308)

Among Orthodox Jews today, redeeming the firstborn son is obligatory, just like circumcision, and, as Ariel (2007) reported, the ritual is celebrated in the United States by non-Orthodox Jews. Has it somehow shed its sacrificial meaning?

13

An Infanticidal Impulse and the Oedipal Paradox

Several authors have offered another version of an Oedipal conflict, in which murderous impulses come from fathers, not sons. It has been suggested that there is a deep strain of paternal enmity toward sons, which creates a specific template of tensions and actions within the family. Here not the patricidal drive is the motive but the infanticidal impulse, coming from the father. Why would it take the form of ritual killing? Why should the gods be involved if we have so many accounts of lethal family conflict without them? Ritual narratives may legitimize paternal hostility but are hardly needed. There is no shortage of horrifying infanticidal narratives, describing family conflicts with no hint of religious sanction.

Bakan (2001), Beiser (1989), and Devereux (1966) suggested that the psychoanalytic focus on the son's hostility toward the father and murderous wishes directed at the father must be a defense against the recognition of the father's hostility against the son and his infanticidal urges.

This suggestion has taken the form of an accusation against Sigmund Freud for his readiness to support the authority of the fathers:

> Why did Freud almost suppress the existence of paedocidal desires? Perhaps Freud had never released himself of the infantile fear of admitting that one's beloved parent who exercises powers of life and death, on whom the infant is dependent, wishes to kill it ... Freud may have been ready to accept the discovery of immoral, guilty, wishes on his own part, but not the guilt of the accusing father. Lastly, though Freud defended bravely many nonconformist positions, he shared the paternalistic cultural values of his historical milieu. Freud may have been unable to assign universal immorality to parents, shaking the ideological basis of parental authority. (Tucker, 1999: 43)

Bakan (1971) points out that religion was created by adults and reflects the experience of the fathers, not of the sons, even though all fathers are also sons.

The myth of Jesus is seen by Bakan as an attempt to make the infanticidal drive conscious, with the mythological Jesus remaining only a son, never a father. In the Roman Catholic Church, priests are "fathers," but are also celibate, thus avoiding the danger of infanticidal impulses.

Against Freud's view of the primal crime as father sacrifice, Lustig (1976) suggested that child sacrifice was much more typical of ancient pre-Judaic cultures. The Passover sacrifice is a substitute for the intended firstborn sacrifice, and this theme is found often in Judaic texts and rituals, though in muted form. Schlesinger (1976) reminds us that the Passover ritual meal, as celebrated by Jews since the Middle Ages, contains many references to child sacrifice.

In the narratives described above involving child sacrifice being bartered for victory in war, calm seas, or a cosmic covenant as in the case of Isaac, Ishmael, or Jesus, there is an implied, hidden indictment of fathers. It is not about an infanticidal impulse but about a transaction, in which a father's love reaches its limits.

Bergmann (1992) presented the development of both Judaism and Christianity as reflecting the struggle against the infanticidal impulse in fathers and assigned to child sacrifice a major role in the history of religion and culture. Offering a critique of Freudian theory, Bergmann modifies the Oedipus complex by introducing the Laius complex, which contains the hostility of fathers toward sons, to explain child sacrifice.

This complex and its sublimation is expressed in the Jewish Passover holiday, in the Christian Eucharist, and in the anti-Semitic Blood Libel against the Jews. Bergmann offers his interpretation as an alternative to Freud's ideas about the development of the two religions, as presented in *Totem and Taboo*, which emphasized the historical development of the two as reactions to the primal patricide.

Bergmann claimed that the ancient Moloch demanded the burning of children, and that the greatest efforts to overcome this ritual can be found in the Biblical accounts of the suspended sacrifice of Isaac by Abraham and of the sacrifice of Christ by God the Father to atone for original sin. Bergmann published his work before the formation of the recent consensus among Bible scholars, who no longer think that Moloch was a god (Noort, 2002). He argued that the development of both Judaism and Christianity was an effort, only partially successful, to ameliorate past sins of child sacrifice through the creation of an entirely loving god.

Still, according to Bergmann, the psychological conflict over child sacrifice haunts the unconscious of modern humanity. Even though there is no archeological evidence to support Bergmann's claims about Moloch worship, the preoccupation with ritual infanticide in Judaism and Christianity is indisputable.

Donovan (1991) suggested that the reality of cruelty inside the family and the active destructiveness of parents toward their children are traditionally hidden and denied. He reminds us that even in *Oedipus Tyrannus*, by Sophocles, it was the mother Jocasta who gave away her son to be killed. Instead of the unpleasant facts of parenting, a cultural ideal is presented as reality. The reality of rejection, then, finds an outlet in popular legends, undermining the myth of the perfect family and the perfect parents.

Infanticide and physical mutilation of children are common themes of mythology all over the world. We find countless historical examples where children make similar claims about (and against) their parents. We find father Chronos in Greek mythology not just killing his children but eating them. The theme of the endangered baby is found everywhere. Krishna, Moses, Jesus, Romulus, and Remus are all a few of the newborn babies in danger of being killed by an evil king in mythical narratives.

Could paternal hostility account for child sacrifice stories? Sometimes a parent may be angry with a child and have a conscious wish about getting rid of him, but this is far from an infanticidal impulse. The fantasy of infanticide is peripheral to most people, a central fantasy in pathological cases, and turns into action in very rare cases.

There are four ways of satisfying the actual infanticidal drive (if it exists):

1. direct action
2. ritual activity (circumcision, Eucharist)
3. art and collective imagination, including myth and folklore
4. individual imagination.

The infanticidal impulse formula, which blames parents, is naturally subject to the same doubts and questions as the Freudian formula it seeks to replace. Given this formula, we may hypothesize that we are going to find some evidence of male filicide by fathers.

The Reality of Filicide

We have encountered many filicide narratives in the context of fantasies about human-gods interaction and many outside a religious context. Parents in such stories are regarded as monsters. The theme will always attract attention, even when it is rare. *Beloved*, by Toni Morrison, tells the story of a girl killed to save her from a life of enslavement. It is based on a true event and leaves us stunned. It reminds us of stories about European Jews in 1096, who slaughtered their children to save them from forced conversion to Christianity.

Because of the shocking nature of filicide, there have been many academic studies that have tried to shed light on the parents involved. They all concluded that while filicide was probably underreported, it is still a rare occurrence. Children who are being violated and threatened are part of everyday reality, but filicide is extremely rare.

Infanticide has been widely practiced among ancient Romans, Australian aborigines, Inuits in North America, and the Yanomamo in South America, among others. Korbin (1991) reported on the extent of child abuse, infanticide, and child abandonment in many societies, from New Guinea to Turkey. Scheper-Hughes (1992) described how poor mothers in Brazil neglected their young children, leading to many deaths. Hausfater and Hrdy (1984) suggested that such phenomena are common in the animal kingdom as well.

In all human societies throughout history, and in some societies today, infanticide has meant mostly female infanticide (Gil'adi, 1992). This glaring fact has often been ignored. While it is females that have been the victims of infanticide, in myths and legends it is mostly males that are under threat. We have clear evidence about the extent of recent female infanticide and the abortion of female fetuses in India and China. In India, female infanticide has been reported since the early nineteenth century. In 2020, the sex ratio in the total population in India is 108.18 males per 100 females. The sex ratio in China was approximately 105.07 males to 100 females. In the United States, the sex ratio is 97 males for 100 females.

Data on actual filicide in modern societies indicate that this crime is unusually rare, and most cases involve biological mothers rather than fathers. In many cases, filicide was followed by attempted suicide (Putkonen et al., 2009).

Oberman (2002) examined mothers who killed their children, using data collected starting in 1870. Less than 20 percent were neonaticide, killed within twenty-four hours after birth. The cases involved poverty, unstable relationships, and mental illness.

With men, some cases of filicide are classified as accidental/discipline, where the child was being physically punished, and too much force was applied (Eriksson et al., 2016).

In a study of 933 filicide cases between 1994 and 2005 in Japan, it was found that mothers were more likely than fathers to kill both sons and daughters.

Only 23 percent of child victims and only 25 percent of the sons were killed by fathers. Twenty-eight percent of the male killers were stepfathers. Fifteen percent of sons and 12 percent of daughters were killed by both parents (Yasumi and Kageyama, 2009).

Filicide rates in this study showed strong correlations with suicide rates and not with homicide rates. Filicide rates also correlated with unemployment rates. We know that infants under one year of age are likely to be killed by their mothers, who may then try to commit suicide (Lester, 1991).

The preponderance of the evidence has shown that filicidal mothers kill biological children, while fathers are more likely to kill nongenetic children in the household (Daly and Wilson, 1994; Liem and Koenraadt, 2008; Temrin, Buchmayer, & Enquist, 2000; Wekes-Shackelford and Shackelford, 2004). The fathers' behavior makes perfect sense in terms of evolutionary logic, but the mothers' less so.

The evidence from non-mythological families is clear. Sons are more valued than daughters, who are considered a burden. In most cases, there is no reason to believe that fathers will threaten their sons' survival. If fathers possess a conscious or unconscious infanticidal impulse, most seem to control it very well.

If we examine the other side, namely patricide, the picture is similar. Such cases are rare, and research shows that among individuals guilty of patricide more than 50 percent have been diagnosed with schizophrenia. Murdered fathers have been described as "domineering," "aggressive," and "cruel." Sons tend to be responsible for 86 percent of parricide, likely to kill both mothers and fathers (Allen, Salari, and Buckner, 2020; West and Feldsher, 2010).

Trying to extrapolate from modern findings, we have no reason to believe that filicide and parricide were common in ancient times, and the infanticidal impulse, if it exists, was blocked in reality by social controls. Some may suggest, however, that that impulse might have found its expression in fantasy, for example, in various Oedipal stories and child sacrifice narratives, in addition to various accusations and projections, such as recent Satanism allegations.

The big question in the debate around Satanism and so-called recovered memories is about judging patterns of action against patterns of imagination. Infanticide myths are very common and infanticidal impulses may be common, while acting them out rarely occurs. While child abuse is very common, and infanticide less common, ritual infanticide has been extremely rare in human history.

Infanticide and Religion Now

Some religious fantasies and rituals present a threat to children, and various practices attract much attention, because of their shocking nature, despite their rarity. Thus, cases of child death caused by exorcism are still reported (Bottoms et al., 1995).

The fantasy of a world without evil in the form of illness has cost the lives of many children and adults (Bottoms et al., 1995; Hughes, 2004; Terhune, 1997; Woolley, 2005). The best-known group that rejects biomedicine has been Christian Science, whose members have lived shorter lives because of this rejection (Simpson, 1989; Wilson, 1956). The group has been in decline for decades, and some have tied it to members' disappointment with its message (Singelenberg, 1999; Stark, 1998; Richardson and Dewitt, 1992). Asser and Swan (1998) reported on 172 child fatalities caused by medical neglect in twenty-three US religious groups. Most of these cases, which occurred between 1975 and 1995, involved Christian Science, the Church of the First Born (an LDS offshoot), and the Faith Assembly.

Hobart Freeman (1920–84), the founder of the Faith Assembly, advocated the complete avoidance of modern medicine, relying instead on prayers "Sickness and disease have been repeatedly defeated by maintaining a positive confession of faith in the face of all apparent evidence to the contrary … When genuine faith is present it alone will be sufficient, for it will take the place of medicines and other aids" (quoted in Beit-Hallahmi, 1998: 130).

This statement represents the view of countless traditions and groups. In the Faith Assembly, 100 members and their children were reported to have died between 1970 and 1990 because of their refusal to seek medical care (Beit-Hallahmi, 1998; Hughes, 1990). Some group members were sent to prison for depriving their children of medical care. When adults decide to expose themselves to danger through avoiding biomedicine, we regard it as their choice. When they deprive their children of medical care, it should be regarded as filicide (Abraham, 1993).

Opposition to vaccinations because of religion can be found all over the world, with tragic consequences (Rodgers et al., 1993). Polio, once known as infantile paralysis, remains endemic in only three countries, Pakistan, Afghanistan, and Nigeria, because of opposition on the part of Islamic religious leaders, who have described it as a plot by Western governments (Antai, 2009; Jegede, 2007; Obadare, 2005). Religion plays a role in the opposition to organ donations, which have become a crucial part of biomedicine, and thus millions of lives are affected (Boulware et al., 2002).

The Oedipal Paradox

Classical psychoanalytic interpretations seem very close to the reality of religion, its rituals, and its myths. Intrafamily violence, child sacrifice, and genital mutilations can fit Oedipal notions very easily.

We may formulate a basic law that summarizes ideas expressed by Freud and others: relations in the family are reproduced in myth, religious beliefs, social groups, formal organizations, culture, and art.

Anthropologist Meyer Fortes expressed this basic law when he stated that "all the concepts and beliefs we have examined are religious extrapolations of the experiences generated in the relationships between parents and children" (Fortes, 1959: 78). Referring to Freud's ideas, he stated,

> I follow him only as far as to see in Tallensi totem animals a symbolic representation of paternity perpetuated in the lineage ... At the same time there is no denying that these taboos stand for unquestioning submission to ancestral, that is magnified paternal, authority. (1987: 142)

This discussion leads us back to the question of the Oedipal matrix, its implications for intrafamily violence, and fantasies about such violence.

Freud defines the Oedipal matrix of the hero's story as follows:

> A hero is a man who stands up manfully against his father and in the end victoriously overcomes him. The myth in question traces this struggle back to the very dawn of the hero's life, by having him born against his father's will and saved in spite of his father's evil intentions. (1939: 9)

The original Oedipus story starts with a crime, as his parents Laius and Jocasta wish their son dead and make sure he is exposed to the elements and disabled. We encounter the same crime on the part of countless evil kings. Newborn sons, whether born to virgins or not, are threatened by Pharaoh in the case of Moses, King Herod in the case of Jesus, and Uncle Kamsa in the case of Krishna, to name just a few.

The baby hero is miraculously saved, just like Isaac and Phrixus. Both Moses and Oedipus, among many others, are raised in a royal court. Our hearts go out to the menaced babies, and we experience the stories as they are told from the victims' point of view.

Freud, in his counterintuitive reading, turns the story on its head, suggesting that this narrative is a denial and a cover-up. The source of threatened and actual violence in the story is the child, not the parents. The son's hostility toward the father is projected on the latter in the myths. The child is not a victim of cruel, blind fate, but a would-be perpetrator, full of criminal schemes. Our identification with the victim is in reality an identification with the schemer's hidden designs. The narratives in which the hero is a parricide or patricide seem to support Freud's view. The spontaneous admiration for patricide has been brilliantly portrayed in the 1907 play, *The Playboy of the Western World*, by John Millington Synge. The hero, Christy Mahon, is on the run after killing his father. He wins universal admiration for being a patricide but loses his appeal when his father shows up alive.

Freud claims that all homicidal intentions come from sons, not fathers, and this calls for added clarifications. In all hero narratives, the son manages to survive the father's hostility and to humiliate him. In many cases, the hero is born to a virgin or through another miraculous birth, and the father is superfluous. This can only be called an Oedipal triumph (Beit-Hallahmi, 2010b).

On top of this victory, the son, who degrades his father, is embraced by all as a victim. Not only does the son humiliate the father but is also regarded as the victim who wins identification and sympathy.

Hero myths are about rebelling against the father and all authority, power, and legitimacy, calling for a rearrangement of power relations. The father is both the one who wields actual power and the symbol of all authority for the child. If the hero is a child threatened with death by his parents (or other family members), who then takes revenge on them, it is a clear accusation against family and authority, and a subversive incitement against parental, and especially paternal, authority. It tells us that parental love is far from being unconditional. This clearly recalls the Satanism fantasies we discussed above.

The *Oedipus Tyrannus* template is one of rebellion against family and paternity, as evidenced first by the two sets of parents, a not unheard-of fantasy that Freud named the *Family Romance* (Freud, 1908), and then by the horrifying presence of patricide and incest. It undermines the conventions and norms of culture and family by telling a story of the ultimate crime. Transgression is exposed and punished only after the unthinkable became a reality. Still, most Oedipal winners, in most cultures, like Zeus and Krishna, remain unpunished, triumphant, and celebrated.

All narratives of alternative paternity are not only subversive of the father and the family, but also of total rejections. All versions of Oedipal triumph fantasies, in which human fathers are demoted in favor of divine fathers, spiritual conceptions, or no conceptions at all, are dethronements of the father. Any enactment of Oedipal triumph undercuts authority (even when followed by punishment) as it begins with the idea that true parental love is far from universal.

Claiming divine paternity implies strong and close contact with great spirits. How and why would a virgin birth add to other claims of superiority for kings, gods, and heroes? Victory over earthly paternity is decisive evidence of superiority, much stronger than other kinds of proof. A resurrection from death is a greater miracle than a virgin birth, but bypassing normal paternity is still a victory over nature and fate. The message in many of the narratives is that having been conceived without sexual intercourse and being born without passing through the vagina is the ideal way to start life, but only a few heroes and gods have experienced this privileged route, bypassing physical paternity (and sometimes even maternity).

What we have here is a doubly subversive story, eroding the authority of all fathers. This subversive story appears in many local versions, as the hero may be Perseus, Romulus, Krishna, or Moses, but it turns out to be the product that humanity loves and is popular in all cultures. But this is only the beginning of what should be called the Oedipal paradox.

We must ask about the cultural processes that have created these narratives everywhere. In every culture, men, who are also fathers, are in control of culture, religion, ritual, and the social order. Popular explanations of culture assume that traditions are preserved when they aid the survival of the established order. How is it that the universal patriarchy has allowed this subversive story, which humiliates all fathers with its messages of showing that sons (1) do not need fathers and (2) are barely saved from being murdered by them?

If we assume that some kind of cultural leadership is in control, and decides on investing resources in particular fantasies, we may wonder why the enacting of Oedipal triumph is supported by so many cultural establishments. Those in positions of power are naturally older males, the fathers of the community, and fathers to their families, and still, we observe them allowing these subversive narratives to become part of collective consciousness. These fathers celebrate the myths that convey not only subversion but also enmity, as rebels are glorified and celebrated.

Where are the old males, who supposedly were in charge, when such stories were created and circulated? It is apparent that the paternal establishment has let this cultural heritage develop.

Why is the story about the hero-victim who overcomes adversity and defeats the imaginary fathers promoted by the real fathers who rule the culture? This subversive version of the father–son relationship undermines paternal authority and power. The fathers, that is, all of us, may be in immense denial about childhood experiences or identifying with helpless babies, who could easily be snuffed out by any father. Despite childhood helplessness, children are capable of fantasies, including hostile ones, and even lethal ones.

What may make the Oedipal paradox possible is that the fathers are also sons, forever involved in the same struggles and fantasies. It is possible that our experiences as children take primacy, and even as adults we view life from a child's perspective. That is why the establishment makes room for such subversive, rebellious, expressions, shared by fathers and sons. We identify with the hero, who kills his father, while we also consciously want to believe that we are victims. The universal celebration of Oedipal winners indicates that Oedipality is stronger than other forces in creating cultural products.

Religious narratives are related to universal childhood experiences, as indicated by the salience of family, parenting, and kinship in cultural heritage. The centrality of kinship idioms may be related to evolution, which leads to kin loyalties, but there are unique patterns of family relations that play a central role in religious traditions, and one basic template is seemingly expressed through many specific narratives.

Psychoanalysis offers an answer and suggests that there is a kernel of truth in mythical stories, but it is solely psychological. The reason myths describe Jesus and Krishna as having a similar childhood lies in universal childhood experiences, shared by all. The constellation of both positive and negative wishes directed at parents is thought to be expressed in a well-known narrative formula, in which miraculous salvation from death is followed by bloody struggles, and triumph often precedes tragedy (Freud, 1915–16).

The Oedipal plot may sound absurd, but its many versions are quite easily produced and entertained by the human imagination. Freud claimed that the Oedipal template, or an Oedipal master narrative, plays a central role in all cultures and all cultural products. This can be tested by assessing the frequency and prevalence of patterns found in cultural traditions.

Even if not everybody is ready to adopt the psychoanalytic framework, the evidence for the recurrence and repetition of certain themes all over the world is incontrovertible (Beit-Hallahmi, 1996, 2010, 2015; Caldwell, 1989; Carroll, 1989; Obeyesekere, 1991). Kluckhohn (1959) presented a survey of global mythology, with the following themes found in all cultures: creation, flood, slaying of monsters, incest, sibling rivalry, castration, hero myths, and "Oedipus type myths." Ubiquitous themes in myths were said to "result from recurrent reactions of the human psyche to situations and stimuli of the same general order" (1959: 268). Brown (1991), in his list of human universals, included religion, mythology, and the "Oedipus complex." Johnson and Price-Williams (1996) described Oedipal themes as globally ubiquitous.

In a denial and projection of the real wish to get rid of the father, children universally blame their parents for being neglected and abused. These narratives are denials of psychological reality, but they are consistent with our conscious preferences to be regarded as innocent victims.

That is why we live close to the legacy of stories about fathers who are determined to kill newborn babies. Contra Freud who claimed that the sons' murderous rebellion was the beginning of tradition, we see hostility flowing both ways. Myths and rituals celebrate the rebellious sons, but also demand sacrifice to maintain the cosmic order. The ambivalence of the patriarchs keeps culture balanced. In the ancient mythological stories reviewed in this book, it is a father, or a father-figure (grandfather, uncle) who kills his son or plans to do that. Pharaoh orders all male babies to be killed, and so does Herod. Abraham is ready to sacrifice his son, and YHWH does kill his only begotten in the New Testament myth.

In the accusations against minority outsiders, Jews, witches, Cathars, or other heretics, they are depicted as killing the children of the majority group. Accusations against the nonexistent Satanists in the late twentieth century go back to mythology in alleging that both parents sacrifice their own children to Satan.

Satanism stories are incredibly subversive. The unique and most striking element in the contemporary Satanism testimonies, dictated by psychiatrists and psychologists, is the role ascribed to the witness' own parents, who are portrayed as Satanists. Unlike many other versions of witchcraft accusations, where outsiders (Christians, Jews, "heretics") play the role of human monsters, here parents and other relatives take the lead in torturing and even killing their own flesh and blood as part of Satanic rituals.

Mother and father are the enemy, in league with Satan. This is an expression of total disillusionment, a uniquely modern, antiauthoritarian point of view, as both mothers and fathers are finally dethroned. Ferenczi (1926) described how disillusionment about the omnipotence and perfection of one's parents and significant others leads to skepticism, which may also take the pathological form of paranoia.

The Satanism conspiracy is of parental hostility squared, but it did not become the dominant pattern in any culture. The classical Oedipal pattern, in which father figures present a threat to a young male, still hovers over all of us.

We described Oedipus as the victim, but, according to Freud, he is an evil schemer. It is the son who wants to kill his father, but the stories we like present sons as victims and fathers as killers. We want to see ourselves as victims, not perpetrators, and these stories are projections and distortions.

It is easy to regard Freud, a dead white male, as being on the side of the fathers, the patriarchy, and the family. The paradox is that the subversive Oedipal template is conservative, and the conservative version (Freud's) is subversive.

14

Conclusion: Back to the Present

The Genealogy of the Modern Satanism Craze

Recent Satanism stories have been told from a stance of protest, denouncing the sacrifice of innocent children, presumably denied or ignored by many. The supposed exposure of Satanism has not led to any change. Those who believe in underground Satanism claim that its horrifying practices are still being carried out and innocents lose their lives or suffer indescribable traumas.

In some mythological narratives, we reach a point of desperation and then a miracle occurs. The Satanism metanarrative expresses total despair, as evil triumphs and children are being sacrificed, despite the exposure by valiant psychotherapists and their clients. Humanity, or the part of humanity that had been exposed to Satanism claims, stands accused of tolerating evil by not stopping these heinous crimes. What happened in the late twentieth century was an eruption of violent fantasies, similar in some ways to apocalyptic visions. In the case of apocalyptic fantasies, the whole world would be destroyed and most of humanity perish. In Satanism stories, most humans survive, except for thousands of children who die during Satanic worship. Where do these stories come from?

Earlier historical cases of the witch crazes and the common phenomenon of witchcraft accusations are similar to the recent Satanism Craze. Claims of horrifying acts, especially cannibalism and child sacrifice, have become attached to contemporary Satanists, the way they did to witches, Jews, and other religious minorities.

The whole craze is about accusations. Just as women accused of being witches in the twenty-first century or in the sixteenth century were not involved in any of the acts attributed to them, stories told about Satanists in recent decades are pure fantasies, expressing the same projection of evil.

Right God, Wrong God

Identity dictates moral judgment. What is obvious is that certain cases of child sacrifice (to the wrong gods) will be denounced, while others (to the right gods) will not. This is no different from what we observe every day in politics.

When Spain established its colonies in the New World, the encounter with other religions raised questions and doubts. The celebrated Bartolomé de las Casas took the position that sincerity counts. If you take the wrong god to be the right god, your sacrifice, be it of a human life, is justified.

The Inca people believed they were negotiating with the right gods and doing the right sacrifice. They were sending children to serve as their emissaries to heaven through sacrifice, and the whole nation stood to gain if the right victim was offered to the right god. Las Casas, quoting what Julius Caesar said about the ancient Gauls: "They think that the only way of placating the sanctity of the immortal gods is to give human life for human life." (MacCormack, 2000: 121). He also stated that "within the limits of the natural light of reason … [people] should sacrifice human victims to the true God or the reputed god, if the latter is taken for the true God" (Lantigua, 2018: 281).

This position justifies all groups and all practices, provided their belief is sincere.

Child Sacrifice and the Family

The fantasies (and sometimes the reality) of child sacrifice start with humanity's earliest ideas about handling misfortune. Flood myths, common around the world, explain imaginary extinctions, and, by inference, other misfortunes, as the gods' response to human iniquity. Disease explanations, like ideas about mortality and immortality, find meaning and moral order where none exist. Both death and disease are turned from individual or collective tragedies into evidence of human fallibility and cosmic justice.

Humanity, by its own admission, does not leave the gods much of a choice: Gen. 6:5

> And God saw that the wickedness of man was great in the earth, and that every imagination of the thoughts of his heart was only evil continually.

This is a universal judgment, appearing in countless flood narratives and other catastrophe narratives.

If misfortunes, such as famine, plague, or military defeat, which consume countless lives, grow out of human sin and the judgments of frustrated deities, then sacrificing a few humans, or just one, to propitiate the angry spirits and save the community seems justified. The best that humans could hope for is a substitution miracle (Staubli, 2015). This very ancient logic is found all over the world, shared by Greeks, Hebrews, Aztecs, Africans, and Asians.

The background to all child sacrifice fantasies is laid by fears about bloodthirsty spirits about to levy a cost in human lives for human transgressions. We may forgive the young child for imagining the authorities on earth to be close to the bloodthirsty deities. We should also forgive them for shouldering the responsibility for losses and conflicts around them.

What is the red thread connecting Satanism allegations to the myths of Isaac and Jesus, in which the father is the actual, or would-be executioner? Any fantasy about a child being killed by its father, which may start as a private experience and then gains public status as an accusation or as myth, threatens the social order.

Let us assume that fantasies of children being killed by their parents, sometimes in response to gods' wishes, reflect children's insecurity and bewilderment, which remains with us for life. This insecurity is not about the human condition, but about our attachments to parents.

Family tensions are real and strong but will rarely lead to actual violence. Murderous fantasies about kin and nonkin are common. Acting them out is rare. Fathers are angry but don't kill their children, and sons may be angry but don't kill their fathers, as research on domestic violence shows.

There are significant differences in stories being told, rituals, and sacrifice fantasies, but the idea of parents killing children is repeated everywhere. The father, like Abraham, is willing to slaughter, but the son is sometimes saved. Satanist fathers are willing, and their children die, because no one saves them. Schultz (1991) correctly shows that mythical stories about infanticide are tied to both real cruelty and to parental ambivalence toward children, easily projected on others.

The image in Satanism accusations and in the Binding of Isaac is identical. It is the father who does the actual killing, and in Satanism narratives he may be aided by his wife. It is not about handing over your child to the priests like fathers in the Inca Empire. The image of a father lifting his knife, getting ready to kill his son, hovers over all our conversations. This image has been assimilated and reconciled with the social order through institutionalization, made possible because of prevalent psychological processes.

Insecurity might lead to a yearning for submission, which is often found in religious discourse, but also to fantasies of perfect love. Is it possible that behind the child sacrifice narratives hides a yearning for a perfect father's love? In Isaac's story, the initial emphasis is on the son being the only one (which he wasn't), who is truly loved. This is what the divine test is about. Such a test is needed when doubts about love keep rising to the surface.

Abraham's test, which is shared by all fathers in these mythological stories, is real because a father's love is real and robust. Otherwise, there is no dilemma and no test; no reward will be conferred.

Much work has been done in academic psychology to develop a general theory of aggression. The consensus seems to be that frustration leads to aggression (Berkowitz, 1993). This may include a variety of frictions and tensions, including subjective insecurity, which may lead to individual or group violence. How relevant are the theories to sacrifice fantasies?

Religious belief systems contain much projected violence. Greater and lesser spirits are imagined as angry and demanding, and attack humans in various ways, causing suffering, misfortune, and death. In addition to anger coming from the gods, there are constant threats coming from lesser spirits. Humans believe that misfortune, coming from angry spirits, is actually caused by human transgression, and is meant as a punishment. Atoning for the sin may involve sacrifice, including human sacrifice.

Most religious traditions include a demonology, that is, a complex of beliefs regarding evil spirits. Religious institutions are expected to provide apotropaic measures to protect us from the demons. These entities are clearly a projection of our own evil wishes and play a role in explaining various events. Humans encounter demons and are possessed by them. Possession fantasies are about violence and describe humans being violated in every way by the spirits.

It is easy to reflect and explain all these manifestations of aggression as resulting from a reservoir of anger inside all of us. That seems elementary but does not predict the realities we are faced with. Internal anger, aggression, or external frictions do not explain the narratives created by religious scribes that have become so central in major traditions. Frustration in any form does not dictate a plot about fathers ready to sacrifice their sons. Why does aggression take this particular form? The origin is family frustrations, and possibly an inherent conflict, which drives child sacrifice narratives.

Behind all this might be a dream of symbiosis, love to the perfect father, or to cosmic paternity, which may lead a child to fantasies of self-sacrifice. Ancient child sacrifice plots give voice to fears of both children and parents but offer resolutions. Their overall message is one of reconciliation, as the cosmic order is salvaged thanks to child sacrifice. The father–child connection is recovered through death or through coming close to its borders.

Mesha's unnamed son in one Biblical story and Jephthah's unnamed daughter in another gave their fathers the victory they needed. They were presumably ready to die for a father's love. Is death and torture the only way to a perfect father's love? That seems to be the message of the mythical Binding of Jesus that united father and son.

We find the themes of child abuse, child rejection, and child sacrifice all over the world in legends and myths. The world of childhood with its many terrors and many hopes is the key to their real meaning.

It reflects the truth of anxieties, desires, and imagined solutions. The eternal and universal fears of children are projected on parents and attributed to them as actions. Fantasies of personal relationship with a parent-like deity or supernatural agent can be found all over the world in all traditions. Love, devotion, and submission fantasies are commonly found in ancestor-worship systems, Buddhist systems, Hindu systems, or among followers of Moses Berg in The Family or Jim Jones in Peoples Temple. Such patterns of submissive identification seem to be panhuman and must have grown out of evolutionary history.

The Parents' Ultimate Responsibility

In the all the cases described above, the need for human sacrifice, or child sacrifice, arose because of human sins. Sometimes the sinner is unknown, but implied. When Stenka Razin throws an unnamed Persian princess into the Volga, she atones for countless sins that may cause the river's ire and threaten sailors.

In all other cases, the gods inflict plagues, famines, or siege on a kingdom because of a king's acts. Athamas was guilty of serious sins, which led to tragedy for his family and descendants, but the punishment was directed first at the common people.

The first act of substitution, done by the gods, is to punish the whole kingdom for one man's act. That this is grossly unfair is not just our modern, democratic reaction. In 2 Sam. 24:17, the Hebrew Bible authors have King David protesting against this injustice:

And David spake unto the Lord when he saw the angel that smote the people, and said, Lo, I have sinned, and I have done wickedly: but these sheep, what have they done? let thine hand, I pray thee, be against me, and against my father's house."

Still, David himself was spared, while 70,000 of his subjects died. The plague ended only when David "built there an altar unto the Lord, and offered burnt offerings and peace offerings" (24:23). The gods may be kings and fathers, and so they are kind toward their earthly peers. Every king is a father to his children and to his subjects, but we see that his compassion is limited vis-à-vis both. Self-sacrifice was an important ideal in Greek culture (Bremmer, 2002, 2015), but was rarely acted upon.

Any king taking the necessary practical steps to be sacrificed for his kingdom would have been eternally praised, but in the mythical narratives we hear only about the mythical King Kodros of Athens, who saved the city by sacrificing himself.

Some of the sacrificed children are praised for their reported willingness to die, and so we hear about Phrixos, Isaac, Ishmael, Iphigenia, Polyxena, and Jephthah's daughter, who were ready to be martyred (to use a possibly anachronistic term).

The case of Andromeda discussed earlier is striking, as she is delivered to the sea monster just because of her mother's arrogance. The queen's subjects die in large numbers before her daughter is offered to the monster, but she is never touched. The mythical message calls upon all of us to accept the ruling hierarchy and prevailing paternal authority, but subversive implications are possible.

If you refuse the message of blind support for the hierarchy in its callous disregard for the rights of the vulnerable, the mythological narratives describe parental cruelty and selfishness. If the father's (or rarely, the mother's) created the problem to be solved by his child's sacrifice, then every narrative is a fateful and shocking accusation. This is despite the praise for the victim's heroism.

There are two cases where the father's sins are never hinted at, of Isaac and of Jesus. It is likely that early versions of the Bindings included references to a problem created by the father, but for modern readers, the intended sacrifice is enough of a sin.

Choosing the Victims

The choice of the human to be sacrificed ranges from the king (or his heir) in mythical stories, members of the royalty and nobility, children chosen for their youthful beauty, to the outcastes and rejects of society, those bereft of any social support. The king or his heir in heroic narratives represents the community in his flesh and blood, but this can be inverted with slaves and abandoned children. The Valdivia quake, the most powerful earthquake in history (9.5 on the Richter Scale), devastated southern Chile on May 22, 1960, causing 1,655 deaths, and making two million homeless. In response, members of the indigenous Mapuche people sacrificed "an abandoned small child" to "calm down deities" (Gonza´lez-Galvez, 2012: 134). Even though it was abandoned, we may assume it came from the Mapuche.

In the most extreme case of distancing the victim from the killers, slaves who came from distant tribes, and were never related to the group, were being sacrificed in northern Burma until 1930, to avert plagues and ensure bountiful crops (Means, 2000). The same idea was followed in West Africa until 1890, where most human victims sacrificed in funerals (in addition to wives) or to the gods were slaves. They were also sacrificed as "substitutes for sick persons" (Ojo, 2005: 387). Sacrificed slaves were always from ethnic outgroups or kidnapped travelers. "An outbreak of smallpox and war with Ikale led to the resumption of human sacrifice in 1891" (Ojo, 2005: 402). This recalls several Greek stories, mentioned in Chapter 7, about heroes and kings, who sacrificed themselves or their daughters to save their people when war, plague, or famine threatened. This quotation refers to West Africa, and those sacrificed were not kings or princesses, but poor slaves, often old and frail. In West Africa of the nineteenth century, "the practice was to sell old slaves who were considered worthless to their owners, for sacrifice" (Ojo, 2005: 392).

Historical evidence shows that poor slaves and war prisoners have been much more likely to be sacrificed than princes. Statistically speaking, the likelihood of the victim to be related by blood to the killer has always been small. In the Aztec empire, mass sacrifices of war captives were carried out in response to natural disasters.

We find the idea that slaves were bought for the sole purpose of being sacrificed shocking, and it seems like the mythical stories of sons being sacrificed are more acceptable. We may feel that the killing of slaves is done in cold blood, while the father–child lethal interaction seems like an emotional affair. We have been seduced by the mythical narratives of fathers ready to sacrifice their sons and daughters, which are, after all, fictional. The reality was much crueller than that.

Should Accusations Be Dismissed?

While the role of actual human sacrifice in human history is variable and debatable, its centrality as an accusatory fantasy is beyond dispute. The basic theme takes the form of a central myth, as in Christianity, but throughout history it appears often as frightening allegations. This happens when the myth, awesome and distant, is described as a concrete act without the correct divine sanction. What we have is a tradition, not of acts but of fantasies and accusations over thousands of years.

Looking at the accusations directed at Christians, Pagans, Jews, witches, Cathars, and modern Satanists, all of which turned out to be pure fictions, forces us to examine again Biblical accusations. Is it possible that the latter are as fictional as the former? (Douglas, 1996). We should be skeptical of any allegations, and ask for evidence, naturally.

Still, the lessons of history should be separate from the protection of children. Any concrete accusation involving a real child deserves to be examined. This is the lesson we should all learn from Lanning (1996).

Generalizations: Religious Fears and Dreams

This book analyzed continuities in images and imaginaries across time and space. The legacy of human sacrifice is universal, but its local manifestations are closer to us and impact us today. The Aztecs are part of human heritage, but Judaic and Christian ideas are more directly implicated, because we are still immersed in them. The issue is both the historical presence of violent imagery and its immense psychological attraction.

One theoretical question raised by the recent case of murderous fantasies (the Satanism Craze) and similar episodes in ancient and contemporary religious traditions is whether the process of denial and projection is useful for humans. As individuals try to adapt to stress, fear, and threat, denial and projection do reduce anxiety. A fundamental law of the human imagination seems to be that our anxieties give rise to fantasies through which we create a distance between the self and experienced threats. Thus, the projection of imaginary cruelty on invisible (or socially invisible) others, which offers emotional release, may be good for individuals and groups. Accuracy in perceiving ourselves and the world around us may not be the best option. Increasing reality distortion and developing paranoid systems, however, may turn out to be too costly and threaten survival.

Contemporary stories that sound crazy lead us to ancient stories of hallowed child sacrifice. Drinking human blood is an arresting image that appears as an accusation in the late twentieth century, and as part of theophagy fantasies in Christianity over two millennia.

The Satanism Craze was a relatively peripheral episode and caused much less suffering than the Blood Libel, which killed countless Jews, or the witch craze, which still kills thousands today. Looking at the historical legacies of major religions shows that modern marginal madness is tied to prehistorical practices and to perennial anxieties, loves, and fears.

Despite secularization, billions still demonstrate an authoritarian respect for tradition. Our job as students of religion is to analyze, dissect, and deconstruct the experiences of believers. We are in Freud's debt for directing our attention to several flesh and blood issues in the practice of religion. These include genital mutilation, the popularity of Oedipal ideas expressed in stories about a virgin birth or other miraculous conceptions, and ritualized fantasy cannibalism. The Freudian way of looking at these traditions and asking direct questions has served us well.

Frankfurter (2006) correctly ridiculed satanism stories and pointed out that cruel Satanic rituals were real but performed in public. Explicit notions of child sacrifice are staring us in the face if we countenance central rites and myths in Christianity and Judaism, but believers will deny any relevance to the fictional stories of Satanic killings. Christian mythology celebrates one narrative of human sacrifice, while Judaism and Islam offer images that are only slightly less shocking. For the believers, the framework of divine history in which they are invested, and the way they look at received traditions does not allow for analysis. Understandably, their identity dominates their reactions.

The satanism craze may be most charitably judged to be a protest against the real suffering of women and children inside the patriarchal family. The reality of human families will range from hell to heaven, and the fantasies it will spawn will repeat the eternal themes of intergenerational conflict, struggle, and reconciliation.

Christian ideas of human sacrifice are privileged, and the fantasy is remote, so no one could accuse Christians of engaging in ritual murder. If we mention the Eucharist or Jewish circumcision in the context of the satanism phenomenon, the reaction is one of shock.

The stories that get repeated thousands of times contain an important and eternal truth. What is it? It is not the truth of the allegations, but the truth of our fantasies, anxieties, desires, problems, and imagined solutions. Family tensions and conflicts, real and imagined, are at the center of most human narratives. Like much of mythology, the battlefield here is that of the family. Satanism stories are tied to difficulties and emotions experienced in early childhood, like much else in human fantasy. The binding of Isaac, the killing of the firstborn in the land of Egypt, as well as the crucifixion, represent our anxious imagination. There is no reality referent, "out there," either for old religious claims or for modern fictions about satanists. The reality is only within us. Good and evil are within us, as well as all other imagined powers: devils, ghosts, angels, and gods.

References

Abraham, H. J. (1993). "Abraham, Isaac and the State: Faith-Healing and Legal Intervention." *University of Richmond Law Review*, 27, 951–88.

Ackermann, S. (1992). *Under Every Green Tree: Popular Religion in Sixth Century Judah*. Atlanta, GA: Scholars Press.

Acocella, J. (1999). *Creating Hysteria. Women and Multiple Personality Disorder*. San Francisco, CA: Jossey-Bass.

Adamczewski, B. (2021). "Abraham and Sanballat." *Old Testament Essays*, 34 (1), 14–26.

Adorno, T. W., Frenkel-Brunswik, E., Levinson, D. J., and Sanford, R. N. (1950). *The Authoritarian Personality*. New York: Harper and Row.

Alexander, K. W., Quas, J. A., Goodman, G. S., Ghetti, S., Edelstein, R. S., Redlich, A. D., Cordon, I. M., and Jones, D. P. (2005). "Traumatic Impact Predicts Long-Term Memory for Documented Child Sexual Abuse." *Psychological Science*, 16 (1), 33–40.

Allen, T., Salari, S., and Buckner, G. (2020). "Homicide Illustrated across the Ages: Graphic Depictions of Victim and Offender Age, Sex, and Relationship." *Journal of Aging and Health*, 32 (3/4), 162–74.

Alonso Serrano, C. A. (2021). "The Name 'Palestine' in Classical Greek Texts." *Journal of Holy Land and Palestine Studies*, 20, 146–79.

Anderson, W. (2014). "Hermannsburg, 1929: Turning Aboriginal 'Primitives' into Modern Psychological Subjects." *Journal of the History of the Behavioral Sciences*, 50 (2), 127–47.

Andrade, G., and Redondo, M. S. C. (2019). "Satanism and Psychopathology: Some Historical Cases." *Journal of Psychohistory*, 47 (2), 126–43.

Andriolo, K. R. (1981). "Myth and History: A General Model and Its Application to the Bible." *American Anthropologist*, 83 (2), 261–84.

Antai, D. (2009). "Faith and Child Survival: The Role of Religion in Childhood Immunization in Nigeria." *Journal of Biosocial Science*, 41 (1), 57–76.

APA (2001). "Lawsuit Raises Questions about APA Liability Insurance Program." *Psychiatric Times*, 18(1). https://www.psychiatrictimes.com/attention-deficit-disorders/lawsuit-raises-questions-about-apa-liability-insurance-program.

Ardren, T. (2011). "Empowered Children in Classic Maya Sacrificial Rites." *Childhood in the Past*, 4 (2), 133–45.

Ariel, Y. (2007). "Still Ransoming the First-Born Sons? Pidyon Haben and Its Survival in the Jewish Tradition." In K. Finsterbusch, A. Lange, and K. F. Diethard Römheld (eds.), *Human Sacrifice in Jewish and Christian Tradition* (pp. 305–19). Leiden: Brill.

Arnold, B. T. (2017). "A Singular Israel in a Pluralistic World." *The Asbury Journal*, 72 (2), 8–20.

Ashforth, A. (2018). *The Trials of Mrs. K.: Seeking Justice in a World with Witches*. Chicago, IL: University of Chicago Press.

Asser, S. M., and Swan, R. (1998). "Child Fatalities from Religion-Motivated Medical Neglect." *Pediatrics*, 101 (4.1), 625–9.

Azize, J. (2014). "'Child Sacrifice' without Children or Sacrifice." *Ancient Near Eastern Studies*, 51 (2014), 263–77.

Baadsgaard, A., Monge, J., and Zettler, R. (2012). "Bludgeoned, Burned, and Beautified: Reevaluating Mortuary Practices in the Royal Cemetery of Ur." In A. M. Porter and G. M. Schwartz (eds.), *Sacred Killing: The Archaeology of Sacrifice in the Ancient Near East* (pp. 125–58). Winona Lake, IN: Eisenbrauns.

Bader, C. D. (1995). "The UFO Contact Movement from the 1950s to the Present." *Studies in Popular Culture*, 17 (2), 73–90.

Bader, C. D., Mencken, F. C., and Froese, P. (2007). "American Piety 2005: Content and Methods of the Baylor Religion Survey." *Journal for the Scientific Study of Religion*, 46, 447–63.

Badouk-Epstein, O., Schwartz, J., and Schwartz, R. W. (eds.). (2018). *Ritual Abuse and Mind Control: The Manipulation of Attachment Needs*. London: Routledge.

Badouk-Epstein, O., Schwartz, J., and Schwartz, R. W. (eds.). (2011). *Ritual Abuse and Mind Control: The Manipulation of Attachment Needs*. London: Routledge.

Badstuebner, J. (2003). "Drinking the Hot Blood of Humans: Witchcraft Confessions in a South African Pentecostal Church." *Anthropology and Humanism*, 28 (1), 8–22.

Baez, J. (1991). "Play Me Backwards." Leopolds randtfilms.https://www.youtube.com/watch?v=AYmvFSmaATM&fbclid=IwAR3kgN-BmEZVozYMYaOpa9kvtGxAud2cwsVQWenJAKOz2G_gxIpIjA7Z6ek.

Bakan, D. (1971). *Slaughter of the Innocents*. San Francisco, CA: Jossey-Bass.

Bakan, D. (2001). "Sacrifice and the Book of Job." In D. Capps (ed.), *Freud and Freudians on Religion: A Reader* (pp. 102–20). New Haven, CT: Yale University Press.

Balcells Gallarreta, José E. (2017). *Household and Family Religion in Persian-Period Judah: An Archaeological Approach*. ANEM 18. Atlanta, GA: Society of Biblical Literature.

Barcelo, P. (1994). "The Perception of Carthage in Classical Greek Historiography." *Acta Classica: Proceedings of the Classical Association of South Africa*, 37, 1–14.

Barnes, R. H. (1993). "Construction Sacrifice, Kidnapping and Head-Hunting Rumors on Flores and Elsewhere in Indonesia." *Oceania*, 64, 146–58.

Barstad, H. (2001). "Deuteronomists, Persians, Greeks, and the Dating of the Israelite Tradition." In L. L. Grabbe (ed.), *Did Moses Speak Attic? Jewish Historiography and Scripture in the Hellenistic Period* (pp. 47–77). London: A&C Black.

Barstow, A. L. (1994). *Witchcraze: A New History of the European Witch Hunts*. New York: HarperOne.

Bar-Yosef, E. (2005). *The Holy Land in English Culture, 1799–1917: Palestine and the Question of Orientalism*. Oxford: Oxford University Press.

Bateson, G., Jackson, D. D., Haley, J., and Weakland, J. (1956). "Toward a Theory of Schizophrenia." *Behavioral Science*, 1, 251–64.

Bauer, S., Boulestin, B., Coupey, A. S., Denaire, A., Haack, F., Jeunesse, C., and Turck, R. (2016). "Human Sacrifices as 'Crisis Management.'" In C. A. Murray (eds.), *Diversity of Sacrifice: Form and Function of Sacrificial Practices in the Ancient World and Beyond Diversity of Sacrifice: Form and Function of Sacrificial Practices in the Ancient World and Beyond* (pp. 171–90). Albany, NY: SUNY Press.

Baum, D. (2013). "Circumcision Anxiety." *Textual Practice*, 27, 695–713.

Becker, E. (1961). "A Note on Freud's Primal Horde Theory." *Psychoanalytic Quarterly*, 30, 413–19.

Becker, E. (1973). *The Denial of Death*. New York: Simon & Schuster.

Beiser, H. R. (1989). "Fatherhood and the Preference for a Younger Child." *Annual of Psychoanalysis*, 17, 203–12.

Beit-Hallahmi, B. (1989). *Prolegomena to the Psychological Study of Religion*. Lewisburg, PA: Bucknell University Press.

Beit-Hallahmi, B. (1996). *Psychoanalytic Studies of Religion: Critical Assessment and Annotated Bibliography*. Westport, CT: Greenwood Press.

Beit-Hallahmi, B. (1998). *The Illustrated Encyclopedia of Active New Religions*. New York: Rosen.

Beit-Hallahmi, B. (2003). "The Return of Martyrdom: Honor, Death and Immortality." *Totalitarian Movements and Political Religions*, 4, 11–34.

Beit-Hallahmi, B. (ed.) (2010a). *Psychoanalysis and Theism: Critical Reflections on the Grünbaum Thesis*. Lanham, MD: Jason Aronson.

Beit-Hallahmi, B. (2010b). "Mapping the Imagination: Heroes, Gods, and Oedipal Triumphs." In B. Beit-Hallahmi (ed.), *Psychoanalysis and Theism: Critical Reflections on the Grünbaum Thesis*. Lanham, MD: Jason Aronson.

Beit-Hallahmi, B. (2011). "The Ambivalent Teaching, and Painful Learning, of the Facts of Life." In V. Talwar, P. Harris, and M. Schleifer (eds.), *Children's Understanding of Death: From Biological to Supernatural Conceptions*. New York: Cambridge University Press.

Beit-Hallahmi, B. (2015). *Psychological Perspectives on Religion and Religiosity*. London: Routledge.

Beit-Hallahmi, B., and Argyle, M. (1997). *The Psychology of Religious Behaviour, Belief, and Experience*. London: Routledge.

Bemporad, E. (2019). *Legacy of Blood: Jews, Pogroms, and Ritual Murder in the Lands of the Soviets*. New York: Oxford University Press.

Bentovim, A. and Tranter, M. (1994). "A Systemic Approach." In V. Sinason (ed.), *Treating Survivors of Satanic Abuse* (pp. 100–12). London: Routledge.

Ben-Yehuda, N. (1980). "The European Witch Craze of the 14th to 17th Centuries: A Sociologist's Perspective." *American Journal of Sociology*, 86, 1–31.

Ben-Zvi, E. (2019). "Exploring the Memory of Moses 'The Prophet' in Late Persian/Early Hellenistic Yehud/Judah." In E. Ben-Zvi (ed.), *Social Memory among the Literati of Yehud* (pp. 199–231). Berlin: de Gruyter.

Berger, B., and Berger, P. L. (1984). *The War over the Family. Capturing the Middle Ground*. Garden City, NY: Anchor Press/Doubleday.

Berger, J. (2011). "Arousal Increases Social Transmission of Information." *Psychological Science*, 22, 891–3.

Bergmann, M. S. (1992). *In the Shadow of Moloch: The Sacrifice of Children and Its Impact on Western Religions*. Irvington, NY: Columbia University Press.

Berkowitz, L. (1993). *Aggression: Its Causes, Consequences, and Control*. New York: McGraw Hill.

Berthelot, K. (2007). "Jewish Views of Human Sacrifice in the Hellenistic and Roman Period." In K. Finsterbusch, A. Lange, and K. F. Diethard Römheld (eds.), *Human Sacrifice in Jewish and Christian Tradition* (pp. 151–73). Leiden: Brill.

Bettelheim, B. (1954). *Symbolic Wounds, Puberty Rites and the Envious Male*. Glencoe, IL: Free Press of Glencoe.

Bettelheim, B. (1967). *The Empty Fortress: Infantile Autism and the Birth of the Self*. New York: Free Press.

Bicknell, J. (1994). "Learning Disability and Ritualistic Child Abuse." In V. Sinason (ed.), *Treating Survivors of Satanic Abuse* (pp. 151–60). London: Routledge.

Birondo, N. (2020). "The Virtues of Mestizaje: Lessons from Las Casas on Aztec Human Sacrifice." *APA Newsletter on Hispanic/Latino Issues in Philosophy*, 19, 2–8.

Black, J., and Green, A. (1992). *Gods, Demons and Symbols of Ancient Mesopotamia: An Illustrated Dictionary*. London: The British Museum.

Blakely, S. (2018). "Images, Merchants, and Mercenaries: Aegeans and Southern Judah in the Eighth Century BCE." In Zev I. Farber and Jacob L. Wright (eds.), *Archaeology and History of Eighth Century Judah* (pp. 35–56). Atlanta, GA: SBL Press.

Blass, R. B. (2004). "Beyond Illusion: Psychoanalysis and the Question of Religious Truth." *The International Journal of Psychoanalysis*, 85, 615–34.

Bliss, E. L. (1980). "Multiple Personalities: A Report of 14 Cases with Implications for Schizophrenia and Hysteria." *Archives of General Psychiatry*, 37, 1388–97.

Bloom, S. L. (1994). "Hearing the Survivor's Voice: Sundering the Wall of Denial." *The Journal of Psychohistory*, 21, 461–77.

Blum, E. (2012). "The Jacob Tradition." In: C. A. Evans, J. N. Lohr, and D. L. Petersen (eds.), *The Book of Genesis: Composition, Reception, and Interpretation* (VT.S 152) (pp. 181-211). Leiden: Brill.

Boaz, D. N. (2019). "The 'Abhorrent' Practice of Animal Sacrifice and Religious Discrimination in the Global South." *Religions*, 10, 160–80.

Boswell, J. (1988). *The Kindness of Strangers: The Abandonment of Children in Western Europe from Late Antiquity to the Renaissance*. New York: Pantheon Books.

Bottoms, B. L., and Davis, S. L. (1997). "The Creation of Satanic Ritual Abuse." *Journal of Social and Clinical Psychology*, 16, 112–32.

Bottoms, B. L., Shaver, P. R., and Goodman, G. S. (1996). "An Analysis of Ritualistic and Religion-Related Child Abuse Allegations." *Law and Human Behavior*, 20, 1–34.

Bottoms, B. L., Shaver, P. R., Goodman, G. S., and Qin, J. (1995). "In the Name of God: A Profile of Religion-Related Child Abuse." *Journal of Social Issues*, 51, 85–111.

Boulware, L. E., Ratner, L. E., Cooper, L. A., Sosa, J. A., LaVeist, T. A., and Powe, N. R. (2002). "Understanding Disparities in Donor Behavior: Race and Gender Differences in Willingness to Donate Blood and Cadaveric Organs." *Medical Care*, 40, 85–95.

Boyer, P. J. (1988). "Program on Satan Worship Spurs Controversy at NBC." *The New York Times*, October 26: D1.

Boyer, P. (2001). *Religion Explained: The Evolutionary Origins of Religious Thought*. New York: Basic Books.

Boyer, P. (2008). "Religion: Bound to Believe?" *Nature*, 455 (7216), 1038–9.

Braun, B. G. (ed.) (1986). *Treatment of Multiple Personality Disorder*. Washington, DC: American Psychiatric Press.

Braun, B. (1988). "Recognition of Possible Cult Involvement in MPD Patients." Paper presented at the Fifth International Conference on Multiple Personality/Dissociative States. Chicago, IL: Audio Transcripts.

Bremmer, J. N. (2001). "The Scapegoat between Hittites, Greeks, Israelites and Christians." In R. Albertz (ed.), *Kult Konflikt und Versöhnung: Beiträge zur kultischen Sühne in religiösen, sozialen und politischen Auseinandersetzungen des antiken Mittelmeerräume* (pp. 175–86). Münster: Ugarit-Verlag.

Bremmer, J. N. (2002). "Sacrificing a Child in Ancient Greece: The Case of Iphigeneia." In E. Noort and E. Tigchelaar (eds.), *The Sacrifice of Isaac. The Aqedah (Genesis 22) and Its Interpretations* (pp. 21–43). Leiden: Brill.

Bremmer, J. N. (2008). "The Myth of the Golden Fleece." In *Greek Religion and Culture, the Bible and the Ancient Near East* (pp. 303–38). Leiden: Brill.

Bremmer, J. N. (2013). "Early Christian Human Sacrifice between Fact and Fiction." In À. A. Nagy and F. Prescendi (eds.), *Sacrifices Humains: Dossiers, Discours, Comparaisons* (pp. 165–76). Geneva: University of Geneva.

Bremmer, J. N. (2015). "The Self-Sacrifice of Menoeceus in Euripides' Phoenissae, II Maccabees and Statius' Thebaid." *Archiv für Religionsgeschichte*, 16, 193–208.

Brenner, C. (1975). "Affects and Psychic Conflict." *The Psychoanalytic Quarterly*, 44, 5–28.

Bromley, D. B. (1991). "Satanism: The New Cult Scare." In J. T. Richardson, J. Best, and D. Bromley (eds.), *The Satanism Scare*. New York: Aldine.

Brown, D. E. (1991). *Human Universals*. Philadelphia, PA: Temple University Press.

Bubandt, N. (2017). "From Head-Hunter to Organ-Thief: Verisimilitude, Doubt, and Plausible Worlds in Indonesia and Beyond." *Oceania*, 87, 38–57.

Bunzl, M. (1997). "Theodor Herzl's Zionism as Gendered Discourse." In R. Robertson and E. Timms (eds.), *Theodor Herzl and the Origins of Zionism* (pp. 74–86). Edinburgh: Edinburgh University Press.
Burkert, W. (1966). "Greek Tragedy and Sacrificial Ritual." *GRBS*, 7, 87–121.
Burkert, W. (1983). *Homo Necans: The Anthropology of Ancient Greek Sacrificial Ritual and Myth*. Berkeley: University of California Press.
Burkert, W. (1985). *Greek Religion*. Cambridge, MA: Harvard University Press.
Byington, J. (2012). *Twenty-Two Faces: Inside the Extraordinary Life of Jenny Hill and Her Twenty Two Multiple Personalities*. Mustang, OK: Tate Publishing.
Cahill, M. J. (2002). "Drinking Blood at a Kosher Eucharist? The Sound of Scholarly Silence." *Biblical Theology Bulletin*, 32, 168–81.
Caldwell, R. (1989). *The Origin of the Gods: A Psychoanalytic Study of Greek Theogonic Myth*. New York: Oxford University Press.
Cameron, N. (1963). *Personality Development and Psychopathology: A Dynamic Approach*. Boston: Houghton Mifflin.
Canessa, R., and Vierci, P. (2016). *I Had to Survive: How a Plane Crash in the Andes Inspired My Calling to Save Lives*. New York: Simon & Schuster.
Carrasco, D. (1999). *City of Sacrifice: The Aztec Empire and the Role of Violence in Civilization*. Boston, MA: Beacon Press.
Carrasco, D. L. (2013). "Sacrifice/Human Sacrifice in Religious Traditions." In M. Juergensmeyer, M. Kitts, and M. Jerryson (eds.), *The Oxford Handbook of Religion and Violence* (pp. 209–25). New York: Oxford University Press.
Carter, E. (2012). "On Human and Animal Sacrifice in the Late Neolithic at Domuztepe." In A. M. Porter and G. M. Schwartz (eds.), *Sacred Killing: The Archaeology of Sacrifice in the Ancient Near East* (pp. 97–124). Winona Lake, IN: Eisenbrauns.
Census Bureau. (1994). *Statistical Abstract of the United States*. Washington, DC: Government Printing Office.
Ceruti, M. C. (2015). "Frozen Mummies from Andean Mountaintop Shrines: Bioarchaeology and Ethnohistory of Inca Human Sacrifice." *BioMed Research International*, 2015, Article 439428. https://doi.org/10.1155%2F2015%2F439428.
Cevasco, C. (2016). "This is My Body: Communion and Cannibalism in Colonial New England and New France." *The New England Quarterly*, 89, 556–86.
Charleson, N., and Corbett, A. (1994). "A Birthday to Remember." In V. Sinason (ed.), *Treating Survivors of Satanic Abuse* (pp. 164–9). London: Routledge.
Chryssides, G. D. (ed.) (2016). *Heaven's Gate: Postmodernity and Popular Culture in a Suicide Group*. London: Routledge.
Claassen, C. (2013). "Infanticide and Sacrifices among Archaic Babies of the Central United States." *World Archaeology*, 45, 298–313.
CNN (2015). "Young Nepalese Boy Slain in Human Sacrifice Ritual." July 27. https://www.cnn.com/2015/07/27/asia/nepal-human-sacrifice/index.html.

Cohen, E. (2012). "Body Piercing in 'Modern Primitivism' and in Thailand's Vegetarian Festival: A Comparative Study." *Tourism Culture & Communication*, 12, 51–68.

Cohen, S. J. (2005). *Why Aren't Jewish Women Circumcised? Gender and Covenant in Judaism*. Berkeley: University of California Press.

Cohn, N. (1975). *Europe's Inner Demons*. New York: Basic Books.

Coleman, J. (1994). "Satanic Cult Practices." In V. Sinason (ed.), *Treating Survivors of Satanic Abuse* (pp. 242–53). London: Routledge.

Collins, J. J. (2003). "The Zeal of Phinehas: The Bible and the Legitimation of Violence." *Journal of Biblical Literature*, 122, 3–21.

Conklin, B. A. (1995). "Thus Are Our Bodies, Thus Was Our Custom: Mortuary Cannibalism in an Amazonian Society." *American Ethnologist*, 22, 75–101.

Conklin, B. A. (2001). *Consuming Grief: Compassionate Cannibalism in an Amazonian Society*. Austin: University of Texas Press.

Cooklin, A., and Barnes, G. G. (1994). "The Shattered Picture of the Family." In V. Sinason (ed.), *Treating Survivors of Satanic Abuse* (pp. 119–32). London: Routledge.

Couch, C. N. C. (1985). *The Festival Cycle of the Aztec Codex Borbonicus*. Oxford: BAR Publishing.

Coudert, A. P. (2012). "The Ultimate Crime: Cannibalism in Early Modern Minds and Imaginations." In A. Classen, and C. Scarborough (eds.), *Crime and Punishment in the Middle Ages and Early Modern Age* (pp. 521–54). Berlin: Walter de Gruyter.

The Council of Trent (1848). *The Thirteenth Session—The Canons and Decrees of the Sacred and Oecumenical Council of Trent*. London: Dolman.

Daly, M., and Wilson, M. I. (1994). "Some Differential Attributes of Lethal Assaults on Small Children by Stepfathers Versus Genetic Fathers." *Ethology and Sociobiology*, 15, 207–17.

Dardick, H. (2004). "Psychiatric Patient Tells of Ordeal in Treatment." *Chicago Tribune*, February 13. https://www.chicagotribune.com/news/ct-xpm-2004-02-13-0402130 313-story.html.

Darshan, G. (2013). "The Reinterment of Saul and Jonathan's bones (II Sam 21, 12–14) in Light of Ancient Greek Hero-Cult Stories." *Zeitschrift für die alttestamentliche Wissenschaft*, 125, 640–5.

Davis, C. G., and Nolen-Hoeksema, S. (2001). "Loss and Meaning: How Do People Make Sense of Loss?" *American Behavioral Scientist*, 44, 726–41.

Day, J. (1989). *Molech: A God of Human Sacrifice in the Old Testament*. Cambridge: Cambridge University Press.

Decker, J. L. (1997). *Made in America: Self-Styled Success from Horatio Alger to Oprah Winfrey*. Minneapolis: University of Minnesota Press.

de Hulster, I. (2012). "Figurines from Persian Period Jerusalem?" *Zeitschrift für die alttestamentliche Wissenschaft*, 124, 73–88.

de Las Casas, B. (1909). *Apologética Historia de las Indias: de Fr. Bartolome de las Casas*. Barcelona: Bailly, Bailliere e hijos.

DeMause, L. (2009). "Child Abuse, Homicide and Raids in Tribes." *The Journal of Psychohistory*, 36, 192–220.

DeMause, L. (1994). "Why Cults Terrorize and Kill Children." *The Journal of Psychohistory*, 21, 505–17.

DeMeo, J. (1997). "The Geography of Male and Female Genital Mutilations." In G. C. Denniston and M. Milos (eds.), *Sexual Mutilations: A Human Tragedy* (pp. 1–15). New York: Plenum Press.

Denniston, G. C., Grassivaro Gallo, P., Hodges, F. M., Milos, M. F., and Viviani, F. (eds.) (2006). *Bodily Integrity and the Politics of Circumcision: Culture, Controversy, and Change*. New York: Springer.

de Pury, A. (2006). "The Jacob Story and the Beginning of the Formation of the Pentateuch." In T. Dozeman and K. Schmid (eds.), *A Farewell to the Yahwist? The Composition of the Pentateuch in Recent European Interpretation* (pp. 51–72). Atlanta, GA: Society of Biblical Literature.

Devereux, G. (1966). "The Cannibalistic Impulses of Parents." *Psychoanalytic Forum*, 1, 114–31.

de Waal, F. (2019). *Mama's Last Hug: Animal Emotions and What They Tell Us about Ourselves*. New York: W. W. Norton.

Dewrell, H. D. (2017). *Child Sacrifice in Ancient Israel*. Winona Lake, IN: Eisenbrauns.

deYoung, M. (1996a). "Breeders for Satan: Toward a Sociology of Sexual Trauma Tales." *The Journal of American Culture*, 19, 111–17.

deYoung, M. (1996b). "A Painted Devil: Constructing the Satanic Ritual Abuse of Children Problem." *Aggression and Violent Behavior*, 1, 235–48.

deYoung, M. (2004). *The Day Care Ritual Abuse Moral Panic*. Jefferson, NC: McFarland.

Dollahite, D. C., Layton, E., Bahr, H. M., Walker, A. B., and Thatcher, J. Y. (2009). "Giving Up Something Good for Something Better: Sacred Sacrifices Made by Religious Youth." *Journal of Adolescent Research*, 24, 691–725.

Dolnick, E. (1998). *Madness on the Couch: Blaming the Victim in the Heyday of Psychoanalysis*. New York: Simon & Schuster.

Donovan, D. M. (1991). "Darkness Invisible." *The Journal of Psychohistory*, 19, 165–84.

Dorahy, M. J. (2017). "Using the Past to Fertilize but not Determine the Future: Reflections on Dissociation in the International Society for the Study of Trauma and Dissociation." *Journal of Trauma & Dissociation*, 18, 1–10.

Dostoevsky, F. (1993). *The Brothers Karamazov*. New York: Penguin Books.

Douglas, M. (1966). *Purity and Danger: An Analysis of Concepts of Pollution and Taboo*. Harmondsworth: Penguin.

Douglas, M. (1972). "Deciphering a meal." *Daedalus*, 101, 61–81.

Douglas, M. (1996). "Children Consumed and Child Cannibals: Robertson Smith's Attack on the Science of Mythology." In L. L. Patton and W. Doniger (eds.), *Myth and Method* (pp. 29–51). Charlottesville: University of Virginia Press.

DSM-V, American Psychiatric Association (2013). *Diagnostic and Statistical Manual of Mental Disorders*, 5th ed. Arlington, VA: American Psychiatric Association.

Dundes, A. (1991). "The Ritual Murder or Blood Libel Legend: A Study of Anti-Semitic Victimization through Projective Inversion." In A. Dundes (ed.), *The Blood Libel Legend: A Casebook in Anti-Semitic Folklore*. Madison: The University of Wisconsin Press.

Economic Times (2015). "Court Grants Bail to Dera Chief Gurmeet Ram Rahim in Castration Case." https://economictimes.indiatimes.com/news/politics-and-nat ion/court-grants-bail-to-dera-chief-gurmeet-ram-rahim-in-castration-case/articles how/66087458.cms.

Edelman, D. V. (ed.) (1995). *The Triumph of Elohim: From Yahwisms to Judaisms*. Leuven: Peeters.

Edelman, D. V. (2013). "Genesis: A Composition for Construing a Homeland of the Imagination for Elite Scribal Circles or for Educating the Illiterate?" In P. R. Davies and T. Römer (eds.), *Writing the Bible: Scribes, Scribalism and Script*. Durham, NC: Acumen.

Edrey, M. (2018). "Towards a Definition of the Pre-Classical Phoenician Temple." *Palestine Exploration Quarterly*, 150, 184–205.

Ehrenreich, B. (1997). *Blood Rites: Origins and History of the Passions of War*. New York: Metropolitan Books.

Eisen, M. L., Goodman, G. S., Qin, J., Davis, S., and Crayton, J. (2007). "Maltreated Children's Memory: Accuracy, Suggestibility, and Psychopathology." *Developmental Psychology*, 43, 1275–94.

Ellis, B. (1983). "De legendis urbis: Modern Legends in Ancient Rome." *The Journal of American Folklore*, 96, 200–8.

Ellis, B. (2014). *Raising the Devil: Satanism, New Religions, and the Media*. Lexington: University Press of Kentucky.

Epiphanius of Salamis (2013). *The Panarion of Epiphanius of Salamis, Books II and III: De Fide*. Leiden: Brill.

Erikson, E. H. (1964). "Identity and Uprootedness in Our Time." In *Insight and Responsibility: Lectures on the Ethical Implications of Psychoanalytic Insight*. New York: W. W. Norton.

Eriksson, L., Mazerolle, P., Wortley, R., and Johnson, H. (2016). "Maternal and Paternal Filicide: Case Studies from the Australian Homicide Project." *Child Abuse Review*, 25, 17–30.

Esterson, A. (2001). "The Mythologizing of Psychoanalytic History: Deception and Self-Deception in Freud's Accounts of the Seduction Theory Episode." *History of Psychiatry*, 12, 329–52.

Feiler, B. S. (2002). *Abraham: A Journey to the Heart of Three Faiths*. New York: HarperCollins.

Feldman, G. C. (1995). "Satanic Ritual Abuse: A Chapter in the History of Human Cruelty." *The Journal of Psychohistory*, 22, 340–52.

Feldt, L. (2021). "Destruction, Death, and Drama: Narratives of Religiocide in the Hebrew Bible." *Numen*, 68, 132–56.

Felsenstein, F. (1995). *Anti-Semitic Stereotypes: A Paradigm of Otherness in English Popular Culture, 1660–1830.* Baltimore, MD: Johns Hopkins University Press.

Fenichel, O. (1946). "Elements of a Psychoanalytic Theory of Anti-Semitism." In E. Simmel (ed.), *Anti-Semitism. A Social Disease.* New York: International Universities Press.

Ferenczi, S. (1926). "The Problem of Acceptance of Unpleasant Ideas: Advances in Knowledge of the Sense of Reality." *International Journal of Psycho-Analysis*, 7, 312–23.

Filihia, M. (1999). "Rituals of Sacrifice in Early Post-European Contact Tonga and Tahiti." *Journal of Pacific History*, 34, 5–22.

Finkelhor, D., and Jones, L. (2006). "Why Have Child Maltreatment and Child Victimization Declined?" *Journal of Social Issues*, 62, 685–716.

Finkelhor, D., and Williams, L. M. (1988). *Nursery Crimes: Sexual Abuse in Day Care.* Newbury Park, CA: Sage.

Finkelstein, I., and Römer, T. (2014). "Comments on the Historical Background of the Abraham Narrative. Between 'Realia' and 'Exegetica.'" *Hebrew Bible and Ancient Israel*, 3, 3–23.

Finsterbusch, K., Lange, A., and Diethard Römheld, K. F. (eds.) (2007). *Human Sacrifice in Jewish and Christian Tradition.* Leiden: Brill.

Firestone, R. (1998). "Merit, Mimesis, and Martyrdom: Aspects of Shi'ite Meta-Historical Exegesis on Abraham's Sacrifice in Light of Jewish, Christian, and Sunni Muslim Tradition." *Journal of the American Academy of Religion*, 66, 93–116.

Firth, Raymond. (2004). *Social Change in Tikopia.* London: Routledge.

Fister, B. (2003). "The Devil in the Details: Media Representation of "Ritual Abuse" and Evaluation of Sources." *Studies in Media & Information Literacy Education*, 3, 1–14.

Florence, R. (2004). *Blood Libel: The Damascus Affair of 1840.* Madison: University of Wisconsin Press.

Fortes, M. (1959). *Oedipus and Job in West African Religion.* Cambridge: Cambridge University Press.

Fortes, M. (1966). "Totem and Taboo." *Proceedings of the Royal Anthropological Institute of Great Britain and Ireland*, 2, 5–22.

Fortes, M. (1980). "Preface: Anthropologists and Theologians: Common Interests and Divergent Approaches." In M. F. C. Bourdillon and M. Fortes (eds.), *Sacrifice* (pp. v–xix). London: Academic Press.

Fox, R. (1967). "Totem and Taboo reconsidered." In E. R. Leach (ed.), *The Structural Study of Myth and Totemism.* London: Tavistock.

Fox, R. (1994). *The Challenge of Anthropology: Old Encounters and New Excursions.* New Brunswick, NJ: Transaction Publishers.

Fox, R. E. (1995). "The Rape of Psychotherapy." *Professional Psychology: Research and Practice*, 26, 147–55.

Frankel, J. (1997). *The Damascus Affair: "Ritual Murder," Politics, and the Jews in 1840.* Cambridge: Cambridge University Press.

Frankfurter, D. (1994). "Religious Studies and Claims of Satanic Ritual Abuse: A Rejoinder to Stephen Kent." *Religion*, 24, 353–60.

Frankfurter, D. (2006). *Evil Incarnate: Rumors of Demonic Conspiracy and Ritual Abuse in History*. Princeton, NJ: Princeton University Press.

Frankfurter, D. (2011). "Egyptian Religion and the Problem of the Category 'Sacrifice.'" In J. W. Knust and Z. Várhelyi (eds.), *Ancient Mediterranean Sacrifice* (pp. 75–93). New York: Oxford University Press.

Frankfurter, D. (2020). "Horrors of the Inner Chamber: Temples, Homes, and Secret Atrocities in Late Antiquity." *Journal of Early Christian History*, 10, 82–107.

Frankfurter, D. (2021). "Religion in the Mirror of the Other: The Discursive Value of Cult-Atrocity Stories in Mediterranean Antiquity." *History of Religions*, 60, 188–208.

Frankish, P., and Sinason, V. (eds.) (2018). *Holistic Therapy for People with Dissociative Identity Disorder*. London: Routledge.

Frazer, J. G. (1913). *The Scapegoat. The Golden Bough: A Study in Magic and Religion*, 3rd ed. Vol. 9. London: Macmillan.

Frazer, J. G. (1922/1981). *The Golden Bough: The Roots of Religion and Folklore*. New York: Macmillan.

Frazer, J. G. (1990). *The Golden Bough*. London: Palgrave Macmillan.

Freeman, D. (1967). "Totem and Taboo: A Reappraisal." *The Psychoanalytic Study of Society*, 8, 9–33.

Freud, S. (1901). "The Psychopathology of Everyday Life." In *The Standard Edition of the Complete Psychological Writings of Sigmund Freud*, Vol. 6 (pp. 1–290). London: Hogarth Press.

Freud, S. (1908). "Family Romances." In *The Standard Edition of the Complete Psychological Works of Sigmund Freud*, Vol. 9 (pp. 235–42). London: Hogarth Press.

Freud, S. (1909). "Analysis of a Phobia in a Five-Year-Old Boy." In *The Standard Edition of the Complete Psychological Works of Sigmund Freud*, Vol. 10 (pp. 1–138). London: Hogarth Press.

Freud, S. (1910). "Leonardo da Vinci and a Memory of His Childhood." In *The Standard Edition of the Complete Psychological Works of Sigmund Freud*, Vol. 11 (pp. 59–137). London: The Hogarth Press.

Freud, S. (1913). "Totem and Taboo." In *The Standard Edition of the Complete Psychological Works of Sigmund Freud*, Vol. 13 (pp. 1–164). London: Hogarth Press.

Freud, S. (1915). "Thoughts for the Times on War and Death." In *The Standard Edition of the Complete Psychological Works of Sigmund Freud*, Vol. 14 (pp. 275–300). London: The Hogarth Press.

Freud, S. (1915–16). "Introductory Lectures on Psycho-Analysis (Parts I and II)." In *The Standard Edition of the Complete Psychological Works of Sigmund Freud*, Vol. 15 (pp. 1–390). London: The Hogarth Press.

Freud, S. (1919). "'A Child Is Being Beaten' A Contribution to the Study of the Origin of Sexual Perversions." In *The Standard Edition of the Complete Psychological Works of Sigmund Freud*, Vol. 17 (pp. 175–204). London: The Hogarth Press.

Freud, S. (1920). "Beyond the Pleasure Principle." In *The Standard Edition of the Complete Psychological Works of Sigmund Freud*, Vol. 18 (pp. 1–64). London: The Hogarth Press.

Freud, S. (1921). "Group Psychology and the Analysis of the Ego." In *The Standard Edition of the Complete Psychological Works of Sigmund Freud*, Vol. 18 (pp. 65–144). London: The Hogarth Press.

Freud, S. (1927). "The Future of an Illusion." In *The Standard Edition of the Complete Psychological Works of Sigmund Freud*, Vol. 21 (pp. 3–56). London: The Hogarth Press.

Freud, S. (1930). "Civilization and Its Discontents." In *The Standard Edition of the Complete Psychological Work of Sigmund Freud*, Vol. 21 (pp. 57–146). London: The Hogarth Press.

Freud, S. (1939/1964). "Moses and Monotheism." In *The Standard Edition of the Complete Psychological Works of Sigmund Freud*, Vol. 23 (pp. 1–138). London: Hogarth Press.

Freud, S. (1985). *The Complete Letters of Sigmund Freud to Wilhelm Fliess, 1887–1904*, Jeffrey M. Masson (ed. and trans.). Cambridge, MA: Belknap Press of Harvard University Press.

Friedman, S. S. (1978). *The Incident at Massena: The Blood Libel in America*. New York: Stein and Day.

Fromm, F. (1961). *Marx's Concept of Man*. New York: Frederick Ungar.

Fromm, E. (1973). *The Anatomy of Human Destructiveness*. New York: Holt, Rinehart and Winston.

Fromm-Reichman, F. (1948). "Notes on the Development of Treatment of Schizophrenics by Psychoanalytic Psychotherapy." *Psychiatry*, 11, 263–73.

Furnham, A., and Grover, S. (2021). "Do You Have to Be Mad to Believe in Conspiracy Theories? Personality Disorders and Conspiracy Theories." *International Journal of Social Psychiatry*. Online ahead of print. https://doi.org/10.1177/00207640211031614.

Ganaway, G. K. (1989). "Historical Truth Versus Narrative Truth: Clarifying the Role of Exogenous Trauma in the Etiology of Multiple Personality Disorder and Its Variants." *Dissociation*, 2, 205–20.

Ganaway, G. K. (1995). "Hypnosis, Childhood Trauma, and Dissociative Identity Disorder: Toward an Integrative Theory." *International Journal of Clinical and Experimental Hypnosis*, 43, 127–44.

Gangelhoff, J. (1995). "Diagnosis." *Houston Press*, July 6. https://www.houstonpress.com/news/diagnosis-6572173.

Garnand, B. K. (2013). "Phoenicians on the Edge: Geographic and Ethnographic Distribution of Human Sacrifice." In P. Xella (ed.), *The Tophet in the Phoenician Mediterranean* (pp. 65–92). Vérone: Essedue edizioni.

Gerard, J. (1989). "Winfrey Show Evokes Protests." *The New York Times*, May 6: 19.

Ghillany, F. W. (1842). *Die Menschenopfer der alten Hebraer*. Nuremberg: Johann Leonhard Schrag.

Gibson, S. (2009). "The Gift of Faith: Rethinking an Ethics of Sacrifice and Decision in Fear and Trembling and the Gift of Death." *Philosophy Today*, 53, 126–35.

Gil'adi, A. (1992). *Children of Islam: Concepts of Childhood in Medieval Muslim Society*. New York: Springer.

Gill, J. R., Rainwater, C. W., and Adams, B. J. (2009). "Santeria and Palo Mayombe: Skulls, Mercury, and Artifacts." *Journal of Forensic Sciences*, 54, 1458–62.

Gilmour, R. (2019). "Remembering the Future: The Topheth as Dystopia in Jeremiah 7 and 19." *Journal for the Study of the Old Testament*, 44, 64–78.

Gnuse, R. K. (2020). *Hellenism and the Primary History: The Imprint of Greek Sources in Genesis–2 Kings*. London: Routledge.

Goldstein, D. I. (1983). *Dostoevsky and the Jews*. Austin: University of Texas Press.

Goldstein, E. (1992). *Confabulations: Creating False Memories-Destroying Families*. Boca Raton, FL: SIRS Books.

González-Galvez, M. (2012). Personal Truths, Shared Equivocations: Otherness, Uniqueness, and Social Life among the Mapuche of Southern Chile. PhD dissertation, Edinburgh University.

Goodman, G. S., Bottoms, B. L., Redlich, A., Shaver, P. R., and Diviak, K. R. (1998). "Correlates of Multiple Forms of Victimization in Religion-Related Child Abuse Cases." *Journal of Aggression, Maltreatment & Trauma*, 2, 273–95.

Goodman, G. S., Ghetti, S., Quas, J. A., Edelstein, R. S., Alexander, K. W., Redlich, A. D., and Jones, D. P. (2003). "A Prospective Study of Memory for Child Sexual Abuse: New Findings Relevant to the Repressed-Memory Controversy." *Psychological Science*, 14, 113–18.

Goodman, G. S., Qin, J., Bottoms, B. L., and Shaver, P. R. (1994). "Characteristics and Sources of Allegations of Ritualistic Child Abuse." Research Report, University of California, Davis.

Goodman, G. S., Quas, J. A., and Ogle, C. M. (2010). "Child Maltreatment and Memory." *Annual Review of Psychology*, 61, 325–51.

Goodwin, M. (2018). "They Couldn't Get My Soul: Recovered Memories, Ritual Abuse, and the Specter(s) of Religious Difference." *Studies in Religion/Sciences Religieuses*, 47, 280–98.

Grabbe, L. L. (ed.) (2001). *Did Moses Speak Attic? Jewish Historiography and Scripture in the Hellenistic Period* (JSOTSup, 317) Sheffield: Sheffield Academic Press.

Granberry, M. (1993). "Ex-school Volunteer Acquitted of Child Abuse Charges." *Los Angeles Times*, November 20, 1993.

Granerød, G. (2019). "Canon and Archive: Yahwism in Elephantine and Āl-Yāhūdu as a Challenge to the Canonical History of Judean Religion in the Persian Period." *Journal of Biblical Literature*, 138, 345–64.

Grant, R. M. (1981). "Charges of 'Immorality' Against Various Religious Groups in Antiquity." In R. Van Den Broek and M. J. Vermaseren (eds.), *Studies in Gnosticism and Hellenistic Religions Presented to Gilles Quispel on the Occasion of His 65th Birthday* (pp. 161–70). Leiden: E. J. Brill.

Grant, S. (1995). *The Passion of Alice*. Boston, MA: Houghton Mifflin.

Graulich, M. (2000). "Aztec Human Sacrifice as Expiation." *History of Religions*, 39, 352–71.

Greaves, G. B., and Faust, G. H. (1996). "Legal and Ethical Issues in the Treatment of Dissociative Disorders." In L. K. Michelson and W. J. Ray (eds.), *Handbook of Dissociation* (pp. 595–615). Boston, MA: Springer.

Green, A. R. W. (1975). *The Role of Human Sacrifice in the Ancient Near East*. Missoula, MT: Scholars Press.

Greer, G. (1970). *The Female Eunuch*. London: MacGibbon & Kee.

Griffith, R. D. (2001). "Sailing to Elysium: Menelaus' Afterlife ('Odyssey' 4.561-569) and Egyptian Religion." *The Phoenix*, 55, 213–43.

Griffiths, J. G. (1980). *The Origins of Osiris and His Cult*. Leiden: E. J. Brill.

Grotstein, J. S. (1997). "Why Oedipus and not Christ? A Psychoanalytic Inquiry into Innocence, Human Sacrifice, and the Sacred—Part I: Innocence, Spirituality, and Human Sacrifice." *American Journal of Psychoanalysis*, 57, 193–218.

Grünbaum, A. (2010). "Psychoanalysis and Theism." In B. Beit-Hallahmi (ed.), *Psychoanalysis and Theism: Critical Reflections on the Grünbaum Thesis* (pp. 5–41). Lanham, MD: Jason Aronson.

Guignebert, C. (1953). *Jesus*. New Hyde Park, NY: University Books.

Guilhem, O. (2004). *Gods and Rituals in The Aztec Empire*. New York: The Solomon R. Guggenheim Foundation.

Gurney, R. (1962). *The Hittites*. Baltimore, MD: Johns Hopkins University Press.

Haaken, J. (1996). "The Recovery of Memory, Fantasy, and Desire: Feminist Approaches to Sexual Abuse and Psychic Trauma." *Signs*, 21, 1069–94.

Hachlili, R. (2013). *Ancient Synagogues: Archaeology and Art: New Discoveries and Current Research*. Leiden: E. J. Brill.

Hacking, I. (1995). *Rewriting the Soul: Multiple Personality and the Sciences of Memory*. Princeton, NJ: Princeton University Press.

Hahn, S. W., and Bergsma, J. S. (2004). "What Laws Were 'Not Good'? A Canonical Approach to the Theological Problem of Ezekiel 20:25-26." *Journal of Biblical Literature*, 123, 201–18.

Hammond, D. C. (1992). "The Greenbaum Speech." http://www.fmsfonline.org/links/usavpeterson_corydon_hammond.html.

Hanson, C. (1998). "Dangerous Therapy: The Story of Patricia Burgus and Multiple Personality Disorder." https://www.chicagomag.com/Chicago-Magazine/June-1998/Dangerous-Therapy-The-Story-of-Patricia-Burgus-and-Multiple-Personality-Disorder/.

Harding, S. F. (1987). "Convicted by the Holy Spirit: The Rhetoric of Fundamental Baptist Conversion." *American Ethnologist*, 14, 167–85.

Harland, P. A. (2007) "'These People are … Men Eaters': Banquets of the Anti-Associations and Perceptions of Minority Cultural Groups. In Z. A. Crook and P. A.

Harland (eds.), *Identity and Interaction in the Ancient Mediterranean Jews, Christians and Others: Essays in Honour of Stephen G Wilson* (pp. 56–75). Sheffield: Sheffield Phoenix.

Harrill, A. J. (2008). "Cannibalistic Language in the Fourth Gospel and Greco-Roman Polemics of Factionalism (John 6:52-66)." *Journal of Biblical Literature*, 127, 133–58.

Harrison, B. G. (1989). "The Importance of Being Oprah." *New York Times Magazine*, 11, 28–30.

Hausfater, G., and Hrdy, S. B. (1984). *Infanticide: Comparative and Evolutionary Perspectives*. New York: Aldine de Gruyter.

Heider, G. C. (1985). *The Cult of Molek: A Reassessment*. Sheffield: Sheffield Academic Press.

Hendrickson, K. M., McCarty, T., and Goodwin, J. (1990). "Animal Alters." *Dissociation*, 3, 218–21.

Henrichs, A. (2019). "Human Sacrifice in Greek Religion: Three Case Studies." In *II Greek Myth and Religion* (pp. 37–68). Berlin: de Gruyter.

Herbert, C. (2002). "Vampire Religion." *Representations*, 79, 100–21.

Hoffman, L. A. (1996). *Covenant of Blood: Circumcision and Gender in Rabbinic Judaism*. Chicago, IL: University of Chicago Press.

Hogg, G. (1966). *Cannibalism and Human Sacrifice*. New York: Citadel Press.

Høgh-Olesen, H. (2006). "The Sacrifice and the Reciprocity-Programme in Religious Rituals and in Man's Everyday Interactions." *Journal of Cognition and Culture*, 6, 499–519.

Holland, J. M., Currier, J. M., and Neimeyer, R. A. (2006). "Meaning Reconstruction in the First Two Years of Bereavement: The Role of Sense-Making and Benefit-Finding." *Omega: Journal of Death and Dying*, 53, 175–91.

Hsia, R. Po-Chia. (1992). *Trent 1475: Stories of a Ritual Murder Trial*. New Haven, CT: Yale University Press.

Hughes, D. D. (1991). *Human Sacrifice in Ancient Greece*. London: Routledge.

Hughes, R. A. (1990). "Psychological Perspectives on Infanticide in a Faith Healing Sect." *Psychotherapy*, 27, 107–15.

Hughes, R. A. (2004). "The Death of Children by Faith-Based Medical Neglect." *Journal of Law and Religion*, 20, 247–65.

Humphrey, N. K. (2018). "The Lure of Death: Suicide and Human Evolution." *Philosophical Transactions of the Royal Society, Sciences*, 373 (1754), 20170269.

Hurston, Z. N. (2006). *Their Eyes Were Watching God*. New York: Harper.

Hutton, R. (1999). *The Triumph of the Moon: A History of Modern Pagan Witchcraft*. Oxford: Oxford University Press.

Illouz, E. (2003). *Oprah Winfrey and the Glamour of Misery: An Essay on Popular Culture*. Irvington, NY: Columbia University Press.

Imhoff, R., & Lamberty, P. (2018). "How Paranoid Are Conspiracy Believers? Toward a More Fine-Grained Understanding of the Connect and Disconnect between

Paranoia and Belief in Conspiracy Theories." *European Journal of Social Psychology*, 48, 909–26.

Irvine, M. (1999). "'Satanic Abuse' Disorder Pioneer Comes under Fire." *Los Angeles Times*, March 7: 17.

Irwin, L. (1992). "Cherokee Healing: Myth, Dreams, and Medicine." *American Indian Quarterly*, 16, 237–57.

Jackson, S. (1948). "The Lottery." *The New Yorker*, June 18, 24–33.

Jacobs, D. M. (1992). *Secret Life: Firsthand Accounts of UFO Abductions*. New York: Simon & Schuster.

Jalahma, U. (2002). "The Jewish Holiday of Purim." *Al-Riyadh*, March 10. http://www.snopes.com/religion/blood.asp.

James, S. E. (2002). "Mimetic Rituals of Child Sacrifice in the Hopi Kachina Cult." *Journal of the Southwest*, 44, 337–56.

Jaroff, L. (1993). "Repressed-Memory Therapy: Lies of the Mind." *Time*, November 29. http://content.time.com/time/subscriber/article/0,33009,979691-8,00.html.

Jáuregui, C. (2009). "Cannibalism, the Eucharist, and Criollo Subjects." In R. Bauer and J. A. Mazzotti (eds.), *Creole Subjects in the Colonial Americas: Empires, Texts, Identities* (pp. 61–100). Chapel Hill: University of North Carolina Press.

Jay, N. (1992). *Throughout Your Generations Forever: Sacrifice, Religion and Paternity*. Chicago, IL: University of Chicago Press.

Jegede, A. S. (2007). "What Led to the Nigerian Boycott of the Polio Vaccination Campaign?" *PLoS Medicine*, 4, 0417–22.

Jegindø, E. M. E., Vase, L., Jegindø, J., and Geertz, A. W. (2013). "Pain and Sacrifice: Experience and Modulation of Pain in a Religious Piercing Ritual." *International Journal for the Psychology of Religion*, 23, 171–87.

Johnson, A. W., and Price-Williams, D. R. (1996). *Oedipus Ubiquitous: The Family Complex in World Folk Literature*. Stanford, CA: Stanford University Press.

Johnson, B. (1977). "Sociological Theory and Religious Truth." *Sociological Analysis*, 38, 368–88.

Jones, I. H. (1969). "Subincision among Australian Western Desert Aborigines." *British Journal of Medical Psychology*, 42, 183–90.

Jones, L. E. (1956). "There Is Power in the Blood." In W. H. Sims (ed.), *The Baptist Hymnal*. Nashville, TN: Convention Press.

Jonker, E., and Jonker-Bakker, P. (1991). "Experiences with Ritualistic Child Sexual Abuse: A Case Study from the Netherlands." *Child Abuse and Neglect*, 15, 191–6.

Kalimi, I. (2010). "Go, I Beg You, Take Your Beloved Son and Slay Him! Binding of Isaac in Rabbinic Literature and Thought." *Review of Rabbinic Judaism*, 13, 1–29.

Kamlah, J., and Michelau, H. (eds.) (2012). *Temple Building and Temple Cult: Architecture and Cultic Paraphernalia of Temples in the Levant (2.-1. Mill. B.C.E.)*. ADPV 41. Wiesbaden: Harrassowitz.

Kanner, L. (1943). "Autistic Disturbances of Affective Contact." *Nervous Child*, 2, 217–50.

Kansa, S. W., Gauld, S. C., Campbell, S., and Carter, E. (2009). "Whose Bones Are Those? Preliminary Comparative Analysis of Fragmented Human and Animal Bones in the 'Death Pit' at Domuztepe, a Late Neolithic Settlement in Southeastern Turkey." *Anthropozoologica*, 44, 159–72.

Kaufmann, W. (1961). *The Faith of a Heretic*. Princeton, NJ: Princeton University Press.

Kelley, S. J. (1989). "Stress Responses of Children to Sexual Abuse and Ritualistic Abuse in Day Care Centers." *Journal of Interpersonal Violence*, 4, 502–13.

Kellner, M. (2014). "And Yet, the Texts Remain." In K. Berthelot, J. E David, and M. Hirshman (eds.), *The Gift of the Land and the Fate of the Canaanites in Jewish Thought* (pp. 153–75). Oxford: Oxford Scholarship Online.

Kempe, C. H., Silverman, F. N., Steele, B. F., Droegemueller, W., and Silver, H. K. (1962). "The Battered Child Syndrome." *Journal of the American Medical Association*, 181, 105–12.

Kierkegaard, S. (1843/1983). *Fear and Trembling*. Princeton, NJ: Princeton University Press.

Kiev, A. (1962). "Ritual Goat Sacrifice in Haiti." *American Imago*, 19, 349–59.

Kihlstrom, J. F. (2005). "Dissociative Disorders." *Annual Review of Clinical Psychology*, 1, 227–53.

Kilgour, M. (2014). *From Communion to Cannibalism*. Princeton, NJ: Princeton University Press.

Kitagawa, J. M. (1961). "Ainu bear festival (Iyomante)." *History of Religions*, 1, 95–151.

Klaits, J. (1985). *Servants of Satan: The Age of the Witch Hunts*. Bloomington: Indiana University Press.

Kletter, R. (1996). *The Judean Pillar-Figurines and the Archaeology of Asherah*. British Archaeological Reports (BAR) International Series 636. Oxford: John and Erica Hedges.

Kletter, R. (2004). "Clay Figurines." In D. Ussishkin (ed.), *The Renewed Archaeological Excavations at Lachish (1973–1994)*. Tel Aviv: Emery and Claire Yass Publications in Archaeology.

Kluckhohn, C. (1959). "Recurrent Themes in Myths and Mythmaking." *Daedalus*, 88, 268–79.

Kluft, R. (1985). *Childhood Antecedents of Multiple Personality*. Washington, DC: American Psychiatric Press.

Kluft, R. P. (1989). "Editorial: Reflections on Allegations of Ritual Abuse." *Dissociation*, 2, 191–3.

Kluft, R. P. (2014). "Noll, R. 'Speak, Memory,'" *Psychiatric Times*, March 21, www.academia.edu/6496435.

Kluft, R. P., Braun, B. G., and Sachs, R. (1984). "Multiple Personality, Intrafamilial Abuse, and Family Psychiatry." *International Journal of Family Psychiatry*, 5, 283–301.

Knauft, B. M. (1987). "Reconsidering Violence in Simple Human Societies: Homicide among the Gebusi of New Guinea." *Current Anthropology*, 28, 467–500.

Korbin, J. E. (1991). "Cross-Cultural Perspectives and Research Directions for the 21st Century." *Child Abuse & Neglect*, 15, 67–77.
Kott, J. (1973). *The Eating of the Gods: An Interpretation of Greek Tragedy.* New York: Random House.
Krappe, A. H. (1923). "The Story of Phrixos and Modern Folklore." *Folklore*, 34, 141–7.
Kroeber, A. L. (1920). "Totem and Taboo." *American Anthropologist*, 22, 48–55.
Kroeber, A. L. (1939). "Totem and Taboo in Retrospect." *American Journal of Sociology*, 45, 446–51.
Kushner, A. W. (1967). "Two Cases of Auto-Castration Due to Religious Delusions." *British Journal of Medical Psychology*, 40, 293–8.
Ladouceur, D. (1980). "Hellenistic Preconceptions of Shipwreck and Pollution as a Context for Acts 27–28." *Harvard Theological Review*, 73, 435–49.
La Fontaine, J. S. (1994). *The Extent and Nature of Organised and Ritual Abuse: Research Findings.* London: HMSO.
La Fontaine, J. S. (1998). *Speak of the Devil.* Cambridge: Cambridge University Press.
Lange, A. (2007). "'They Burn Their Sons and Daughters. That Was No Command of Mine' (Jer 7: 31): Child Sacrifice in the Hebrew Bible and in the Deuteronomistic Jeremiah Redaction." In K. Finsterbusch., A. Lange, and K. F. Diethard Römheld (eds.), *Human Sacrifice in Jewish and Christian Tradition* (pp. 109–32). Leiden: Brill.
Langmuir, G. I. (1990). *History, Religion, and Antisemitism.* Berkeley: University of California Press.
Lanning, K. V. (1992). *Investigators' Guide to Allegations of "Ritual" Child Abuse.* Quantico, VA: FBI Academy.
Lanning, K. V. (1996). "The 'Witch Hunt,' the 'Backlash,' and Professionalism." *The APSAC Advisor*, 9 (4), 8–11.
Lantigua, D. (2018). "Religion within the Limits of Natural Reason: The Case of Human Sacrifice." In D. T. Orique O. P. and R. Roldán-Figueroa (eds.), *Bartolomé de las Casas, O.P.: History, Philosophy and Theology in the Age of European Expansion* (pp. 280–309). Leiden: Brill.
Laungani, P. (2007). "Counseling the Dead." *Counselling Psychology Quarterly*, 20, 81–95.
Lavin, T. (2020). QAnon, Blood Libel, and the Satanic Panic. *The New Republic*, September 29. https://newrepublic.com/article/159529/qanon-blood-libel-satanic-panic.
Law, R. (1985). "Human Sacrifice in Pre-Colonial West Africa." *African Affairs*, 84, 53–87.
Lawrence, B. B. (1976). *Shahrastani on the Indian Religions.* Berlin: Walter de Gruyter.
Lawrence, D. H. (1922). *Studies in Classic American Literature*, rpt. 1977, New York: Penguin.
Laycock, J. P. (2014). "The Trial of the West Memphis Three: Rival Visions of Evil." In S. Packer and J. Pennington (eds.), *The Devil We Know: Evil in American Pop Culture* (pp. 245–66). Santa Barbara, CA: ABC-CLIO.

Leavy, B. F. (1994). *In Search of the Swan Maiden: A Narrative on Folklore and Gender*. New York: New York University Press.

Leith, M. J. W. (2020). "New Perspectives on the Return from Exile and Persian-Period Yehud." In B. Strawn and B. Kelle (eds.), *The Oxford Handbook of the Historical Books of the Hebrew Bible* (pp. 147–72). Oxford: Oxford University Press.

Lemański, J. (2021). "Abraham—a Canaanite? Tracing the Beginnings of the Literary Tradition of Abraham." *The Biblical Annals*, 11, 185–230.

Leslie, D., and Adamski, G. (1953). *The Flying Saucers Have Landed*. New York: The British Book Centre.

Lester, D. (1991). "Murdering Babies." *Social Psychiatry and Psychiatric Epidemiology*, 26, 83–5.

Levack, B. P. (2015). *The Witch-Hunt in Early Modern Europe*. London: Routledge.

Levenson, J. D. (1993). *The Death and Resurrection of the Beloved Son: The Transformation of Child Sacrifice in Judaism and Christianity*. New Haven, CT: Yale University Press.

Levenson, J. D. (1998). "Abusing Abraham: Traditions, Religious, Histories, and Modern Misinterpretations." *Judaism*, 47, 259–78.

Lewis, B. (1984). *The Jews of Islam*. Princeton, NJ: Princeton University Press.

Lewontin, R. C. (1995). "Sex, Lies, and Social Science." *The New York Review of Books*, 42(7), 24–9.

Lichtenthal, W. G., Currier, J. M., Neimeyer, R. A., and Keesee, N. J. (2010). "Sense and Significance: A Mixed Methods Examination of Meaning Making After the Loss of One's Child." *Journal of Clinical Psychology*, 66, 791–812.

Lidz, T., Cornelison, A. R., Fleck, S., and Terry, D. (1957). "The Intrafamilial Environment of the Schizophrenic Patient." *Psychiatry*, 20, 329–50.

Lime, M., and Koenraadt, F. (2008). "Filicide: A Comparative Study of Maternal Versus Paternal Child Homicide." *Criminal Behaviour and Mental Health*, 18, 166–76.

Lipschits, O., Römer, T., and Gonzalez, H. (2017). "The Pre-Priestly Abraham Narratives from Monarchic to Persian Times." *Semitica*, 59, 261–96.

Littlewood, R. (2004). "Multiple Personality Disorder: A Clinical and Cultural Account." *Psychiatry*, 3, 11–13.

Loeb, E. M. (1923). "The Blood Sacrifice Complex." *Memoirs of the American Anthropological Association*, 30, 3–28.

Loftus, E. F. (1993). "The Reality of Repressed Memories." *American Psychologist*, 48, 518–37.

Logan, A. (2009). "Rehabilitating Jephthah." *Journal of Biblical Literature*, 128, 665–85.

Lombaard, C. (2008). "Isaac Multiplex: Genesis 22 in a New Historical Representation." *HTS: Theological Studies*, 6, 907–19.

Lombaard, C. (2019). "Testing Tales: Genesis 22 and Daniel 3 and 6. In S. Gillmayr-Bucher and M. Häusl (eds.), *Prayers and the Construction of Israelite Identity* (pp. 113–23). Atlanta, GA: Society of Biblical Literature.

Lorenz, K. (1966). *On Aggression*. New York: Harcourt, Brace & World.

Lotto, D. (1994). "On Witches and Witch Hunts: Ritual and Satanic Cult Abuse." *The Journal of Psychohistory*, 21, 373–9.

Lowney, K. S. (1995). "Teenage Satanism as Oppositional Youth Subculture." *Journal of Contemporary Ethnography*, 23, 453–84.

Luckert, K. W. (1975). *The Navajo Hunter Tradition*. Tucson: University of Arizona Press.

Lundberg-Love, P. K. (1988). "Update on Cults, Part I: Satanic Cults." *Family Violence Bulletin*, 5, 9–10.

Lustig, E. (1976). "On the Origin of Judaism: A Psychoanalytic Approach." *The Psychoanalytic Study of Society*, 7, 331–57.

Luther, M. (1971). "On the Jews and Their Lies, 1543." In *Luther's Works* (Vol. 47, pp. 123–306). Philadelphia, PA: Fortress.

MacCormack, S. (2000). "Processions for the Inca: Andean and Christian Ideas of Human Sacrifice, Communion and Embodiment in Early Colonial Peru." *Archiv für Religionsgeschichte*, 2, 110–40.

Mack, J. E. (1994). *Abduction: Human Encounters with Aliens*. New York: Macmillan.

Magness, J. (2005). "Heaven on Earth: Helios and the Zodiac Cycle in Ancient Palestinian Synagogues." *Dumbarton Oaks Papers*, 59, 1–52.

Maler, M. (1966). "The Jewish Orthodox Circumcision Ceremony: Its Meaning from Direct Study of the Rite." *Journal of the American Psychoanalytic Association*, 14, 510–7.

Manring, R. J. (2018). "Child Sacrifice in Rūparāma's Dharmamaṅgala." *The Journal of Hindu Studies*, 11, 187–206.

Manuel, F. (1983). *The Changing of the Gods*. London: University Press of New England.

Marks, J. D. (1991). *The Search for the "Manchurian Candidate": The CIA and Mind Control*. New York: W. W. Norton.

Martinez, R. (2011). "The Trokosi Tradition in Ghana: The Silencing of a Religion." *History in the Making*, 4, 5–11.

Masson, J. M. (ed.) (1985). *The Complete Letters of Sigmund Freud to Wilhelm Fliess, 1887–1904*. Cambridge, MA: Harvard University Press.

Matheson, T. (1998). *Alien Abductions: Creating a Modern Phenomenon*. Buffalo, NY: Prometheus Books.

Matthew, L., and Barron, I. G. (2015). "Participatory Action Research on Help-Seeking Behaviors of Self-Defined Ritual Abuse Survivors: A Brief Report." *Journal of Child Sexual Abuse*, 24, 429–43.

Matthews, D. (2015). "Revisiting the Satanic Panic Television Specials of the 1980s and '90s." October 29. https://splinternews.com/revisiting-the-satanic-panic-television-specials-of-the-1793852408

Matthews, L., and Marwit, S. J. (2003). "Examining the Assumptive World Views of Parents Bereaved by Accident, Murder, and Illness." *Omega: Journal of Death and Dying*, 48, 115–36.

Matthiessen, P. (1962). *Under the Mountain Wall: A Chronicle of Two Seasons in the Stone Age*. New York: Viking.

Mayer, D. E. B. Y., Vandermeersch, B., and Bar-Yosef, O. (2009). "Shells and Ochre in Middle Paleolithic Qafzeh Cave, Israel: Indications for Modern Behavior." *Journal of Human Evolution*, 56, 307–14.

Mayer, R. S. (1991). *Satan's Children*. New York: Avon.

McDonough, S. P., and Holoyda, B. (2018). "Ritualistic Animal Killing. In *Veterinary Forensic Pathology*, Vol. 2 (pp. 129–38). Cham: Springer.

McGowan, A. (1994). "Eating People: Accusations of Cannibalism against Christians in the Second Century." *Journal of Early Christian Studies*, 2, 413–42.

McGowan, A. (2010). "Rethinking Eucharistic Origins." *Pacifica*, 23, 173–91.

McGrath, A. (2001). *Christian Theology: An Introduction*. Oxford: Blackwell.

McHugh, P. R. (2008). *Try to Remember: Psychiatry's Clash over Meaning, Memory, and Mind*. Washington, DC: Dana Press.

McLeod, S. (2018). "Human Sacrifice in Viking Age Britain and Ireland." *Journal of the Australian Early Medieval Association*, 14, 71–88.

Mead, M. (1963). "Totem and Taboo Reconsidered with Respect." *Bulletin of the Menninger Clinic*, 27, 185–99.

Means, G. P. (2000). "Human Sacrifice and Slavery in the 'Unadministered' Areas of Upper Burma during the Colonial Era." *Journal of Social Issues in Southeast Asia*, 15, 184–221.

Merskey, H. (1992). "The Manufacture of Personalities: The Production of Multiple Personality Disorder." *The British Journal of Psychiatry*, 160, 327–40.

Meyer, C., Kürbis, O., Dresely, V., and Alt, K. W. (2018). "Patterns of Collective Violence in the Early Neolithic of Central Europe." In A. Dolfini, R. J. Crellin, C. Horn, and M. Uckelmann (eds.), *Prehistoric Warfare and Violence* (pp. 21–38). Cham: Springer.

Miguel, E. (2005). "Poverty and Witch Killing." *Review of Economic Studies*, 72, 1153–72.

Miles, G. B., and Trompf, G. (1976). "Luke and Antiphon: The Theology of Acts 27–28 in the Light of Pagan Beliefs about Divine Retribution, Pollution, and Shipwreck." *The Harvard Theological Review*, 69, 259–67.

Miller, A. (2018). *Healing the Unimaginable: Treating Ritual Abuse and Mind Control*. London: Karnac Books.

Mishel, L., and Bernstein, J. (1994). "The Joyless Recovery." *Dissent*, 41, 136–8.

Mol, H. (1979). "The Origin and Function of Religion: A Critique of, and Alternative to, Durkheim's Interpretation of the Religion of Australian Aborigines." *Journal for the Scientific Study of Religion*, 18, 379–89.

Mollon, P. (1994). "The Impact of Evil." In V. Sinason (ed.), *Treating Survivors of Satanic Abuse* (pp. 136–47). London: Routledge.

Monroe, L. A. (2013). "Disembodied Women: Sacrificial Language and the Deaths of Bat-Jephthah, Cozbi, and the Bethlehemite Concubine." *The Catholic Biblical Quarterly*, 75, 32–52.

Mordeniz, C., and Verit, A. (2009). "Is Circumcision a Modified Ritual of Castration?" *Urologia Internationalis*, 82, 399–403.

Moriarty, A. (1992). *The Psychology of Adolescent Satanism*. Westport, CT: Greenwood Press.
Morris, E. F. (2014). "(Un)dying Loyalty: Meditations on Retainer Sacrifice in Ancient Egypt and Elsewhere." In R. B. Campbell (ed.), *Violence and Civilization: Studies of Social Violence in History and Prehistory* (pp. 61–93). Oxford: Oxbow.
Morris, S. (1994). "You Will Only Hear Half of It and You Won't Believe It." In V. Sinason (ed.), *Treating Survivors of Satanic Abuse* (pp. 302–26). London: Routledge.
Mosse, G. L. (1985). *Toward the Final Solution: A History of European Racism*. Madison, WI: University of Wisconsin Press.
Mulhern, S. (1991). "Satanism and Psychotherapy: A Rumor in Search of an Inquisition." In J. T. Richardson, J. Best and D. G. Bromley (eds.), *The Satanism Scare* (pp. 145–72). Hawthorne, NY: Aldine de Gruyter.
Mulhern, S. (1994). "Satanism, Ritual Abuse, and Multiple Personality Disorder: A Sociohistorical Perspective." *International Journal of Clinical and Experimental Hypnosis*, 42, 265–88.
Mullin, J. (1995). "Fear of 'Demon Forces' Drove Mother to Kill Children." *The Guardian*, May 12: 2.
Murray, J. B. (1994). "Dimensions of Multiple Personality Disorder." *The Journal of Genetic Psychology*, 155, 233–46.
Murray, J. (2019). "The Battle for Chastity: Miraculous Castration and the Quelling of Desire in the Middle Ages." *Journal of the History of Sexuality*, 28, 96–116.
Nathan, D. (1994). "Dividing to Conquer? Women, Men, and the Making of Multiple Personality Disorder." *Social Text*, 40, 77–114.
Nathan, D. (2011). *Sybil Exposed: The Extraordinary Story Behind the Famous Multiple Personality Case*. New York: Simon & Schuster.
Nathan, D., and Snedeker, M. (1995). *Satan's Silence: Ritual Abuse and the Making of a Modern American Witch Hunt*. New York: Basic Books.
Nathan, G. J., and Mencken, H. L. (1921). *The American Credo: A Contribution Toward the Interpretation of the National Mind*. New York: Alfred A. Knopf.
Neria, Y., Roe, D., Beit Hallahmi, B., Neimneh, M., and Balaban, A. (2005). "The Al Qaeda 9/11 Instructions: A Study in the Construction of Religious Martyrdom." *Religion*, 35, 1–11.
Newman, A. (1994). "Feminist Social Criticism and Marx's Theory of Religion." *Hypatia*, 9, 15–37.
Niditch, S. (1995). *War in the Hebrew Bible: A Study in the Ethics of Violence*. New York: Oxford University Press.
Niehr, H. (2008). "Phoenician Cult in Palestine after 586 BCE." In I. Cornelius and L. Jonker (eds.), *From Ebla to Stellenbosch: Syro-Palestinian Religions and the Hebrew Bible* (pp. 13–24). Wiesbaden: Harrassowitz.
Noegel, S. B. (2007). "Greek Religion and the Ancient Near East." In D. Ogden (ed.), *The Blackwell Companion to Greek Religion* (pp. 21–37). London: Blackwell.

Noegel, S. B. (2016). "Corpses, Cannibals, and Commensality." *Journal of Religion and Violence*, 4, 255–304.

Noll, R. (2013). "When Psychiatry Battled the Devil." *Psychiatric Times*. https://www.garygreenbergonline.com/w/wp-content/uploads/2013/12/Psychiatric_Times_-_When_Psychiatry_Battled_the_Devil_-_2013-12-06.pdf.

Noort, E. (2002). "Genesis 22: Human Sacrifice and Theology in the Hebrew Bible." In E. Noort and E. Tigchelaar (eds.), *The Sacrifice of Isaac. The Aqedah (Genesis 22) and Its Interpretations, Themes in Biblical Narrative, Jewish and Christian Traditions* (pp. 1–20). Leiden: Brill.

Noritake, T. (1918). "Human Sacrifice in Japan." *The Open Court*, 32, 760–7.

Norris, P., and Inglehart, R. (2004). *Sacred and Secular: Religion and Politics Worldwide*. Cambridge: Cambridge University Press.

Nunberg, H. (1947). "Circumcision and Problems of Bisexuality." *International Journal of Psycho-Analysis*, 28, 145–79.

Oates, J. C. (2010). "Lost Daddy." In *Sourland: Stories* (pp. 292–323). New York: Harper Collins.

Obadare, E. (2005). "A Crisis of Trust: History, Politics, Religion and the Polio Controversy in Northern Nigeria." *Patterns of Prejudice*, 39, 265–84.

Oberman, M. (2002). "Understanding Infanticide in Context: Mothers Who Kill, 1870–1930 and Today." *Journal of Criminal Law and Criminology*, 92, 707–38.

Obeyesekere, G. (1990). *The Work of Culture: Symbolic Transformation in Psychoanalysis and Anthropology*. Chicago, IL: University of Chicago Press.

O'Flaherty, W. D. (1995). *Other Peoples' Myths: The Cave of Echoes*. Chicago, IL: University of Chicago Press.

Ofshe, R., and Watters, E. (1994). *Making Monsters: False Memories, Psychotherapy, and Sexual Hysteria*. New York: Charles Scribner.

Ojo, O. (2005). "Slavery and Human Sacrifice in Yorubaland: Ondo, c. 1870–94." *Journal of African History*, 46, 379–404.

Olivier, K. (2000). "Theoretical Explanations for Parent Abuse." *Acta Criminologica*, 13, 46–56.

Orne, M. T., Whitehouse, W. G., Dinges, D. F., and Orne, E. C. (1988). "Reconstructing Memory Through Hypnosis: Forensic and Clinical Implications." In H. M. Pettinati (ed.), *Hypnosis and Memory* (pp. 21–63). New York: Guilford.

Osofsky, M. J., Bandura, A., and Zimbardo, P. G. (2005). "The Role of Moral Disengagement in the Execution Process." *Law and Human Behavior*, 29, 371–93.

Otgaar, H., Howe, M. L., Patihis, L., Merckelbach, H., Lynn, S. J., Lilienfeld, S. O., and Loftus, E. F. (2019). "The Return of the Repressed: The Persistent and Problematic Claims of Long-Forgotten Trauma." *Perspectives on Psychological Science*, 14, 1072–95.

Owens, B. M. (1993). "Blood and Bodhisattvas: Sacrifice among the Newar Buddhists of Nepal." In C. Ramble and M. Brauen (eds.), *The Anthropology of Tibet and the Himalayas* (pp. 258–69). Kathmandu: Vajra Publications.

Parker, R. (2016). "Sacrifice, Greek." In *Oxford Research Encyclopedia of Classics*. Oxford: Oxford University Press.

Parren, N. (2017). "The (Possible) Cognitive Naturalness of Witchcraft Beliefs: An Exploration of the Existing Literature." *Journal of Cognition & Culture*, 17, 396–418.

Parsons, T. (1937). *The Structure of Social Action*. New York: Macmillan.

Parsons, T. (1951). *The Social System*. Glencoe, IL: The Free Press.

Patihis, L., and Pendergrast, M. H. (2019). "Reports of Recovered Memories of Abuse in Therapy in a Large Age-Representative US National Sample: Therapy Type and Decade Comparisons." *Clinical Psychological Science*, 7, 3–21.

Paul VI (1965). *Mysterium Fidei*, September 3. See https://www.vatican.va/content/paul-vi/en/encyclicals/documents/hf_p-vi_enc_03091965_mysterium.html

Pepper, S. C. (1942). *World Hypotheses*. Berkeley: University of California Press.

Peterson, C. A. (2015). "Military Service as Child Sacrifice: Oedipal and Odyssean Perspectives." *International Journal of Applied Psychoanalytic Studies*, 12, 36–52.

Peto, A. (2009). "About the Narratives of a Blood Libel Case in Post-Shoah Hungary." In L. O. Vasvari and S. Totosy de Zepetnek (eds.), *Comparative Central European Holocaust Studies* (pp. 40–9). West Lafayette, IN: Purdue University Press.

Pew Research Center (2010). "U.S. Religious Knowledge Survey Executive Summary." https://www.pewforum.org/2010/09/28/u-s-religious-knowledge-survey/.

Piaget, J. (1929). *The Child's Conception of the World*. London: Routledge & Kegan Paul.

Pongratz-Leisten, B. (2012). "Sacrifice in the Ancient Near East: Offering and Ritual Killing." In A. M. Porter and G. M. Schwartz (eds.), *Sacred Killing: The Archaeology of Sacrifice in the Ancient Near East* (pp. 291–304). Winona Lake, IN: Eisenbrauns,

Pope Francis (2013). "How to Rout the Demon's Strategy." October 11. https://www.vatican.va/content/francesco/en/cotidie/2013/documents/papa-francesco-cotidie_20131011_demon-strategy.html.

Pope Francis (2015). "An Address to Children and Young People in Turin, Italy." https://www.vatican.va/content/francesco/en/speeches/2015/june/documents/papa-francesco_20150621_torino-giovani.html.

Popenoe, D. (1988). *Disturbing the Nest: Family Change and Decline in Modern Society*. New York: de Gruyter.

Prag, J. (2010). "Tyrannizing Sicily: the Despots Who Cried 'Carthage!'" In A. Turner, J. K. O. Chong-Gossard and F. Vervaet (eds.), *Private and Public Lies: The Discourse of Despotism and Deceit in the Graeco-Roman World* (pp. 51–71). Leiden: Brill.

Precin, P. (2011). "Return to Work: A Case of PTSD, Dissociative Identity Disorder, and Satanic Ritual Abuse." *Work*, 38, 57–66.

Price, M. L. (2004). *Consuming Passions: The Uses of Cannibalism in Late Medieval and Early Modern Europe*. London: Routledge.

Prince, R. (1961). "The Yoruba Image of the Witch." *Journal of Mental Science*, 107, 795–805.

Provost, G. (1989). *Across the Border: True Story of Satanic Cult Killings in Matamoros, Mexico*. New York: Pocket Books.

Pseudo-Plutarch. (2008). *De Fluviorum et Montium Nominibus IX. MAEANDER (About the Names of Rivers and Mountains/on Rivers)*. http://www.perseus.tufts.edu/hopper/text?doc=Perseus%3Atext%3A2008.01.0400%3Achapter%3D9.

Pullella, P. (2021). "Pope, on Palm Sunday, Says Devil Taking Advantage of Pandemic." https://www.reuters.com/article/uk-religion-easter-pope-palmsunday-idUKKBN2BK0A0c.

Punt, J. (2008). "Jude and the Others. Hermeneutics. Identity, Conflict." *SABJT*, 17, 149–62.

Punt, J. (2009). "The Aqedah in the New Testament-Sacrifice, Violence and Human Dignity." *Scriptura: Journal for Contextual Hermeneutics in Southern Africa*, 102, 430–45.

Putkonen, H., Amon, S., Almiron, M. P., Cederwall, J. Y., Eronen, M., Klier, C., Kjelsberg, E., and Weizmann-Henelius, G. (2009). "Filicide in Austria and Finland: A Register-Based Study on All Filicide Cases in Austria and Finland 1995–2005." *BMC Psychiatry*, 9, 1–9.

Putnam, F. W. (1993). "Diagnosis and Clinical Phenomenology of Multiple Personality Disorder: A North American Perspective." *Dissociation*, 7, 80–6.

Putnam, F. W., Guroff, J. J., Silberman, E. K., Barban, L., and Post, R. M. (1986). "The Clinical Phenomenology of Multiple Personality Disorder: Review of 100 Recent Cases." *Journal of Clinical Psychiatry*, 47, 285–93.

Rabi, Y. (1985). "Pro-Nazi Arab's Anti-Semitic Tirades at UN Seminar Denounced by U.S. Jewish Telegraphic Agency." January 14. https://www.jta.org/archive/special-to-the-jta-u-s-protests-to-the-un-about-anti-semitic-remarks-at-a-un-forum-by-an-arab-nazi.

Raine, S. (2005). "Reconceptualising the Human Body: Heaven's Gate and the Quest for Divine Transformation." *Religion*, 35, 98–117.

Rank, O. (1914). *The Myth of the Birth of the Hero*. New York: Nervous and Mental Disease Publishing.

Ransel, D. L. (1988). *Mothers of Misery. Child Abandonment in Russia*. Princeton, NJ: Princeton University Press.

Raphael, F. (1972). "Le Juif et le Diable dans la civilisation de l'Occident." *Social Compass*, 19, 549–66.

Raschke, C. (1990). *Painted Black: Satanic Crime in America*. San Francisco, CA: Harper and Row.

Raveenthiran, V. (2018). "The Evolutionary Saga of Circumcision from a Religious Perspective." *Journal of Pediatric Surgery*, 53, 1440–3.

Read, P. P. (1974). *Alive: The Story of the Andes Survivors*. Philadelphia, PA: J. B. Lippincott.

Reik, T. (1951). *Dogma and Compulsion: Psychoanalytic Studies of Religion and Myths*. New York: International Universities Press.

Reik, T. (1961). *The Temptation*. New York: George Braziller.

Reinhard, J., and Ceruti, C. (2005). "Sacred Mountains, Ceremonial Sites, and Human Sacrifice Among the Incas." *Archaeoastronomy*, 19, 1–43.

Rempel, M. (2010). "Nietzsche, Mithras, and "Complete Heathendom." *Comparative and Continental Philosophy*, 2, 27–43.

Reynolds, A. (1993). *Jesus Versus Christianity*. London: Open Gate Press.

Reynolds, B. H. (2006). "What Are Demons of Error? The Meaning of אתועט ידיש and Israelite Child Sacrifices." *Revue De Qumrân*, 22, 593–613.

Richardson, J. T., Best, J., and Bromley, D. (eds.) (1991). *The Satanism Scare*. New York: Aldine.

Richardson, J. T., and Dewitt, J. (1992). "Christian Science, Spiritual Healing, the Law, and Public Opinion." *Journal of Church and State*, 34, 549–61.

Richter, L. M., Dawes, A., and Higson-Smith, C. (eds.) (2004). *Sexual Abuse of Young Children in Southern Africa*. Cape Town: HSRC Press.

Rieber, R. (1998). "Hypnosis, False Memory and Multiple Personality: A Trinity of Affinity." *History of Psychiatry*, 10, 3–11.

Riehl, A. (2019). "'God Is a Man Eater': Consumption Rituals and the Creation of Christianity under Roman Persecution." *Constellations*, 10, 1–13.

Rivera, G. (1988). "Devil Worship: Exposing Satan's Underground." https://www.imdb.com/title/tt1136645/.

Rives, J. (1995). "Human Sacrifice among Pagans and Christians." *The Journal of Roman Studies*, 85, 65–85.

Rodgers, D. V., Gindler, J. S., Atkinson, W. L., and Markowitz, L. E. (1993). "High Attack Rates and Case Fatality during a Measles Outbreak in Groups with Religious Exemption to Vaccination." *Pediatrics Infectious Disease Journal*, 12, 288–92.

Roheim, G. (1945). *The Eternal Ones of the Dream: A Psychoanalytic Interpretation of Australian Myth and Ritual*. New York: International Universities Press.

Römer, T. C. (1998). "Why Would the Deuteronomist Tell about the Sacrifice of Jephthah's Daughter?" *Journal for the Study of the Old Testament*, 77, 28–34.

Römer, T. C. (2007). "Israel's Sojourn in the Wilderness and the Construction of the Book of Numbers." In R. Rezetko, T. Lim and B. Aucker (eds.), *Reflection and Refraction: Studies in Biblical Historiography in Honour of A. Graeme Auld* (pp. 419–45). Leiden: Brill.

Römer, T. (2012). "Abraham's Righteousness and Sacrifice: How to Understand (and Translate) Genesis 15 and 22." *Communio Viatorum*, LIV, 3–15.

Römer, T. (2015). "The Hebrew Bible and Greek Philosophy and Mythology—Some Case Studies." *Semitica*, 57, 185–203.

Ronen, A. (2012). "The Oldest Burials and Their Significance." In S. C. Reynolds and A. Gallagher (eds.), *African Genesis: Perspectives on Hominin Evolution* (pp. 554–70). Cambridge: Cambridge University Press.

Roose, K. (2020). "What is QAnon, the Conspiracy Swarm?" *The New York Times*, August 19: B1–B4.

Rose, E. S. (1993). "Surviving the Unbelievable: A First-Person Account of Cult Ritual Abuse." *Ms,* January/February: 40–5.

Rose, P. L. (1990). *Revolutionary Antisemitism in Germany from Kant to Wagner.* Princeton, NJ: Princeton University Press.

Rosica, T. (2015). "Why Is Pope Francis So Obsessed with the Devil?" *CNN*, July 20. https://www.cnn.com/2015/07/20/living/pope-francis-devil/index.html.

Ross, C. A. (1991). "Epidemiology of Multiple Personality Disorder and Dissociation." *Psychiatric Clinics of North America*, 14, 503–18.

Ross, C. A. (1998). "Evidence." See https://archive.org/details/EvidenceAgainstDr.Col inA.RossVol.1.

Ross, C. A. (2000). *Bluebird: Deliberate Creation of Multiple Personality by Psychiatrists.* Richardson, TX: Manitou Communications.

Ross, C. (2017). "Treatment Strategies for Programming and Ritual Abuse." *Journal of Trauma & Dissociation*, 18, 454–64.

Rowe, L., and Cavender, G. (1991). "Caldrons Bubble, Satan's Trouble, but Witches Are Okay: Media Constructions of Satanism and Witchcraft." In J. T. Richardson, J. Best, and D. Bromley (eds.), *The Satanism Scare* (pp. 263–76). New York: Aldine.

Roy, M. (ed.) (1977). *Battered Women: A Psychosociological Study of Domestic Violence.* New York: Van Nostrand Reinhold.

Ruane, N. J. (2013). *Sacrifice and Gender in Biblical Law.* Cambridge: Cambridge University Press.

Sachs, R. G. (1990). "The Role of Sex and Pregnancy in Satanic Cults." *Journal of Prenatal and Perinatal Psychology and Health*, 5, 105–14.

Sales, R. H. (1957). "Human Sacrifice in Biblical Thought." *Journal of Bible and Religion*, 25, 112–7.

Sarna, N. M. (1989). *The JPS Torah Commentary: Genesis.* Philadelphia, PA: JPS.

Sartre, J. P. (1967). *The Words.* Harmondsworth: Penguin.

Sasser, M. T. (2017). "The Binding of Isaac: Jewish and Christian Appropriations of the Akedah (Genesis 22) in Contemporary Picture Books." *Children's Literature*, 45, 138–63.

Schatz, J. (1991). *The Generation: The Rise and Fall of the Jewish Communists of Poland.* Berkeley: University of California Press.

Scheper-Hughes, N. (1992). *Death without Weeping: The Violence of Everyday Life in Brazil.* Berkeley: University of California Press.

Schlesinger, K. (1976). "Origins of the Passover Seder in Ritual Sacrifice." *The Psychoanalytic Study of Society*, 7, 369–99.

Schlossman, H. H. (1966). "Circumcision as Defense: a Study in Psychoanalysis and Religion." *The Psychoanalytic Quarterly*, 35, 340–56.

Schmuttermaier, J., and Veno, A. (1999). "Counselors' Beliefs about Ritual Abuse: An Australian Study." *Journal of Child Sexual Abuse*, 8, 45–63.

Schreiber, F. R. (1973). *Sybil: The True Story of a Woman Possessed by 16 Separate Personalities.* New York: Grand Central Publishing.

Schröder, J., Nick, S., Richter-Appelt, H., and Briken, P. (2020). "Demystifying Ritual Abuse-Insights by Self-Identified Victims and Health Care Professionals." *Journal of Trauma & Dissociation*, 21, 349–64.

Schultz, C. E. (2010). "The Romans and Ritual Murder." *Journal of the American Academy of Religion*, 78, 516–41.

Schultz, M. (1991). "The Blood Libel: A Motif in the History of Childhood." In A. Dundes (ed.), *The Blood Libel Legend: A Casebook in Anti-Semitic Folklore* (pp. 273–303). Madison, WI: The University of Wisconsin Press.

Schuster, D. B. (1970). "The Holy Communion: An Historical and Psychoanalytic Study." *The Bulletin of the Philadelphia Association for Psychoanalysis*, 20, 223–36.

Schwartz, G. M. (2013). "Memory and Its Demolition: Ancestors, Animals and Sacrifice at Umm el-Marra, Syria." *Cambridge Archaeological Journal*, 23, 495–522.

Schwartz, J. H., Houghton, F. D., Bondioli, L., and Macchiarelli, R. (2017). "Two Tales of One City: Data, Inference and Carthaginian Infant Sacrifice." *Antiquity*, 91, 442–54.

Scott, S., and Snelling, O. (1994). "Report on the Channel 4 Dispatches Documentary on Satanic Ritual Abuse 19 February 1992, and a Helpline after Transmission of the Programme." In V. Sinason (ed.), *Treating Survivors of Satanist Abuse* (pp. 70–89). London: Routledge.

Scrivner, C., 3Holbrook, C., Fessler, D. M., and Maestripieri, D. (2020). "Gruesomeness Conveys Formidability: Perpetrators of Gratuitously Grisly Acts Are Conceptualized as Larger, Stronger, and More Likely to Win." *Aggressive Behavior*, 46, 400–11.

Seeman, D. (2007). "Ritual Practice and Its Discontents." In C. de Conerly and R. B. Edgerton (eds.), *A Companion to Psychological Anthropology: Modernity and Psychocultural Change* (pp. 339–54). Hoboken, NJ: Wiley-Blackwell.

Sherwood, Y. (2004). "Binding–Unbinding: Divided Responses of Judaism, Christianity, and Islam to the 'Sacrifice' of Abraham's Beloved Son." *Journal of the American Academy of Religion*, 72, 821–61.

Shoemaker, S. J. (2008). "Epiphanius of Salamis, the Kollyridians, and the Early Dormition Narratives: The Cult of the Virgin in the Fourth Century." *Journal of Early Christian Studies*, 16, 371–401.

Shullenberger, G. (2010). "Analogies of the Sacrament in Sixteenth Century French and Spanish Ethnography: Jean de Léry and José de Acosta." *Romance Studies*, 28, 84–95.

Shulman, D. (1993). *The Hungry God: Hindu Tales of Filicide and Devotion*. Chicago, IL: University of Chicago Press.

Sigel, D. (2009). "Was Isaac Sacrificed in the End?" Reading Midrash in Elementary School." *Journal of Jewish Education*, 75, 47–78.

Simmel, E. (1946). "Anti-Semitism and Mass Psychopathology." In E. Simmel (ed.), *Anti-Semitism: A Social Disease*. New York: International Universities Press.

Simon, A., Hauari, H., Hollingworth, K., and Vorhaus, J. (2012). *A Rapid Literature Review of Evidence on Child Abuse Linked to Faith or Belief*. London: Childhood Wellbeing Research Centre.

Simpson, W. F. (1989). "Comparative Longevity in a College Cohort of Christian Scientists." *Journal of the American Medical Association*, 262, 1657–58.

Sinason, V. (1994a). Introduction. In V. Sinason (ed.), *Treating Survivors of Satanic Abuse*. London: Routledge.

Sinason, V. (ed.) (1994b). *Treating Survivors of Satanic Abuse*. London: Routledge.

Sinason, V. (ed.) (2011a). *Attachment, Trauma and Multiplicity: Working with Dissociative Identity Disorder* (2nd ed.). London: Routledge.

Sinason, V. (2011b). "What Has Changed in Twenty Years?" In O. Epstein, J. Schwartz, and R. Schwartz (eds.), *Ritual Abuse and Mind Control: The Manipulation of Attachment Needs* (pp. 1–37). London: Karnac Books.

Sinason, V., Galton, G., and Leevers, D. (2008). "Where Are We Now? Ritual Abuse, Dissociation, the Police and the Media." In R. Noblitt and P. Perskin-Noblitt (eds.), *Ritual Abuse in the Twenty First Century: Psychological, Forensic, Social and Political Considerations* (pp. 363–80). Bandon, OR: Robert Reed Publishers.

Singelenberg, R. (1999). "Comments on Rodney Stark's 'The Rise and Fall of Christian science." *Journal of Contemporary Religion*, 14, 127–32.

Ska, J. L. (ed.) (2009). "Essay on the Nature and Meaning of the Abraham Cycle (Gen 11, 29-25, 11)." In *The Exegesis of the Pentateuch: Exegetical Studies and Basic Questions* (pp. 23–45). Tübingen: Mohr Siebeck.

Ska, J. L. (2013). "Genesis 22: What Question Should We Ask the Text?" *Biblica*, 94, 257–67.

Smelser, N. J. (1962). *Theory of Collective Behavior*. London: Routledge & Kegan Paul.

Smith, M. (1975). "A Note on Burning Babies." *Journal of the American Oriental Society*, 95, 477–79.

Smith, M. (1993). *Ritual Abuse: What It Is, Why It Happens, How to Help*. London: Harper Collins.

Smith, M., and Pazder, L. (1980). *Michelle Remembers*. New York: Congdon & Lattes.

Smith, P., Avishai, G., Greene, J. A., and Stager, L. E. (2011). "Aging Cremated Infants: the Problem of Sacrifice at the Tophet of Carthage." *Antiquity*, 85, 859–74.

Snow, B., and Sorensen, L. (1990). "Ritualistic Child Abuse in a Neighborhood Setting." *Journal of Interpersonal Violence*, 5, 474–87.

Sokolowski, R. (1994). *Eucharistic Presence: A Study in the Theology of Disclosure*. Washington, DC: The Catholic University of America Press.

Spanos, N. P. (1996). *Multiple Identities & False Memories: A Sociocognitive Perspective*. Washington, DC: American Psychological Association.

Sparks, K. L. (2007). "'Enūma Elish' and Priestly Mimesis: Elite Emulation in Nascent Judaism." *Journal of Biblical Literature*, 126, 625–48.

Stacey, J. (1998). *Brave New Families: Stories of Domestic Upheaval in Late-Twentieth-Century America*. Berkeley, CA: University of California Press.

Stark, R. (1998). "The Rise and Fall of Christian Science." *Journal of Contemporary Religion*, 13, 189–214.

Staubli, T. (2015). "The 'Pagan' Prehistory of Genesis 22: 1–14: The Iconographic Background of the Redemption of a Human Sacrifice." In I. J. De Hulster, B. A. Strawn, and R. P. Bonfiglio (eds.), *Iconographic Exegesis of the Hebrew Bible/Old Testament: An Introduction to its Method and Practice* (pp. 77–102). Göttingen: Vandenhoeck & Ruprecht.

Stavropoulos, F. (2004). *King Manasseh and Child Sacrifice: Biblical Distortions of Historical Realities.* Berlin: de Gruyter.

Stein, C. H., Abraham, K. M., Bonar, E. E., McAuliffe, C. E., Fogo, W. R., Faigin, D. A., Abu Raiya, H., and Potokar, D. N. (2009). "Making Meaning from Personal Loss: Religious, Benefit Finding, and Goal-Oriented Attributions." *Journal of Loss and Trauma*, 14, 83–100.

Steinem, G. (1993). *Revolution from Within: A Book of Self-Esteem.* New York: Little, Brown.

Stern, E. (2003). "The Phoenician Source of Palestinian Cults at the End of the Iron Age." In W. G. Dever and S. Gitin (eds.), *Symbiosis, Symbolism, and the Power of the Past: Canaan, Ancient Israel, and Their Neighbors, from the Late Bronze Age through Roman Palaestina* (pp. 309–22). Winona Lake, IN: Eisenbrauns.

Stern, E. (2021). "The Religious Revolution in Persian-Period Judah." In O. Lipschits and M. Oeming (eds.), *Judah and the Judeans in the Persian Period* (pp. 199–206). Winona Lake, IN: Eisenbrauns.

Storr, W. (2011). "The Mystery of Carole Myers." *The Guardian*, December 10. http://www.theguardian.com/society/2011/dec/11/carole-myers-satanic-child-abuse.

Strenski, I. (2003). "Sacrifice, Gift and the Social Logic of Muslim 'Human Bombers.'" *Terrorism and Political Violence*, 15, 1–34.

Strieber, W. (1987). *Communion: A True Story.* New York: Avon.

Stroumsa, G. G. (2004). "Christ's Laughter: Docetic Origins Reconsidered." *Journal of Early Christian Studies*, 12, 267–88.

Stroumsa, G. G. (2008). "Sacrifice and Martyrdom in the Roman Empire." *Archivio di Filosofia*, 76, 145–54.

Stroumsa, G. G. (2009). *The End of Sacrifice: Religious Transformations in Late Antiquity.* Chicago, IL: University of Chicago Press.

Stroumsa, G. G. (2015). *The Making of the Abrahamic Religions in Late Antiquity.* Oxford: Oxford University Press.

Swenson, E. (2014). "Dramas of the Dialectic: Sacrifice and Power in Ancient Polities." In R. B. Campbell (ed.), *Violence and Civilization: Studies of Social Violence in History and Prehistory* (pp. 28–60). Oxford: Oxbow.

Swetnam, J. (1981). *Jesus and Isaac: A Study of the Epistle to the Hebrews in the Light of the Aqedah.* Rome: Biblical Institute Press.

Tamney, J. B., and Johnson, S. D. (1998). "The Popularity of Strict Churches." *Review of Religious Research*, 209–23.

Tannahill, R. (1975). *Flesh and Blood: A History of the Cannibal Complex.* New York: Stein and Day.

Tate, T. (1991). *Children for the Devil: Ritual Abuse and Satanic Crime*. London: Methuen.
Tatlock, J. (2006). How in Ancient Times They Sacrificed People: Human Immolation in the Eastern Mediterranean Basin with Special Emphasis on Ancient Israel and the Near East. PhD dissertation, The University of Michigan.
Tatlock, J. (2019). "Human Sacrifice and Propaganda in Popular Media: More Than Morbid Curiosity." *Dialogue: The Interdisciplinary Journal of Popular Culture and Pedagogy*, 6, 43–59.
Temrin, H., Buchmayer, S., and Enquist, M. (2000). "Step-Parents and Infanticide: New Data Contradict Evolutionary Predictions." *Proceedings of the Royal Society of London. Series B: Biological Sciences*, 267, 943–5.
Terhune, C. (1997). "Cultural and Religious Defenses to Child Abuse and Neglect." *Journal of the American Academy of Matrimonial Lawyers*, 14, 152–92.
Test, E. M. (2011). "A Dish Fit for the Gods": Mexica Sacrifice in De Bry, Las Casas, and Shakespeare's Julius Caesar." *Journal of Medieval and Early Modern Studies*, 41, 93–115.
Teter, M. (2020). *Blood Libel: On the Trail of an Antisemitic Myth*. Cambridge, MA: Harvard University Press.
Thigpen, C. H., and Cleckley, H. M. (1984). "On the Incidence of Multiple Personality Disorder: A Brief Communication." *International Journal of Clinical and Experimental Hypnosis*, 32, 63.
Thomas, D. E. (2005). *African Traditional Religion in the Modern World*. Jefferson, NC: McFarland.
Thompson, S. (1955). *Motif-index of Folk-Literature: A Classification of Narrative Elements in Folktales, Ballads, Myths, Fables, Mediaeval Romances, Exempla, Fabliaux, Jest-books, and Local Legends*. Bloomington, IN: Indiana University Press.
Tiverios, M. (2014). "Phrixos' Self-Sacrifice and His 'Euphemia.'" In A. Avramidou and D. Demetriou (eds.), *Approaching the Ancient Artifact: Representation, Narrative, and Function* (pp. 105–16). Berlin: Walter de Gruyter.
Toczek, N. (2015). *Haters, Baiters and Would-Be Dictators: Anti-Semitism and the UK Far Right*. London: Routledge.
Trachtenberg, J. (1966). *The Devil and the Jews: A Medieval Conception of the Jew and Its Relation to Modern Antisemitism*. New York: Harper & Row.
Travis, T. (2009). *The Language of the Heart: A Cultural History of the Recovery Movement from Alcoholics Anonymous to Oprah Winfrey*. Chapel Hill: University of North Carolina Press.
Tucker, A. (1999). "Sins of Our Fathers: A Short History of Religious Child Sacrifice." *Zeitschrift für Religions-und Geistesgeschichte*, 51, 30–47.
Turina, I. (2011). "Consecrated Virgins in Italy: A Case Study in the Renovation of Catholic Religious Life." *Journal of Contemporary Religion*, 26, 43–55.
Twitchell, J. (1985). *Dreadful Pleasures: An Anatomy of Modern Horror*. New York: Oxford University Press.

Tylor, E. B. (1871). *Primitive Culture: Researches into the Development of Mythology, Philosophy, Religion, Art and Custom*. London: John Murray.

Ullucci, D. (2015). "Sacrifice in the Ancient Mediterranean: Recent and Current Research." *Currents in Biblical Research*, 13, 388–439.

Ulreich, J. C. (2009). "Isaac as the Lamb of God: A Hermeneutic Crux in the Re-Reading of Jewish Texts." In R. S. Sabbath (ed.), *Sacred Tropes: Tanakh, New Testament, and Qur'an as Literature and Culture* (pp. 421–34). Leiden: Brill.

Urban, H. B. (2015). "The Branch Davidians: Millenarian Movements, Religious Freedom, and Privacy." In *New Age, Neopagan, and New Religious Movements* (pp. 265–80). Berkeley: University of California Press.

Uttley, R. M. (1993). *The Lance and the Shield: The Life and Times of Sitting Bull*. New York: Henry Holt.

Vandiver, E. (2012). "'Strangers Are from Zeus': Homeric Xenia at the Courts of Proteus and Croesus." In E. Baragwanath and M. de Bakker (eds.), *Myth, Truth and Narrative in Herodotus* (pp. 143–66). Oxford: Oxford University Press.

Van Seters, J. (2003). "From Child Sacrifice to Paschal Lamb: A Remarkable Transformation in Israelite Religion." *Old Testament Essays*, 16, 453–63.

Vilaça, A. (2000). "Relations Between Funerary Cannibalism and Warfare Cannibalism: the Question of Predation." *Ethnos*, 65, 83–106.

Wajdenbaum, P. (2010). "Is the Bible a Platonic Book?" *Scandinavian Journal of the Old Testament*, 24, 129–42.

Walsh, M. J., Moen, M., O'Neill, S., Gullbekk, S. H., and Willerslev, R. (2020). "Who's Afraid of the S-Word? Deviants' Burials and Human Sacrifice." *Norwegian Archaeological Review*, 53, 154–62.

Warner, M. (2017). "Back to the Future: Reading the Abraham Narratives as Prequel." *Biblical Interpretation*, 25, 479–96.

Watts, J. (2011). "The Rhetoric of Sacrifice." In C. Eberhart (ed.), *Ritual and Metaphor: Sacrifice in the Bible* (pp. 3–16). Atlanta, GA: Society of Biblical Literature.

Watts, J., Sheehan, O., Atkinson, Q. D., Bulbulia, J., and Gray, R. D. (2016). "Ritual Human Sacrifice Promoted and Sustained the Evolution of Stratified Societies." *Nature*, 532 (7598), 228–31.

Wax, A. (2021). "Snuff: The Biggest Myth in Film: It's Time to Demystify This Scare Tactic." https://www.fangoria.com/original/snuff-the-biggest-myth-in-film/

Weber, J. A. (2012). "Restoring Order: Death, Display, and Authority." In A. M. Porter and G. M. Schwartz (eds.), *Sacred Killing: The Archaeology of Sacrifice in the Ancient Near East* (pp. 159–90). Winona Lake, IN: Eisenbrauns.

Weber, M. (1920/1993). *The Sociology of Religion*. Boston, MA: Beacon Press.

Weddle, C. (2013). "The Sensory Experience of Blood Sacrifice in the Roman Imperial Cult." *Making Senses of the Past: Toward a Sensory Archaeology*, 40, 137–59.

Weekes-Shackelford, V. A., and Shackelford, T. K. (2004). "Methods of Filicide: Stepparents and Genetic Parents Kill Differently." *Violence and Victims*, 19, 75–81.

Weiler, G. (2007). "Human Sacrifice in Greek Culture." In K. Finsterbusch, A. Lange, and K. F. Diethard Römheld (eds.), *Human Sacrifice in Jewish and Christian Tradition* (pp. 35–64). Leiden: Brill.

Weiss, C. (1966). "Motives for Male Circumcision among Preliterate and Literate Peoples. *Journal of Sex Research*, 2, 69–88.

Werbner, P. (2015). "Sacrifice, Purification and Gender in the Hajj: Personhood, Metonymy, and Ritual Transformation. In L. Mols and M. Buitelaar (eds.), *Hajj. Global Interactions through Pilgrimage* (pp. 27–39). Leiden: Sidestone Press.

Werlein, E., Jr. (1999). United States of America v. Judith A. Peterson, et al., Crim. No. H-97-237, U.S. Dist. Ct., So. Dist. Texas, Houston Div. https://law.justia.com/cases/federal/district-courts/FSupp2/71/695/2515367/.

West, A. M., and Hill, V. (1995). *Out of the Shadows: Fred West's Daughter Tells Her Harrowing Story of Survival*, London: Hodder & Stoughton.

West, S. G., and Feldsher, M. (2010). "Parricide: Characteristics of Sons and Daughters Who Kill Their Parents." *Current Psychiatry*, 9, 20–38.

White, A. D. (1896/1993). *A History of the Warfare of Science with Theology in Christendom*. Buffalo, NY: Prometheus Books.

Wilbur, C. B. (1984). "Multiple Personality and Child Abuse: An Overview." *Psychiatric Clinics of North America*, 7, 3–7.

Wilkomirski, B. (1996). *Fragments. Memories of a Wartime Childhood*. New York: Schocken Books.

Wilks, I. (1975). *Asante in the Nineteenth Century: The Structure and Evolution of a Political Order*. Cambridge: Cambridge University Press.

Willerslev, R. (2009). "The Optimal Sacrifice: A Study of Voluntary Death among the Siberian Chukchi." *American Ethnologist*, 36, 693–704.

Williams, P. R. (1968). A Commentary to Philo Byblius "Phoenician History." PhD thesis, University of Southern California.

Wilson, G. E. (1956). "Christian Science and Longevity." *Journal of Forensic Sciences*, 1, 43–60.

Winkelman, M. (2014). "Political and Demographic-Ecological Determinants of Institutionalised Human Sacrifice." *Anthropological Forum*, 24, 47–70.

Woodrow, J. C. (2011). *Rose West: The Making of a Monster*. London: Hodder & Stoughton.

Woolley, C. L. (1934). *The Royal Cemetery: A Report on the Predynastic and Sargonid Graves Excavated between 1926 and 1931*. Oxford: Oxford University Press.

Woolley, S. (2005). "Children of Jehovah's Witnesses and Adolescent Jehovah's Witnesses: What Are Their Rights?" *Archives of Disease in Childhood*, 90, 715–19.

Wortzman, H. (2008). "Jewish Women in Ancient Synagogues: Archeological Reality vs. Rabbinical Legislation." *Women in Judaism: A Multidisciplinary e-Journal*, 5, 1–17.

Wrangham, R. (2019). *The Goodness Paradox: The Strange Relationship between Virtue and Violence in Human Evolution*. New York: Pantheon.

Wright, L. (1994). *Remembering Satan*. New York: Alfred A. Knopf.

Wunn, I., and Grojnowski, D. (2016). *Ancestors, Territoriality, and Gods.* Berlin: Springer.

Wyatt, N. (2009). "Circumcision and Circumstance: Male Genital Mutilation in Ancient Israel and Ugarit." *Journal for the Study of the Old Testament*, 33, 405–31.

Xella, P. (2017). "Pourquoi tous ces enfants? Quelques réflexions sur les sanctuaires infantiles à incinération de tradition phénicienne («tophet»). Pallas." *Revue d'études antiques*, 104, 345–57.

Yapko, M. D. (1994). *Suggestions of Abuse: True and False Memories of Childhood Sexual Trauma.* New York: Simon & Schuster.

Yasumi, K., and Kageyama, J. (2009). "Filicide and Fatal Abuse in Japan, 1994–2005: Temporal Trends and Regional Distribution." *Journal of Forensic and Legal Medicine*, 16, 70–5.

Young, W. C., Sachs, R. G., Braun, B. G., and Watkins, R. T. (1991). "Patients Reporting Ritual Abuse in Childhood: A Clinical Syndrome. Report of 37 Cases." *Child Abuse and Neglect*, 15, 181–90.

Yuval, I. J. (2008). *Two Nations in Your Womb: Perceptions of Jews and Christians in Late Antiquity and the Middle Ages.* Berkeley: University of California Press.

Zatelli, I. (1998). "The Origin of the Biblical Scapegoat Ritual: the Evidence of Two Eblaite Texts. *Vetus Testamentum*, 48, 254–63.

Zivkovic, T. M. (2014). "Consuming the Lama: Transformations of Tibetan Buddhist Bodies." *Body & Society*, 20, 111–32.

Index

abductees 67
Abraham 1, 4, 87, 143, 152–5, 168
  animal sacrifice 131
  bound son of 106
  condemnation in Satanism 95
  covenants 153
  descendants of 127, 139, 151, 163
  faith and decision 147
  family of origin 151
  Genesis 22 163
  grandson Jacob 152
  miracle of 143
  monotheistic revolution 161
  motivation 142
  readiness to sacrifice 130
  reference in Gen. 21:8-21 146
  reference in Gen. 22:1-19 140
  reference in Genesis 22 169
  religious myth 91
  sacrifice of his son Ishmael 86, 145, 154, 172
  sacrifice of sons Moses and Aaron 80, 154
  self circumcision of 122, 132, 148, 154
academic psychology 15, 18, 210
accusation 131–2
  child abuse 33
  of child sacrifice and cannibalism 84
  dismissal of 213–14
  of Jews 83, 89
  against minority outsiders 205
  ritual-murder 78
  Satanism 37, 49, 74, 78, 85, 209
  witchcraft 73, 75–6, 137, 205
Achilles 125, 128
Adamczewski, B. 149
Adamski, George 66
Aeschylus 122, 125
Agamemnon 123, 125, 127
Agathocles of Syracuse 119
Akiki, Dale 37
Al-Dawalibi, Ma'aruf 82

aliens 67, 90
Alkis 120
altruism 100, 183
Ammonites 126, 131
Anaxibia 126
Androkleia 120
Andromeda 120, 132
animal mutilation 30, 38, 42
animal sacrifice 33, 38, 87, 102, 104, 106, 141–2, 174, 182
animism 12, 20
Anobret 122
Antipoinos 120
antiquity 58, 78, 80, 85–6, 102, 168, 184
anti-Semitism 25, 78–81, 191
anxieties 16, 57–8, 61, 87, 90, 93, 214–15
Applewhite, M. 188
aquifer hypothesis 76
Archelaus 126
archeological finds 160
Argonauts 121
Asser, S. M. 200
Athamas 120–2, 130, 131, 152–5
atheist intellectuals 22
atoning blood of Christ 182
Aun (King) 111
autochthonous Canaanites 158
Aztecs 91, 112, 115

Babylonia 150
Baez, Joan 48
Barnes, R. H. 109
Battered Women: A Psychosociological Study of Domestic Violence (Roy) 27
Becker, Ernest 182
Beilis, Mendel 81
beliefs
  about end of life/world 9
  Catholic 177
  desires and 149
  historical legacy of 96
  imaginary religions 31

imaginations and 3
in immortality 10
para-religious 66
religious 4, 19–21, 40, 64–6, 115, 178, 181, 201
religious rituals and 8
Ben-Zvi, E. 149
Bergmann, M. S. 196–7
Bergsma, J. S. 134
Bettelheim, B. 68
Beyond the Pleasure Principle (Freud) 27
Biblical ban *(Herem)* 134
Bicknell, Jean 74
Biden, Joseph R. 55
Bikel, Ofra 63
Binding
  appearance of Jewishness and 156–62
  to Christian 144
  dating and motives 148–52
  father–child dynamic 145
  of Isaac 139, 140–8
  of Ishmael 171–2
  of Jesus 163–7
  to Jewish 144
  narrative of 139, 144
  video game 144
Black, J. 101
Black Mass fantasy 74
Blood Covenant 187
blood drinking 58, 74–5, 84, 88–9
Blood Libel 73, 75, 78–83, 84–5
Blood of Christ 167
blood rituals 7
blood sacrifices 101, 148, 167–71
Bottoms, B. L. 30
brainwashing 25
Braun, Bennet G. 29–30, 34, 41, 43–4, 48, 51, 57, 68–9, 84, 135
Bremmer, J. N. 119, 121, 137
Breuer, Josef 46
Bromley, David 60
The Brothers Karamazov (Dostoevsky) 80
Brown, D. E. 205
Buddhism 4, 8, 101, 104, 211
Burgus, Pat 67
Burgus, Patricia 44, 50
burials 10, 11, 132
Burkert, Walter 105–6
Byington, Judy 52–3

cabalism 25
Cadmus 120
cannibalism 31, 46, 74, 75, 136–7, 178, 180
Cannibalistic fantasies 178
Cargo Cults 8
Carter, E. 109
Casas, Bartolome de Las 181
Cassiopeia 120
castration 188–9
catechism 175
Catholicism 80, 82, 175, 177, 179
Cepheus, King 120
Cercaphus 126
Cetus 120
Cevasco, C. 180
Chemosh 129
child abuse 27, 33, 42, 48–9, 53, 198–9, 211
child as victim 95–7
childhood
  abuse 30
  experiences 17, 204
  fantasies 17
  fears and nightmares 13
  histories 63
  in-group favoritism 9
  traumas 27, 29
  unfulfilled desires 16
child of promise 165
child sacrifice 2–3, 75, 87–97, 118, 131, 208–11
  archeological evidence of 134
  as atonement offering 133
  child as victim 95–7
  commands 133
  condemnations of 142
  fantasies 5, 187–8
  fantasy 95–7, 110–12
  individual response level 89–95
  Israelites 134
  justification of 180
  narratives 131–2
  reality and fantasy 95–7
  in West Asia 118
child sexual abuse 43
Christianity 2, 4, 7–8, 74, 85, 88, 166–8, 174
Christian myth 169
Christian theology 166

circumcision
  anti-semitism and 191
  ceremony in Rome 189
  as form of sacrifice represents 188
  Jewish ritual 189–90
Civilization and Its Discontents (Freud) 20
Cleckley, H. M. 29
clinical hypnosis 25
Clinton, Hillary 55
cognitive skills 11–12
Colchis (Georgia) 121
collective memory 3
conflict
  father–son 131
  intergenerational 215
  intrafamily 77
  Oedipal 145, 195
  psychological 196
  sexual identity 189
conscious identity 1
conscious message 13
conspiracy therapists 53
Constanzo, Adolfo 33
contacts and spirits 8–10
cooperation 99–100
Council of Trent 175
Covenant Blood 189
Creon 119
Crete 128
Crucifixion 167
Cult Programming 26
cultures 4–5, 8, 118
  blood shedding 101
  Greek and Roman 185
  Mediterranean 102
  West Asian pastoral 104

Dalai Lama 55
Damascus 82
Damascus Affair 80
dating and motives 148–52
Daumer, Georg Friedrich 80
David (King) 3–4, 129–30, 131
Davis, S. L. 30
dead
  investment in future of 11
Dead Sea 134
death 79, 162
  Christianity and 79

denial of 10
firstborn sacrifice and 162
reality of 18
threats 24, 26
unnatural 137
DeGeneres, Ellen 55
de hulster, I. J. 160
Delphian oracle 120
DeMeo, J. 187
de Montaigne, Michel 189
Demophon, King 119
demystification 17–18
denunciations of Canaanites 158
Der Feuer- und Molochdienst der alten Hebräer (Daumer) 80
Devil Worship: Exposing Satan's Underground (Rivera) 61
devotion 188–9
de Waal, F. 183
Die Menschenopfer der alten Hebräer (Ghillany) 80
Die Phoenizier (Movers) 80
dissociative disorders 28
Dissociative Identity Disorder (DID) 29, 43
Divided Memories (Bikel) 63
divine mercy 154
Donovan, D. M. 197
Dössekker, Bruno 62
Dostoevsky, F. 80
Douglas, Alfred 82
Douglas, M. 100, 137, 178–9
Dulles, Allen 24
Dundes, A. 83
Durkheim, Emile 9

Egyptian pharaohs 109
The Elementary Forms of the Religious Life (Durkheim) 9
Eleusis 119
Elisha 128
elite writings 160
el-Marra, Umm 107
Elos 122
Enlightenment 15, 17, 20, 82
Epiphanius of Salamis 128
Erechtheus 119
Eucharist 173–6, 179
  in Catholicism 175
  similar rituals 184–6

Eurystheus, King 119
Eusebius 122
exile 121, 128, 134, 150–1, 157
existential insecurity hypothesis 5
Exodus 3, 156
exquisite mental torture 147
externalization 15, 19

false consciousness 20
fantasies 99–116
   about afterlife 8
   about spirits and contacts 8–10
   child sacrifice 5, 95–7, 110–12
   dreams of purity 112–16
   human sacrifice as a necessity 110
   politics and human sacrifice 107–9
   reality of human sacrifice 106–7
father's double culpability 131–2
father–son conflict 131
Federal Bureau of Investigation (FBI) 32
feminism 45–8
filicide 197–9
Finkelstein, I. 149
firstborn formula 118
firstborn reversal 155–6
firstborn sacrifice 134–5, 154, 162
first-person accounts 37–8
First World War 18
Firth, Raymond 72–3
foreign gods 134
Fortes, Meyer 101, 182, 183, 201
Fourth Lateran Council 174
Fox, Ronald 26, 183
Frank, Jacob 80
Frankfurter, David 58, 78, 89, 114
Frazer, James George 82, 121, 186
Frederick II (Roman Emperor) 79
Freeman, Derek 183
Freeman, H. 200
Freud, Sigmund 9–1, 15–16, 20, 22, 27, 46, 68, 71, 87, 181–5, 186, 188, 191, 201
   fantasies 72
   impatience 21–2
   subjective relief 20
   on truth claims 21
   writings of 16–18
Friend-of-a Friend (FOAF) 37
Fromm-Reichmann, Frieda 68

F Scale questionnaire 59
The Future of an Illusion (Freud) 20

Gale, Elizabeth 44, 50, 67
Gallarreta, Balcells 160
Garnand, B. K. 137
generalizations 214–16
genital mutilation 96, 187–8
Ghillany, F. W. 80
Gibson, S. 147
Gnuse 127
Gonzalez, H. 149
Goodman, G. S. 33
Goodwin, J. 29
Gorky, Maxim 80
Gospels 79, 164
gratification 35, 54, 89–90, 92–3
grave goods 109
Greaves, George 45
Greek and Roman cultures 185
Green, A. 101
Grotstein, J. S. 178
group loyalty 9, 139, 159
group of Wendat (Huron) 180
gruesome violence 108
Grünbaum, A. 184

Hacking, Ian 43, 53–4, 87, 92, 94
Hagar 146–8
Hahn, S. W. 134
Hammond, D. Corydon 23–6, 34, 44, 51
Hanks, Tom 55
Harding, S. F. 166
Hart, Roma E. 52
Hassidic Jews 105
headhunters 57
Hebrew Bible 4–5, 58, 121, 129, 130, 132, 134–7, 140, 145, 149, 152, 156, 158, 161, 163, 168
Helle 120–1
Hendrickson, K. M. 29
henotheism 131
Heracles/Herakles 119–20
hidden holocaust 26
Hill, Jenny 52–3
Hindu 143, 179
Hinduism 4, 8
Hittite 148
homosexuality 82

Hughes, D. D. 136
human animism 20
human sacrifice 58, 75
   Andromeda 120
   Athamas 120-2
   colonial encounter 179-81
   control nature and human threats through 130
   David 129-30
   distinguished citizen 120
   Greek case 136-8
   historicity question 132-6
   Idomeneus 128
   Indian mythology 142
   Jephthah 126-8
   Jonah 123-5
   justification of 180
   King 119-20
   Mesha 128-9
   as necessity 110
   Phoenician 118-19, 122
   politics and 107-9
   reality of 106-7
   Saul 129-30
   virgins 119-20
   in West Asia 117-38
human victim 148
Humphrey, N. K. 11
Hurston, Z. N. 106
Hyacinthus 120

identity 208
Idomeneo 128
Idomeneus 128
Idumea 150
Ieoud 122
imaginary religion 23-55
   feminism 45-8
   first-person accounts 37-8
   Satanism 35-7, 38-9, 45-8
immortality 10-11, 18-19, 186, 208
impatience 21-2
Inca empire 112-13
individualism 59, 66
infancy 16, 47
infanticidal impulse 195-7
infanticide and religion 200
Ingram, Ericka 49
Ingram, Julie 49

Ingram, Paul 49-50
Ingram, Sandy 49
Innocence Lost: The Plea (Bikel) 63
Innocence Lost: The Verdict (Bikel) 63
Innocent IV (Pope) 79
Ino 120
internalization 15
International Society for the Study of Multiple Personality and Dissociation (ISSMPD) 29, 45
International Society for the Study of Trauma and Dissociation (ISSTD) 53
interpreting religion 11-13. *See also* religion
interpreting theophagy 178-9
Iphigeneia 123, 125-7
Isaac-Ishmael-Jesus story 172
Ishmael 5, 146-8
Islam 4, 7-8
Italicus, Silius 118

Jackson, Shirley 77
Jacob-Israel 152
Jacob story cycle 152
Jalahma, Umaya 82
Japan 124
Jehovah 130
Jephthah 126-8, 130-1, 134, 135, 170
Jesus Christ 1, 4-5, 101
Jewish circumcision ritual 189-90
Jewishness 156-62
Jews 78-85, 89, 106, 158-9, 189, 193-4
Johnson, A. W. 205
Jonah 123-5, 131, 134
Judaic culture 135
Judaic identity 151
Judaism 4, 78, 84, 88, 166, 174

Kanner, L. 68
Kansa, S. W. 107
Kaufmann, W. 147
Kiev, A. 104-5
kingdom of priests 161
King James Bible 4
King Lear (Edmund) 145
Kipling, Rudyard 72
Kluckhohn, C. 204
Kluft, Richard 84
Knauft, B. M. 73

Kodros, King 119–20
Korbin, J. E. 198
Koresh, David 58
Kosmon Era 4–5
Kott, J. 179
Kroeber, A. L. 182, 183
Kronos 122, 130, 132
Kronos Phoenician template 154

La Fontaine, J. S. 42, 77
Laius 119
Lanning, K. V. 49, 214
Laungani, P. 102
Lawrence, D. H. 180
Learchus 121
Leos 120
Lessing, Doris 32, 94
Levi, Raphael 79
Lindsey, Hal 66
Lipschits, O. 149
Little Red Riding Hood 178
Loeb, E. M. 192
Lombaard, C. 149
Lorenz, Konrad 91
"The Lottery" (Jackson) 77
loving daughter 125–6

Macaria 119
MacKinnon, Catharine 48
Maeander 126
Mahabharata 135
Marx, Karl 15, 19
Mason, Shirley 28
mass beliefs 160. *See also* beliefs
The Matza of Zion (Tlass) 83
McCarty, T. 29
McHugh, Paul 30
Mead, M. 183
Mecca 171
Meda 128
media 61–4
Melicertes 121
Melito of Sardis 163
Melville, Herman 180
memory enhancement 28
memory work 27
Mencken, H. L. 66
Menelaus 123
Menoeceus 119

Mesha 128–9, 131
Mesopotamia 117, 151
Mesopotamian art 118, 141
Michelle Remembers (Smith and Pazder) 34
Middle Ages 73, 81, 84, 102, 192, 196
Middle Paleolithic in West Asia 10
Miguel, E. 73
mind control 25, 75
Mithras religion 185
Moab 129
Moloch 72
moral panic 57
Mormonism 4
Moses 4, 19, 80, 88, 141, 151, 190, 197, 201, 211
Moses and Monotheism (Freud) 19
Moslems 65, 78, 82, 101, 139
Mount Laphystion 120
Movers, F. C. 80
Mozart 128
Mulhern, S. 33
Multiple Personalities: The Search for Deadly Memories (Steinem) 48
multiple personality 34
Multiple Personality Disorder (MPD) 26, 29, 47
Muslims 143, 171–2
al-Muttalib, 'Abd 172
My Life on the Road (Steinem) 48
mythical sacrifice 173–8
myth/mythologies 3, 85
  Biblical 4
  Christian 4, 169, 182
  Crucifixion 2, 174
  Exodus 159
  impersonal 90
  infantocentric 96
  Ishmael 2

Near-Death Experiences (NDEs) 63
Nephele 120
Nereids 120
New Bible 4
Newbrough, John Ballou 4
New Testament 4–5, 132, 135, 149–50, 155, 161, 163, 173
Niditch, S. 134
Noll, Richard 45

nonacademic psychoanalysis 15
Norse mythology 137
North America 32
Nunberg, H. 189

Oates, J. C. 145
Obama, Barack 55
obedience 139, 161
Oberman, M. 198
objectification 15
objective stress 60
Oedipal mythology 85
Oedipal paradox 201–6
Oedipal triumph 202
Oedipus complex 119, 205
O'Flaherty, W. D. 179
On the Jews and Their Lies 79
Oprah Winfrey Show 62
oracle of Delphi 120. *See also* Delphian oracle
Orkhomenos 120
Orpheus 120
Orthodox Jewish 116
Orthodox Judaism 104
Ouranos 122
Owen, Wilfred 144–5

Palestine Exploration Fund (PEF) 4
Palestine War 82
Palo Mayombe 33
Panarion 128
paranormal beliefs 8. *See also* beliefs
parental hostility and cruelty 72
parental insecurity 60–1
parents' ultimate responsibility 211–12
Parker, R. 136
Parsons, Talcott 20–1
Passover sacrifice 135, 167
Pazder, Lawrence 34
Pepper, S. C. 12
Perseus 120
Persian-Hellenistic era 157
Pessinuntines 126
pharmakos 77
phenomenon of religion 7–8
Philo Byblius 122
Phoenician 122
Phoenician child sacrifice 118–19
Phrixos 120–1

Piaget, Jean 17, 22
Polin, Vicki 62
Polish Roman Catholic 80
politics and human sacrifice 107–9
Polyxena 123, 128
Pongratz-Leisten, B. 109
Pope Francis 55, 65
Pope Gregory IX 74
Poseidon 120, 128
Poznanski, Elva 44
practices evident 160
Praeparatio Evangelica (Eusebius) 122
Praxithea, Queen 119
Price-Williams, D. R. 205
primal crime 181, 183–4
primal horde 183
Prince of Darkness 71
psychoanalytic theory 93
psychologists 11, 20, 26, 32, 55
psychotherapists 7, 30, 33, 35–6, 38, 61, 66, 68, 207
psychotherapy 27, 29–31, 43, 51, 68–9
public sacrifice 130
"Punica" 118
Punt, J. 89
purity in fantasy 112–16

QAnon 55

Rabbinic Judaism 174
Rais, Gilles de 74
Razin, Stenka 123
reality
    child sacrifice 95–7
    of human sacrifice 106–7
reciprocity 100
recovered memory 28, 30
recovered memory therapy (RMT) 27, 33
Reik, T. 143, 190
religion 7–13
    academic psychology of 18
    defined 13
    as false consciousness 20
    fantasies about spirits and contacts 8–10
    before interpretation 13
    interpreting 11–13
    phenomenon 7–8
    sociology of 159
    universals in 10–11

religious apologists 17
religious beliefs 19–21, 64–6
religious fears and dreams 214–16
religious ideation 19
religious praxis 8–9
religious rituals 8, 72
religious salvation 20
religious texts 3, 5
repressed abuse 30
repressed memory 51
Resurrection 167
Revolution from Within: A Book of Self-Esteem (Steinem) 45–6, 48
Rinpoche, Bokar 184
rituals 184–6
  abuse 23–4, 35, 76
  infanticide 88
  killing 77, 107
  violence 109
Rivera, Geraldo 61–2, 63
Rives, J. 136
Roman Catholic Church 101
Römer, T. 127, 149
Ross, Colin 43, 51–2
Roy, M. 27

Sachs, Roberta 44
sacred killing 106, 118
sacrifice, defined 101
sacrifice narratives 5
sacrifice of distress 167
sacrificial-cannibalistic complex 134
Samaria 150
Santa Claus 9
Sartre, J. P. 21
Satanic churches 40
Satanic Conspiracy 58
Satanic cults 50
Satanic Ritual Abuse (SRA) 26, 29, 32, 35
Satanic sacrifice 13, 86
Satan Is Alive and Well on Planet Earth (Lindsey) 66
Satanism 35–7, 38–9, 45–8
  special powers 75
  stories 38–9
  victims of 49–55
Satanism Craze 5, 27, 57–69
  individualism 66

media 61–4
objective stress 60
parental insecurity 60–1
religious beliefs 64–6
Satanism fantasies 64–6
secularization 66
testimonies 66–9
therapists 66–9
Satanism fantasies 64–6
Satanism narratives 71–86
  antiquity 85–6
  Blood Libel 78–83
  psychological origins 83–5
  witchcraft 72–7
Satanists 26, 41, 43, 75
  blood-drinking 84
  Blood Libel 85
  cannibalism 178
  goat-sacrificing 94
  intergenerational network 29
Satan's Underground: The Extraordinary Story of One Woman's Escape (Willson) 62
Saul, King 129–30, 131
scapegoating 10, 73, 75, 77, 91
Scheper-Hughes, N. 198
Schlesinger 192, 196
Schlossman, H. H. 192
Schreiber, F. R. 28
Schreiner, Olive 123
Schultz, M. 78
Schuster, D. B. 182
scribal elite 160
scriptures 3–5, 40
The Search for Satan (Bikel) 63
Second World War 81
secularization 66
Selden, Johannis 80
self-castration 188
self-esteem 2, 10, 22, 48, 150
shockingly violent fantasy 171
Siculus, Diodorus 119
Sigel, D. 144
Simmel, E. 83
Sinason, Valerie 35, 38, 52, 93–4
Singh, R. R. 189
Sioux Sun Dance 101
Sizemore, Chris Costner 28
Ska, J. L. 142, 149

Smith, Joseph 4
Smith, Michelle 20, 34, 95
smooth sailing 125–6
social problems 57, 61
Society for Psychical Research 8
sociology of religion 159
Solomon 3
Sophocles 122
Soros, George 55
spirits and contacts 8–10
Staubli, T. 5, 117, 135, 140
Steinem, Gloria 45–8
Stop Mind Control and Ritual Abuse Today (S.M.A.R.T.) 53
substitution hypothesis 192–4
Swan, R. 200
Syria 117

Tatlock, J. 135, 179
telepathy 25
Tell en-Nasbeh 160
Ten Commandments 53
testimonies 66–9
Theban citizen 120
Thebes 119
theophagy 178–9
therapists 26–8, 30–1, 36, 66–9
Thigpen, C. H. 29
Third World 8
Thomas of Monmouth 79
Thompson, S. 110, 126
Thyestes 111
Tlass, Mustafa 83
Totem and Taboo (Freud) 18, 181, 183
totem feast 182
totemic meal 182
trauma 27–30, 51, 53, 66, 144, 151
traumatists 27
Trump, Donald 55
truth claims 20–1
Twitchell, J 90
Tylor, E. B. 76

Ulreich, J. C. 166
unconscious identification 1
undisguised cannibalism 175
United States
  breeders 39
  empirical science 20
  Europe and 60
  killing of children 12–13, 72
  military hospitals in 24
  Satanism coalitions 65
  sex ratio 198
  systematic survey 67
  television audiences 61
universals in religion 10–11. *See also* religion

Vajrayana Buddhist teachings 184
Van Seters, J. 134
victimization 5, 76, 85, 96, 171
victims 106–7, 109, 212–13
  of abuse 37
  of alien abduction 67
  Jewish 81
  perpetrators 26
  of Satanism 67
  of SRA 32
Victor, Jeffrey S. 60
VIP tomb 132
virgin birth doctrine 64, 184
virgins 119–20
Volga river 123

warrior father 125–6
Watts, J. 108, 136
Weber, J. A. 109
Weber, Max 9
Weiler, G. 136
Wellhausen 149
Werlein, Ewing 50–1, 68
West, Fred 54
West, Rosemary 54
West Asia 168
  child sacrifice in 118
  cultural climate around 118
  human sacrifice in 117–38
Wilbur, Cornelia 28–30, 57, 69
Wilde, Oscar 82
Wilkomirski, Binjamin 62
Willerslev, R. 106–7
Willson, Laurel Rose 62
Winfrey, Oprah 55, 62, 63
Winkelman, M. 108, 134, 179
witchcraft 72–7
  accusation 73, 75–6, 137, 205

witch killing 73
Wrangham, R. 183
Wyatt, N. 190

Young, W. C. 30, 42

Yuval, I. J. 79

Zeus 120–1
Zionism 82
Zivkovic, T. M. 184

www.ingramcontent.com/pod-product-compliance
Lightning Source LLC
Chambersburg PA
CBHW062128300426
44115CB00012BA/1850